Breathless

Rutgers Films in Print

Charles Affron, Mirella Jona Affron, and Robert Lyons, editors

Breathless

Jean-Luc Godard,
director

Dudley Andrew, editor

Rutgers University Press

New Brunswick, New Jersey

Breathless is volume 9 in the *Rutgers Films in Print* Series

Third paperback printing, 1995

Library of Congress Cataloging-in-Publication Data

Breathless.

(Rutgers films in print ; v. 9)

Filmography: p.

Bibliography: p.

1. A bout de souffle (Motion picture)
I. Godard, Jean Luc, 1930–
II. Andrew, James Dudley,
1945–   III. A bout
de souffle (Motion picture)   IV. Series.
PN1997.A23   1987   791.43′72   87-4596
ISBN 0-8135-1252-2
ISBN 0-8135-1253-0 (pbk.)

British Cataloging-in-Publication information available

The continuity script and the original treatment for *Breathless* first appeared in *L'Avant-Scène Cinéma*, no. 79 (March 1968) and are reprinted by permission of Jean-Luc Godard and *L'Avant-Scène Cinéma*.
The stills on pages 36, 45, 50, 51, 56, 57, 63, 67, 73, 79, 84, 91, 103, 105, 109, 116, 135, 142, 143, and 145 are reproduced courtesy of the Museum of Modern Art/Film Stills Archive.

Interview with Yvonne Baby and review by Jean de Baroncelli, *Le Monde* (March 18, 1960), courtesy of *Le Monde*. "I'm Not Out of Breath," *Arts* (March 1960) and "But 'Wave' Adds Brightness," *Films and Filming* (September 1961), courtesy of Jean-Luc Godard. "An Interview with Jean-Luc Godard" (December 1962) and Luc Moullet, "I Want You . . . To Not Want You" (April 1960), courtesy of *Cahiers du Cinéma*. Statements by Georges de Beauregard, Producer, Raoul Coutard, Director of Photography, and François Truffaut from Jean Collet, *Jean-Luc Godard* (Paris: Editions Seghers, 1963). Review by Pierre Marcabru, *Arts* (March 19, 1960), courtesy of *Arts*. Reviews by Claude Mauriac (March 19, 1960) and Louis Chauvet (March 18, 1960), courtesy of *Le Figaro Littéraire*. Review by Gene Moskowitz (January 27, 1960), courtesy of *Variety*. Review by Louis Marcorelles, *Sight and Sound* (Spring 1960), courtesy of the British Film Institute. Review by Bosley Crowther (February 8, 1961), copyright © 1961 by *The New York Times Company*. Review by Stanley Kauffmann (February 13, 1961), courtesy of *The New Republic*. Excerpts from review (February 17, 1961), copyright © 1961 by *Time, Inc.*, all rights reserved. Review by Arlene Croce, *Film Quarterly* 14 (Spring 1961): 55–56, copyright © 1961 by The Regents of the University of California; reprinted by permission of The Regents and Arlene Croce. Review by Dwight MacDonald (July 1961) copyright © 1961 and reprinted by permission of *Esquire, Inc.* Review (July 7, 1961), courtesy of *The Times* (London). Review by Gordon Gow, *Films and Filming* (August 1961), courtesy of Brevet Publishing Ltd. Jean Carta, "On *Breathless*" (April 8, 1960), courtesy of *Témoignage Chrétien*. Charles Barr, "*A Bout de Souffle*" (1970) courtesy of Henry Holt & Company. Extracts from her essay, "The Graphic in Filmic Writing," *Enclitic* (Fall 1981/Winter 1982), courtesy of Marie-Claire Ropars.

Acknowledgments

I am deeply indebted to Laura Baratto for clearing the way for this book at the library, at the Movieola, and at the computer. She was a model of thoroughness and accuracy to which I have labored to be faithful. Philip Benz and Dory O'Brien helped with translations while, in breathless summer, Brigid and Nell Andrew groomed the final text.

Contents

Introduction

Breathless:
Old as New

Dudley Andrew

F ew innovative films are hailed in their own day. *Citizen Kane, Greed,* and *Rules of the Game* were recognized as exceptional when they appeared, but exceptional in the sense of aberrant. Neither the public nor the critical establishment was prepared to pay them serious attention. On the other hand, most of the "breakthroughs" that stud the pages of *Variety* every year end up as only fads. Remember *Easy Rider* or the *I Am Curious* films. Their novelty wears thin. *Breathless* belongs to that very short list of films that stunned audiences in their own time and continue to stun us today. Like *Open City,* it was recognized immediately both as a sundering with the recent past, and as an absolutely apt expression of the current sensibility.

Such works are not generated in a vacuum, although I do not discount in advance the role played by sheer creativity. In any case, propitious conditions are required: the felt need for a new kind of film, the availability of models for inspiration and direction, the existence of an audience to engage, if not welcome the film, and of course the material means to produce it. Like most introductions, this one sets a dramatic stage for the entrance of the artwork it announces. But despite or because of hindsight, and despite the clarity that our filtering of history permits, we should never forget the fundamentally illogical eruption in 1960 that was *Breathless.*

In his long personal involvement with the cinema, Jean-Luc Godard calculates that his first phase lasted from 1949 to 1960, that is, from his first encounter with the film clubs of Paris until *Breathless,* a film he has always claimed to be the culmination of a "decade's worth of making movies in my head."[1] His true beginning as a "professional" filmmaker he would mark with *Une Femme est une femme* in 1961. This year would also mark his growing estrangement from the *équipe* at *Cahiers du Cinéma* (François Truffaut, Jacques Rivette, Claude Chabrol, and Eric Rohmer are its best-known members) and the kind of cinema they promoted. But before that break, Godard relished his status as a precocious student of the medium, precocious and arrogant. Let us examine Godard, then, during his amateur phase up to *Breathless,* taking it as an opportunity to see the forces of culture at work in an intensely productive moment. A revolution would occur with the ascendancy of Chabrol, Truffaut, and Godard in 1959–60, but the struggle that climaxed then is to me more exhilarating than the short-lived success of the New Wave. A well-known story, it is nonetheless so edifying as to be worth going over again, this time with a single character in mind, Jean-Luc Godard.

Today Truffaut stands for the sincerity of the Nouvelle Vague; Rohmer for its cool intelligence. Godard, one might think, lit the fuse to set off this volatile concoction. In fact, however, it was the young Truffaut whose famous "Certain Tendency of the French Cinema" was only the loudest and smokiest bomb he dropped in what became an incessant, nearly indiscriminate strafing of the established film industry.[2] Godard carried the ammunition, admired his friend from the sidelines, and soon tested out his own weapons. If, later, he would bitterly scorn Truffaut's softened militancy, one might hear in his tone the hurt of betrayal, as though his older brother had joined forces with the domineering father both had conspired and rebelled against. The script of *Breathless,* we must recall, was a fraternal gift from Truffaut, flushed with the success of his *400 Blows,* to his eager sibling. No matter what he did with that brief script, Godard most likely was proud of its source.[3] It had a New Wave pedigree.

Godard has never concealed the immaturity of his ideas in those years. Indeed it took the pretentiousness of youth, his and Truffaut's, to flaunt the idea of a revivified cinema in the stone face of an even more pretentious establishment. One finds in his writings and memoirs of this period a winning mixture of the brash, pugnacious smart ass (proud of petty thefts from stores, from friends) and

1. Jean-Luc Godard, *Introduction à une véritable histoire du cinéma* (Paris: Albatros, 1980), 36.
2. François Truffaut, "A Certain Tendency of the French Cinema," in *Movies and Methods,* ed. Bill Nichols (Berkeley: University of California Press, 1976), 224–236.
3. François Truffaut, in *L'Avant-Scène Cinéma,* no. 79 (March 1968), 47–49, translated in this volume.

of the young romantic, dreaming of the purity of artistic expression. Poe, Baude-
laire, and Rimbaud were his models, and perhaps (uncredited) the medieval outlaw poet François Villon.

He could write without irony, "What is difficult is to advance into unknown
lands, to be aware of the danger, to take risks, to be afraid."[4] Early in *Breathless*
Michel Poiccard walks by a movie poster that blares the same message: "To Live
Dangerously until the End." Godard was obsessed by personal courage in life
and in art. Even someone as uncompromising as the Marxist aristocrat Luchino
Visconti came under attack for dressing up his mise-en-scène, putting on airs,
relying on good taste when what was needed was "courage."[5] Courage—or the
appearance of it—he found, like so many people, in Ingmar Bergman. The
lonely Swede could show the whole French industry that, as Godard said,

> The cinema is not a craft. It is an art. It does not mean teamwork. One is
> always alone on the set as before the blank page. And to be alone . . . means
> to ask questions. And to make films means to answer them. Nothing could
> be more classically romantic.[6]

"Alone on the set as before a blank page," Godard saw himself and the directors he admired as heirs to a literary tradition: "Tell me whether the destiny of
the modern cinema does not take the same form as it did for the belated partisans
of romanticism. Yes, *with new thoughts let us make old verses.*"[7] The cinema
with its images, visual rhymes, and editing rhythm would reinvent the old verses
of poetry. The surrealist Jean Cocteau had already shown this (Godard's first
short was an homage to that poet). And the new thoughts expressed in this authentic language would be the thoughts of the age. Cinema would respond to the
traditional destiny of art by addressing its own era, not by emulating the past.

Here we come close to Godard's central intuition, one I am sure he took from
Jean-Paul Sartre, the dominant moral presence in the Paris he inhabited. Authentic art comes from sincere artists who extend the sacred tradition only when they
forget tradition and forge the present with contemporary tools of expression.
Every true thought must be reinvented or else it lies dead on the library shelf.
Citing Sartre, Godard says that cinema is the medium where "reticence, as it
were, is unable to hide its secrets; the most religious of arts, it values man above

4. Jean-Luc Godard, *Godard on Godard,* ed. Tom Milne (New York: Viking, 1972), 80.
5. Ibid.
6. Ibid., 76.
7. Ibid., 28.

the essence of things and reveals the soul within the body."[8] And so, ingenuously, he can compare Nicholas Ray to Goethe:

> *Bitter Victory* [is] a kind of Wilhelm Meister 1958. No matter. It would mean little enough to say that *Bitter Victory* is the most Goethian of films. What is the point of redoing Goethe, or of doing anything again—*Don Quixote* or *Bouvard et Pécuchet*, *J'accuse* or *Voyage au bout de la nuit*— since it has already been done? . . . There was theater (Griffith), poetry (Murnau), painting (Rossellini), dance (Eisenstein), music (Renoir). Henceforth there is cinema. And the cinema is Nicholas Ray.[9]

In the auteur idiom of the day he absolved Ray from an earlier failure, *Hot Blood*, by blaming the weakness of the script, and appealing again to literature and what it might have offered him instead.

> Nicholas Ray is *morally* a director, first and foremost. This explains the fact that in spite of his innate talent and obvious sincerity, a script which he does not take seriously will remain superficial. . . . No one who shares my opinion that D. H. Lawrence's *The Plumed Serpent* is the most important novel of the 20th century will be surprised when I say that here, had he so chosen, Nicholas Ray could have found a subject even more modern in its overtones than the ones he prefers.[10]

The subject of *The Plumed Serpent,* we might note, concerns someone who, like Michel Poiccard, "weary of adventure, returns to the people to whom he belongs."

In other places Godard claims that Joseph Mankiewicz is the reincarnation of the famous French playwright Jean Giraudoux and that his script for *The Quiet American* is superior to its source, Graham Greene's celebrated novel.[11] Thus the cinema need not feel inferior. It will have its Stendhal and its Proust; though, he concludes, in order to be faithful to our epoch and this new art, cinéastes must drive beyond the intelligence of such authors and "go for the instant."

From the very outset Godard was certain that the defining characteristics of modern life had to be speed, boldness, and ingenuity. He was infatuated with André Malraux's early novels for precisely these qualities. He admired as well the

8. Ibid., 26.
9. Ibid., 64, 66.
10. Ibid., 43.
11. Ibid., 82.

man himself, who left literature to take on a political destiny that must at first have seemed to be of the same high order. Malraux reinforced his modernity by filming *L'Espoir* and by writing a key essay on the cinema. For Godard this made him the prototype of the modern intellectual. He would echo Malraux's philosophy in his selection of Alfred Hitchcock as one of the most serious thinkers of our time: Of *Strangers on a Train* (but perhaps already thinking of the movies he himself would make) he said, "I know of no other recent film which better conveys the condition of modern man, who must escape his fate without the help of the gods." [12]

If any artistic expression were to be equal to this existentialist view of life, it would have to rely on swiftness, chance, and reflex, forgoing the elegance and even the intelligence of an earlier age. The modern-day cinematic Stendhal must sacrifice precision, form, and clarity to render the vigor and anxiety of the age, for our age is not Stendhal's. Although he loved John Ford, Godard felt him to be a cinéaste of an earlier aesthetic. "The force of Ford's camera movement," he wrote in contrasting the modern and classical western, "arises from its plastic and dynamic beauty. [Anthony] Mann's shot is, one might say, of *vegetal* beauty. Its force springs precisely from the fact that it owes nothing to any planned aesthetic." [13] Speaking not of filmmakers but of genres, he made the same point: "If the emergence of American comedy is as important as the advent of sound, it is because it brought back swiftness of action, and allowed the moment to be savoured to the full. . . . It is pointless to kill one's feelings in order to live longer." [14] Michel Poiccard would utterly agree. When Patricia reads him William Faulkner's conclusion to *The Wild Palms,* "between grief and nothingness, I choose grief," Michel rebuts: "Grief is a compromise. I'd choose nothingness. . . . You've got to have all or nothing."

What is so astonishing is that Godard routinely calls on maligned genres, the Western and the musical, to help address the most serious philosophical issues of the day. Indeed, he implies that the late twentieth-century philosopher, like the writer, must work through the cinema or be out of touch with the problems of our world. Naturally he is thinking of the existentialist philosopher. Sartre had attended Bazin's ciné-club during the Occupation, had written the first serious critique of *Citizen Kane,* and had worked on several scripts. [15] In a 1953 address

12. Ibid., 23.
13. Ibid., 119.
14. Ibid., 27.
15. Dudley Andrew, *André Bazin* (New York: Oxford University Press, 1978), esp. pp. 70–80.

from the chair he held at the Collège de France Maurice Merleau-Ponty had proclaimed that henceforth the work of philosophy and that of cinema were parallel.[16]

One might point to the question of "authenticity" as the key ethical concept of the era. It certainly was central to Godard's judgments. From André Bazin he learned to subsume this issue to the linked terms of spontaneity and sincerity. He would attack his former ally Roger Vadim in the late fifties for having given up spontaneity and intuition in the demeaning search for respect by aiming at calculated effects.[17] Godard preferred the immediacy, and even the bad taste, of the American cinema. "I love the moment in *Fallen Angel* when the camera, in order not to lose sight of Linda Darnell as she walks across a restaurant, rushes so fast through the customers that one sees the assistants' hands seizing two or three of them by the scruff of the neck and pulling them aside to make way for it." [18] How much this description is like Bazin's review of *Kon Tiki,* which ecstatically recounts that moment when the cameraman must lay down the camera to help defend the raft from a charging shark.[19] The film, even in its blemishes and gaps, is a true record of the scene, for here it visibly records the danger, the energy of the moment in which it is engaged. "Clumsiness," Godard said, "attempts to fix simplicity straight in the eye. It is not a mark of incompetence but of reticence." [20] No film would try harder than *Breathless* to fix simplicity straight in the eye. No film so joyously and cavalierly disregards finesse and technical competence in the pursuit of direct expression.

While Bazin promoted the unique virtues of cinematic mise-en-scène, virtues that owed far more to the recording rather than the shaping powers of the medium, Godard stands ready to turn to editing strategies when the frenzy on the set fails to convey the turmoil of the plot, characters, or theme. More important, he is ready to rethink the relation of editing to mise-en-scène, hoping to go beyond accepted strategies to describe more aptly (and in *Breathless* to produce) a distinctively cinematic pulse of energy.

> In *Les Mauvaises Rencontres* [Alexandre] Astruc was still using this sort of effect, this premeditated violence, in the manner of Bardem: as a shot changed, a door opened, a glass shattered, a face turned. In *Une Vie,* on

16. Maurice Merleau-Ponty, "The Psychology of Film," in *Sense and Nonsense* (Evanston: Northwestern University Press, 1964), 48–59. Originally published in French in 1948 by Nagel (Paris).
17. *Godard on Godard,* 194.
18. Ibid., 133–134.
19. André Bazin, *What Is Cinema?* (Berkeley: University of California Press, 1967), 161.
20. *Godard on Godard,* 151.

the other hand, he uses it within a shot, pushing the example of Richard Brooks—or, more especially, Nicholas Ray—so far that the *effect becomes almost the cause.* The beauty is not so much in Marquand's dragging Maria Schell out of the château as in the abruptness with which he does it. This abruptness of gesture which gives a fresh impulse to the suspense every few minutes, this discontinuity latent in its continuity, might be called the tell-tale heart of *Une Vie.*[21]

"Discontinuity in continuity," a "heart" beating within an "abstraction." With *Une Vie* we are, in 1958, almost at the New Wave. A new aesthetic has replaced the tired cinema of quality that had dominated France with its prettified, innocuous adaptations since the war. Truffaut finally delivers the needed push and Godard, in one of his most quoted litanies, chants: "*Les Quatre Cents Coups* [*The 400 Blows*] will be a film signed Frankness. Rapidity. Art. Novelty. Cinematography. Originality. Impertinence. Seriousness. Tragedy. Renovation. Ubu-Roi. Fantasy. Ferocity. Affection. Universality. Tenderness."[22]

As Truffaut began actively making films, Godard leaped into the first rank of the insurgents. Irate that his friend had won only the director's prize, not the Palme d'or at the Cannes film festival, he lashed out against the film that did win, *Black Orpheus,* by Marcel Camus, that chic pretender to originality:

What would the "Concerto for Clarinet" be without Mozart? What would the "Head of a Girl" be without Vermeer? [Louis] Aragon's prose without Aragon? What in short would Orpheus' song (have you seen [Cocteau's] *Orphée* again recently?) be without Orpheus? Or what would poetry be without a poet? Well, it would be *Orfeu Negro. . . . Orfeu Negro* is . . . totally unauthentic.[23]

And the critical world agreed with him. He thought the whole world agreed. In a shameless victory speech he announced a revivified film culture under the new cultural minister of France:

The face of French cinema has changed. . . . Malraux [who confirmed *The 400 Blows* as France's entry at Cannes] made no mistake. He could hardly help recognizing that tiny inner flame, that reflection of intransigence, shin-

21. Ibid., 98. Juan Antonio Bardem was a noted Spanish filmmaker. His *Death of a Cyclist* was a hit in France in 1955.
22. Ibid., 121. *Ubu Roi,* literally "King Shit," is an 1896 play by Alfred Jarry that still represents the ultimate in social and artistic rebellion.
23. Ibid., 151.

ing in the eyes of Truffaut's Antoine . . . for it is the same as that which glittered twenty years ago on Tchen's dagger on the first page of *La Condition humaine.* . . . We won the day in having it acknowledged in principle that a film by Hitchcock, for example, is as important as a book by Aragon. Film *auteurs,* thanks to us, have finally entered the history of art. But you whom we attack have automatically benefited from this success. And we attack you for your betrayal, because we have opened your eyes and you continue to keep them closed. Each time we see your films we find them so bad, so far aesthetically and morally from what we had hoped, that we are almost ashamed of our love for the cinema. . . . We cannot forgive you for never having filmed girls as we love them, boys as we see them every day, parents as we despise or admire them, children as they astonish us or leave us indifferent; in other words, things as they are. Today, victory is ours. It is our films which will go to Cannes to show that France is looking good, cinematographically speaking. Next year it will be the same again, you may be sure of that. Fifteen new, courageous, sincere, lucid, beautiful films will once again bar the way to conventional productions.[24]

Of course, the next year one of those fifteen films would be Godard's. What kind of film would it be? Godard may not have been sure of his subject, but he had certainly settled on a style. It would be "American," with speed, reflex, and a character who could go to the limit. In short, it would have directness and honesty in theme and style, as opposed to the good taste (or what Godard felt was the congenital mendacity) of the ruling French cinema of quality. The relation between aesthetics and ethics could be no closer than it was in 1960.

Godard was measuring spiritual depth when he reviewed films. The New Wave was a club of distinction where a mentality of heroism prevailed and where it was presumed that vibrant lives could produce only vibrant films. Great souls are fashioned when a filmmaker's drive toward originality is guided, but not hampered, by tradition. The proof of this lies in the films themselves. And so Godard confidently could propose Claude Chabrol as one of the elect. "When I say that Chabrol gives me the impression of having invented the pan—as Alain Resnais invented the track, Griffith the close-up, and Ophuls reframing—I can speak no greater praise."[25] Godard planned to invent the cinema in its entirety. He hoped to do so even in his first feature, *Breathless.*

24. Ibid., 146–147.
25. Ibid., 129.

Breathless is crammed with reinvention, as was evident to its incredulous first audiences. The jump cuts were the most blatant celebration of technique, occurring seemingly in disregard to the story, to the dialogue, and to the construction of cinematic illusion. While they often excise dead time from a conversation, at other times (as in shot 108 for example) they produce a pulse to the image and nothing more, actually working against the scene they exist within.

Less remarked upon than the jump cut is what I term the technique of the quick cut. Here Godard butts the image of a static figure up against one (often the same one) in full motion. Occasionally the screen direction of the two shots will be opposed to further jar the viewer, propelling the film in some cases or breaking all sense of flow in other cases. When Patricia finally resolves to turn in Michel, her trip to the café telephone consists of three shots (376–378), each reversing her screen direction and the speed of her gait. Unlike the rapid flow of motion that the New Wave taught Madison Avenue how to use in the stylish TV ads of the 1960s, *Breathless* stutters and spurts in scenes like this, jolting the viewer nervously and unpredictably. The effect of the quick cut is heightened by other contributing factors. Enormous changes in scale keep us off our guard, as, for example, the extreme closeup pan of Michel's revolver cut against the long-shot figure of the policeman already in the act of falling backwards into the bushes (shots 47, 48).

In contrast to such cinematic hyperactivity is the static wordiness of much of the rest of the film, particularly the scene in Patricia's hotel room that takes up virtually a third of the movie. This scene contains numerous jump cuts, a few quick cuts, and several closeup pans and tilts; however, its overall effect is to establish an unusual duration in which lengthy pauses cushion sessions of the incessant jockeying of the two characters. Godard endeavors to present in a single overlong scene the formula of the Hollywood love story, confining it to one location and forcing it to run its course in real time without the slightest interruption from the outside.

The true antithesis of the jump and quick cuts is not, however, the film's extended dialogue sequence but rather its extraordinary long takes. The first promenade Michel and Patricia take down the Champ Elysées is justly celebrated for its documentary evidence, but it is only a prelude to the tour de force of camerawork displayed in the travel agency, in the *Herald Tribune* office, and in the Swedish model's apartment at the end of the film. In all three of these cases, the camera weaves a broadly circular path 360 degrees or more as it follows a main character, only to retrace the path with another character. Thus the dramatic opposition of two characters is figured by the overlaying of one trajectory immediately on another without a cut. These three shots, 85, 285, and 384, are among the most beautiful and audacious in film history. They proclaim the tracking camera to be a moral as well as an aesthetic force, a way of seeing and representing life that was born with the cinema and is reborn now.

Breathless directs its play and replay of technique along the line of a story that may in itself be thought of as play and replay, that is, as fundamentally generic. Since the cinema has always shaped itself into genres, and since Godard, for all his belief in authenticity, doubts the possibility of radical originality, his first feature models itself on that tradition. The theme of the film, like the essence of its hero, is precisely the futile struggle to be original "in the manner of" something or someone else. The notion of individuality and of forthrightness is as American as the movies, and as fully processed. Since there can be no escaping genre, since freedom is attainable only within or against genre, Godard the cinéphile embraces it. And he chooses the genre that most promoted and problematized freedom, the film noir.[26]

Film noir was itself a marginal genre, almost an experimental one in relation to the Hollywood system of the 1940s and 1950s. It spoke forbidden secrets (murder, betrayal, incest) that continue to obsess film addicts. And it spoke them in a murky way whose very indirection was a sign of its deeper, darker truth: the mumbled dialogue, at times aggressive, at times utterly irrelevant; the spontaneous violence; the inventive sets and more inventive camerawork establishing a space at once urban and psychological; the overly dramatic musical scores and the abrupt sound cuts. Its contradictory tone, both hushed and hysterical, expressed unconsciously the existential angst of the times. The disillusioned young French people who haunted the Paris Cinémathèque after the war felt that these films spoke directly to them.

> Even before *Cahiers* [*du Cinéma*], Bazin, Doniol-Valcroze, and others created a ciné-club called Objectif 49 which showed film noir, like *Gilda* and *Fallen Angel*. I thought of *Mark McPherson, Detective* [*Laura*] with Dana Andrews also in it while I was making *Breathless*. . . . *Fallen Angel* and its type became a model for *Breathless*.[27]

---

26. The French were the first to define and to admire this genre. See Raymond Borde and E. Chaumeton, *Panorama du film noir* (Paris: Editions du Minuit, 1955).
27. Godard, *Introduction à une véritable histoire*, 25.

Godard packed his film with direct and glancing citations to this genre. "I remember I had put in a poster of an Aldrich film whose subtitle was 'To live dangerously until the end' simply because at that time [Robert] Aldrich was part of our cinéphile references." [28] A plethora of other such references quickly surface. Belmondo's ruse in the public toilet, for instance, where he pretends to wash his hands before attacking the unsuspecting gentleman, comes directly from *The Enforcer* (1951, Bretaigne Windust). Jack Palance's name appears on the poster for *Ten Seconds to Hell* (1959, Aldrich), just as Humphrey Bogart's full photo arrests Belmondo in front of a lobby card for Mark Robson's 1956 *The Harder They Fall,* a film about the lowlife of the boxing world. Belmondo, before acting, had been a boxer. Now, as actor, he wipes his thumb across his lips mimicking one of the authentic (unstaged) tics of "Bogey" and then worshipfully he lives out his life like an American gangster, slapping his pal Berutti on the shoulder in greeting, sporting just the right style hat, keeping a cigarette constantly in his mouth as part of his costume, and driving flashy cars. In the most ostentatious reference to the genre, Jean Seberg runs right through a theater playing a film noir in her escape from the clumsy "dick." Although the screen is not visible to us, the English dialogue is plain: Gene Tierney and Richard Conte in another Preminger film, *Whirlpool.* [29]

The casting of Jean-Pierre Melville as the noted writer Parvulesco is a gesture of dubious homage to the greatest exponent of film noir working in France, dubious because his name is the Roumanianization of the Latin term for "puny." Nevertheless the savant holds forth, wearing in the film his signature American-style hat, the same hat he no doubt wore on the set of *Deux hommes dans Manhattan,* a thriller he was filming at that very moment. Melville's influence on the whole New Wave is well documented. Godard is happy to acknowledge it in his script. In an early scene the detectives pressure Belmondo's contact, Tolmatchoff, at the Inter-America Travel Agency, saying, "Remember when you tipped us off to your friend Bob? You're going to repeat the performance." Michel has in fact already learned that "Bob's in the cooler." And he should have known it, for Bob is none other than Michel's prototype, a small-time gangster with plenty of style, the star of Melville's precocious 1956 *Bob the Gambler* [*Bob le flambeur*].

Beyond such direct citation one feels everywhere the general "film noir tone"

---

28. Ibid., 26.
29. Let me thank Marc Vernet for helping me identify many of the citations to American films. Craig Sapir pointed out the particular relation to *Gun Crazy.*

of *Breathless*. Belmondo's dream of going south to Italy with his girl and his swag recalls the "escape over the border" dreams of so many forties' antiheroes, like the fated couple of *Gun Crazy*, a 1949 film that displays one of the earliest extended-take scenes in Hollywood cinema. This scene, a bank robbery filmed entirely from the back of the getaway car, may very well have inspired the taxi scenes in *Breathless*. Belmondo's anecdote to Seberg about the bus driver who stole a pile of dough to impress a girl seems to rewrite *Gun Crazy*, for that couple too goes deeper into crime as their love grows. One can hardly forget, moreover, that the director of *Gun Crazy*, Joseph H. Lewis, worked frequently for Monogram Pictures, a specialist in this genre; this was the company to which Godard, in a remarkable gesture of mixed homage and irony, dedicated *Breathless*.

The noir tone is equally sustained by the jazz score flamboyantly inserted in unpredictable, though not arbitrary places throughout the film, and by the countless gestures of all the actors, including Godard himself who peeks over his dark glasses and his newspaper before denouncing his hero. More than these individual moments, the film's dramatic flow unmistakably recalls a whole battery of films, all of whose doomed and passionate couples "live dangerously until the end." *Gun Crazy* is a B-variation on the theme eloquently initiated by Fritz Lang in *You Only Live Once* (1936). Lang has always been one of Godard's heroes. In 1962 the German master literally played himself in *Contempt* as a sophisticated and moral filmmaker set off against an unscrupulous and crass producer, Jack Palance. *Breathless* replays Lang's perpetual theme and method in the dragnet that closes around Belmondo. That net of plot might best be symbolized (in Lang's films as well as in *Breathless*) as a maniacal system of roads. The highway where the crime takes place harbors no hiding places. One drives forward or is caught. Later this narrow trajectory fans into the confusion of the metropolis with its infinitely intersecting streets. Michel will be gunned down at last at one such intersection, tired of running.

Three other driven heroes of the forties whose fate Belmondo wants to share come from Raoul Walsh. In *High Sierra* (with Bogart, 1941), *Colorado Territory* (with Joel McCrea, 1949), and *White Heat* (James Cagney, 1949) tormented gangsters are cornered by the law and wiped out, leaving the audience to wonder if this has been a merciless or merciful extermination. Critics of the time were quick to note the attraction to death expressed by these characters.[30] Godard and Belmondo have made this urge explicit. Indeed, the filmmaker mentioned that the whole interest of the script lay in the umbrella of death hovering above Bel-

30. Pierre Marcabru, review in *Arts*, March 19, 1960.

mondo, one Jean Seberg refused, or knew not how, to share.[31] Her ingenuous question standing over Belmondo's corpse, "Qu'est-ce que c'est 'dégueulasse?'" is modeled precisely on Ida Lupino's blank stare at Bogart's riddled body in the final scene of *High Sierra:* "What does it mean to crash out?" Both women are fascinated by the death-drive of their men.

Because of this instinct for death and because of his complete alienation, Michel Poiccard became, for certain French critics, a reincarnation of Sartre's Roquentin, Albert Camus's Meursault, and Jean Genet's perverse heroes.[32] *Breathless,* after all, was a French film and one could search for cinematic references beyond Hollywood.[33] Belmondo's gestures may come from Jean Gabin, in Marcel Carné's *Daybreak* (*Le Jour se lève,* 1939), for both men measure out their final hours chain smoking, often lighting one cigarette from the butt of another and playing with the teddy bears of their winsome girlfriends. A more pertinent source is Carné's *Port of Shadows* (*Quai des brumes,* 1938). There, a deserter, Gabin hopes to escape on a ship with Michèle Morgan but is gunned down in the final moments, survived, like Bogart in *High Sierra,* not only by his distraught woman but by a sad little mutt that has followed him throughout the film foretelling his death in its yelps.

The film historian Georges Sadoul thumbed through his notes to find other Gabin vehicles of romantic pessimism, linking Belmondo's scene in front of the movie poster with one in Julien Duvivier's *They Were Five* (*La Belle Equipe,* 1936) where Gabin, out of work, stares at a poster advertising winter holidays. Gabin in Duvivier's *Pépé le Moko* (1937) is also a trapped criminal, though the strongest rapport here would be between the Algerian detective Slimane and Godard's slimy detective, Vital (Daniel Boulanger), whose dull determination is like the working of fate.[34]

This exchange between France and America follows what I believe to be a historical pattern. Gabin did indeed initiate a strong, silent acting style in the pessimistic films preceding World War II. He played out his roles on sets largely adopted from German expressionism, but he restrained his own body, allowing it to burst into anger once per film. He is the model Bogart would bring to life in America during the war, passing down his reticence to Dana Andrews, Fred

---

31. Cited in Yvonne Baby, "Propos recueillis," *Le Monde,* March 18, 1960.

32. René Guyonnet, review in *L'Express,* March 17, 1960.

33. See, among others, Marcel Martin, review in *Cinéma,* no. 46 (May 1960) and Claude Mauriac, review in *Le Figaro Littéraire,* March 19, 1960.

34. Sadoul, review in *Lettres Françaises,* no. 828 (March 31, 1960).

MacMurray, and the catatonic Richard Widmark. This is the tradition that comes back to France in *Breathless*. If the moral stakes have changed, the position of the character in society has not budged at all.[35]

What has changed, though, is the filmmaker's attitude to this character. Walsh and even Lang uphold, though do not condone, the established order their heroes defy; Godard, however, not only backs his hero's nihilism, but limes the film with half-serious references to very serious artists. In the apartment where he spends his last night, Belmondo picks up a Nouvelle Revue Française book. It is Maurice Sachs's *Abracadabra*. Sachs can be thought of as a predecessor of Jean Genet, a cultured gangster and defiant homosexual who was imprisoned before his death at the end of World War II. More important is the para-reference one can read on the book cover: "Nous sommes des morts en permission [We're all dead men on leave]." This is Lenin. Godard, I think, is more interested in death than in Lenin at this time, interested at least in clothing his hero with it. He ostentatiously includes Mozart's Clarinet Concerto in the film's final sequence because, he once claimed, he believed (erroneously) that this was Mozart's final composition before his early death.[36] Big thinkers find their way into the dialogue as well: aphorisms about death by Faulkner and about love by Rainer Maria Rilke add to the film's philosophical aura.

Other references are made less ponderously, indeed so lightly that they glide off the edges of the film. Paul Klee appears (via a postcard reproduction stuck on Patricia's wall) perhaps because he is, like Godard, Swiss. Dylan Thomas comes up, it seems, only because Godard loved the title of his book, *Portrait of the Artist as a Young Dog*. Godard allows himself this privilege his predecessors never dreamed of, the privilege of arbitrary citation.

> People in life quote as they please, so we have the right to quote as we please. Therefore I show people quoting, merely making sure that they quote what pleases me. In the notes I make of anything that might be of use for a film, I will add a quote from Dostoievsky if I like it. Why not? If you want to say something, there is only one solution: say it. . . . Moreover, *Breathless* was the sort of film where anything goes: that was what it was all about. Anything people did could be integrated in the film. As a matter of fact, this was my starting-point.[37]

35. My ideas concerning the history of this acting style come from Randy Wood, unpublished seminar paper, University of Iowa, 1980.
36. In Baby, *Le Monde*, March 18, 1960.
37. *Godard on Godard*, 173.

Naturally friends sneak into the film. Laszlo Kovacs, now an important cine-matographer, lent his name to Michel as an alias, simply because Godard liked the man and the name. Parvulesco draws on Cocteau to answer one reporter; Patricia looks at Michel through a rolled-up poster. . . . a Renoir! This is a double-citation, for the telescope may be Renoir, but the scene itself comes right out of Sam Fuller's *Forty Guns* (1957). Godard again strikes twice with the ques-tion launched at Parvulesco, "Aimez-vous Brahms?" His violent "No" may be read first of all as a rejection of Françoise Sagan's novel of that title and second as a condemnation of romantic music. Chopin is the next victim: "dégueulasse"; whereas Mozart and Bach are both ratified. On the other hand, Patricia and Michel do make love to Chopin and Sagan did originally author Patricia's very character, if we care to believe Godard when he claims that "Jean Seberg was a continuation of the role she played in *Bonjour Tristesse.*"[38]

Godard, it seems, had at least two uses for intertextual references. The first, stronger use, deepens the aesthetic and philosophical thrust of his own effort by linking it to the low-art film noir with its excruciating ruminations about death and love. The second use, paradoxically involving elite novelists, composers, and painters, is textural rather than structural. Godard splashes these names on his canvas to vary the tone and interest of his scenes, to keep his drama within a live and lively cultural space. Just as he presumptuously (and wrongly) claimed he was the first filmmaker to shoot on the Champs Elysées, bringing De Gaulle and Eisenhower in as an international backdrop to a petty low-life melodrama, so he thought himself the first to drop names like Renoir and Faulkner, the first to show Picasso's *The Lovers*, the first to play disrespectfully, because offhandedly, with art. In the film's most blatant fabrication of "culture" Patricia and Michel kiss long and lovingly in a theater where Budd Boetticher's 1956 *Westbound* is playing. But the voices we hear dubbing the English actors are not reciting Boetticher's script at all; they pour out poems by Louis Aragon and Guillaume Apollinaire. Marie-Claire Ropars takes this moment as a key, not to unlock the mystery of the meaning of the film but to open up her own playful dialogue with the movie, using *Breathless* as irresponsibly and ingeniously as Godard used the film noir.[39]

An older form of criticism might have wrestled some of these references into

38. Ibid. Actually Godard makes reference to several novels by Sagan in his film. See notes 26 and 48 to the Continuity Script. She was unquestionably the most popular author of the day, representing the new youth culture.

39. Marie-Claire Ropars, "The Graphic in Filmic Writing: *A bout de souffle* or the Erratic Alpha-bet," *Enclitic* 6 (Fall 1981/Winter 1982), 147–161.

an allegorical frieze. For instance, when Patricia explicitly calls on Shakespeare and Godard provides a cutaway to Picasso's drawing of the lovers, one might suggest that Godard is rendering the cultural history of love, citing love's greatest literary source, Shakespeare, then its modernist reprise by Picasso, as criteria for his own ultramodern version of love. But years ago Susan Sontag waged war against this sort of interpretation, holding up *Breathless* as a film whose sheer speed and casual structure must ridicule every attempt at a consistent reading of its images. She proposed an erotics, not a hermeneutics of art.[40] This spirit is the one Marie-Claire Ropars has breathed as she dallied rather perversely with parts of the film. Her goal, perhaps Godard's goal in making the film, is the pleasure of language and images, the pleasure of citation, contradiction, and feigned innovation. This brings us to the aesthetics of pastiche where any element can lead for a time. This film begs to be savored in parts.

Pastiche. Naive and optimistic about the cinema in this first phase of his career, Godard felt he could incorporate the past in the elastic volume of a film whose contours were arbitrary because conventional. He was sure of success because in his iconoclasm and his posing he was as authentic as his hero. We have itemized some of the numerous and heterogenous indices of culture pulled into the vortex of *Breathless*. The spiral of that vortex is not Godard's either, but spins down to him from B-films and existential literature. What is original, what can only be original, is the film's energy. Citation, parody, homage . . . devices that depend on the past . . . are thrust into a discursive moment and used in the present tense. *Breathless* of all films insists on its presentness. Godard called it "reinvention" so that everything would appear to be expressed as if for the first time.

What makes *Breathless* a quintessential New Wave film is not a particular technique or techniques but the energy with which it speaks. The French had a word for this, a word once again made popular by Sartre: "authenticité." At the end of his first period of a life in film, Godard could maintain that optimism about his medium that permitted him to incorporate whatever he wanted of the past in a film which would mobilize those traces and thrust them into the future. The lone auteur in front of the blank page, solitary on the set, wanders through the storehouse of his memory in order to begin to write and to direct. When he rubs his thumb across his lips, he means it.

Can we confidently accept in a postmodern work such qualities as "spontaneity," "immediacy," and "life"? These days innovative style is more likely to

40. Susan Sontag, *Against Interpretation* (New York, Dell, 1969), 23.

be thought of as a symptom of market forces than of authenticity. We look to Pepsi commercials for the most ingenious discoveries in shooting and editing. Even if our general cultural cynicism were not enough to put the significance of *Breathless* in grave doubt, Jim MacBride's 1983 remake of the film blows up the issue of originality in its very project. In an intricately argued essay on both films Pamela Falkenberg upends such notions as "original" and "realist" by turning them into marketing strategies required in the capitalist film industry, where every product must be at once new and reliable, different and the same.[41] This is as true of the art world as it is of pop music.

Both Jim MacBride and Jean-Luc Godard sought to overturn the current cinema by getting outside it, onto the margins. Godard called on an older Hollywood tradition of B-films to help fashion the New Wave art film (because, in part, the French cinema of quality against which he railed had consciously differentiated itself from precisely those Hollywood genres like the gangster film). These odd reversals are themselves reversed in 1983, when MacBride hoped to rewrite "the commercial Hollywood cinema . . . through the rewriting of the French art cinema." [42] Both films acknowledge the need for mediation, for intertextuality, and forthrightly insist that the truth of any new cinema (New Wave or New American) is not established by looking at life in the streets or in a director's psyche, but by looking at other movies, at books, songs, and representations of all sorts.

Here we reach the necessary commonplace concerning Godard's postmodernism. Utterly opposed to the organicism and moralism of the cinema of quality, Godard would deliberately emphasize the heterogeneity of culture, of its texts and artifacts, and of its social organization. If literature is to appear in his films (and it always makes many appearances), it is as a thing apart. The hard edge of words confronts the engulfing image without being swallowed up. Literature sticks out of Godard's films, the way pieces of newspaper stick out of cubist collages. In short, Godard incorporates literary material in the ongoing dialectical purpose of his heterodox style.

Today Godard would say that "style" itself, even a heterodox style, is but an element in an impersonal dialectic of enunciation. But in 1960 it was supreme, the controlling vision capable of knowing what to throw in, what to cite, what to invent on the spot, what tone to take, and so on. Godard now apologizes for the

---

41. Pamela Falkenberg, "Hollywood and the 'Art Cinema' as a Bipolar Modeling System: *A bout de souffle* and *Breathless*," *Wide Angle* 7, no. 3 (1985), 44–53.

42. Ibid., 51–52.

flagrant individualism of *Breathless,* particularly in its glorifying of the freedom of its characters or of the models they base themselves upon.[43] Today Michel Poiccard, and even Bogart and Dana Andrews, seem less heroic, for they achieved at best an incoherent and local freedom, whereas what is required, Godard feels, is the systematic comprehension of social forces and contradictions. We experience with Belmondo the excitement of the outlaw life, and the greater excitement of indifference. Like his hero, the Godard of 1960 is an outlaw, throwing obscene gestures at the cinema of his day. In flailing about for new directions, in escaping traps laid for him by producers, censors, the establishment, he is both inventive and plagiaristic, inventive *as* plagiaristic. Belmondo has his Bogart, Godard his Preminger.

Godard, we have noted, labeled his gesture to the cultural heritage "a cinema of reinvention."[44] "To reinvent the cinema as though for the first time" is a phrase that recurs like a refrain in his criticism of the 1950s. It is also how he described his ambitions for his first film. What can this mean? First of all, it does not mean that he feels capable of changing the course of cinema altogether, of pretending that 1960 is 1895 and all doors are open. Reinvention means precisely the reappropriation of the history of cinema as one's own: the *authentic* laying down of the lessons of the past for the present. The iris that closes down on the distant, confused detectives when Belmondo goes to find Jean Seberg is not a homage to or citation of D. W. Griffith. It is the spontaneous discovery of the value of cinematic punctuation. Godard's pleasure in employing this technique is amplified by, was perhaps triggered by, the fact that the detectives are not seen directly but as reflected in a movie theater door, and this only after Belmondo has had his face-to-face exchange with a film noir movie poster. We who have entered the theater after ogling production stills of Belmondo and Seberg must find our interest deflected from the story of the chase to the mythology of representation, since the detectives become in effect framed behind glass, another paper-thin publicity photo promising whatever it is that the movies can deliver. *Breathless* is an attempt to fulfill that promise in its own terms.

43. Godard, *Introduction à une véritable histoire,* 29.
44. *Godard on Godard,* 173.

Jean-Luc Godard
A Biographical Sketch

Born in Paris in 1930 into an upper-crust Swiss family, Jean-Luc Godard spent his formative years in Geneva, capital city of capitalism. The rest of his life he has spent fighting that background, criticizing the ideas that underpin it and then criticizing his own critical stance. By his own account, life seriously began for him in 1948 when he left Switzerland for the vibrant culture of Paris. This was the era of existentialist cafés and of burgeoning ciné-clubs, and Godard spent far more time at these locations than at the Sorbonne where he was ostensibly pursuing a degree in ethnology. Here begins what he calls his first phase of life with the cinema, a phase that lasted a dozen years through the production of *Breathless.*

The days and nights he spent with François Truffaut, Claude Chabrol, Jacques Rivette, and Eric Rohmer at Henri Langlois's Cinémathèque are fabled: a thousand films viewed a year is the estimate, if you include films seen at commercial theaters. In 1949 he crashed the Biarritz festival with the blessing of its indulgent master of ceremonies, Jean Cocteau. The next year he helped start the short-lived *Gazette du Cinéma* edited by Rohmer. Soon he was writing reviews, under the pseudonym Hans Lucas, for *Cahiers du Cinéma,* perhaps because its founding editor, Jacques Doniol-Valcroze, was a family friend. In short, he insinuated himself deeply into a cinema subculture that was already making waves.

From 1953 to 1956 Godard was less visible. Family problems took him back to Switzerland, where, it is rumored, he got in trouble with the law for theft. When in Paris, he kept up his relations with Truffaut and through him struck up a friendship with Roberto Rossellini. A job at Twentieth Century-Fox in Paris, secured for him by Chabrol, led him to the producer Georges de Beauregard. Meanwhile he completed a few short films and prepared a number of scripts. After Truffaut's success, Beauregard was willing to take a chance on his friend as director of *Breathless,* no doubt because the film project stemmed from a treatment by Truffaut and because Chabrol agreed to be assistant director. The reception of this film was utterly sensational.

Godard's second phase began when he awoke suddenly as a director of promise with resources. It ended in 1968 during the political manifestations in France. During those eight years, he produced fourteen features and five shorts, ranging in genre from musical comedy (*Une Femme est une femme*) to Brechtian allegory (*Les Carabiniers*). An international audience awaited each new production for the inevitable surprise it would bring. And they had not long to wait. There was the bizarre science-fiction detective film, *Alphaville;* the mock homage to the gangster genre, *Band of Outsiders;* and the lush Cinemascope *Contempt,* an expensive production featuring Brigitte Bardot, Jack Palance, and Fritz Lang.

Increasingly there was the use of the cinematic essay format. This would be Godard's central contribution. Already in 1962 with *My Life to Live* he addressed his audience directly, confronting them with sociological facts, with the discourse of a philosopher (Brice Parain), and with a drama brutally dissected into a dozen tableaux, labeled as such. The topic? Prostitution. Prostitution and acting, for the film starred his wife Anna Karina and included, as one of its tableaux, her watching tearfully the great actress Falconetti in Dreyer's *Passion of Joan of Arc.* In 1965 he would divorce Karina, only to marry another of his actresses, Anne Wiazemsky, two years later. His turbulent domestic and political life is evident in *Masculine/Feminine,* which pitted Jean-Pierre Léaud against his bubble-gum singer of a girlfriend. Léaud's search for sincerity in modern Paris is both tragic and revealing.

With *The Married Woman, Made in U.S.A.,* and *Two or Three Things I Know about Her* Godard's sociological inquiries became less personal. He freely intercut small dramatic vignettes with sociological statistics, random shots of advertising posters, and cosmic speculation, concluding one film with an immense closeup of a coffee cup framed so that the bubbles whirling in the black liquid appeared like great galaxies. Such aesthetic improvisation took its toll, annoying those critics who had been partisans of his early inventiveness. The fact that he shot the latter two films simultaneously (one in the morning, one in the afternoon) provoked doubts about the seriousness of his work or at least about the nature of cinema as an art form.

But Godard did not hesitate to go further. Beyond sociology was the political film and with *La Chinoise* he fashioned an unforgettable discourse on Vietnam and international capitalism. *Weekend* did not just investigate French bourgeois society; it satirized it, assaulted it, predicting and demanding its demise. He was indisputably arrogant and successful, even if he had left a large number of supporters behind.

Having relentlessly riddled the modern world and its cinema during his second phase, Godard next turned the gun on himself. The autocriticism implied in a film like *Le Gai Savoir* is often overlooked because of the coincidence of its production with the great uprisings in 1968. Certainly this is a militant film, but it militates less against its culture than against the cinema that represents that culture, including the arrogant art films Godard had made his name with. Sitting against a black background, Jean-Pierre Léaud and Juliet Berto carry on a dialogue about language, image, and truth that in its minimal form criticizes spectacle and demands a cinema of personal and political honesty. While editing this film, Godard involved himself in the campaign to save Henri Langlois from being deposed as head of the Cinémathèque, an early skirmish in what became a cultural civil war. Godard was at the forefront of the manifestations closing the Cannes film festival, although his participation in the clashes in Paris in late May was token.

In any case, whether as part of the general upheaval of that year or because of a dead end he sensed in his earlier work, Godard vowed to rethink completely the cinema, to refuse, for example, conventional production and distribution mechanisms, all of which he felt were completely compromised. In other words, he took his own corpus as nothing more than the response of a bourgeois intellectual to bourgeois culture, a response that, while critical, helped both him and the system to prosper. With Jean-Pierre Gorin he formed the so-called Dziga Vertov group, named after the revolutionary Soviet documentarist and dedicated to the use of cinema for directly political aims. The austerity of *Le Gai Savoir* was already a start in this direction. Next came his *Sympathy for the Devil*, where he seemed to take pleasure in frustrating and alienating not only the Rolling Stones, its subject, but most of their fans. Godard seemed glad to have retreated out of the spotlight so that he and Gorin could devote themselves to inexpensive, but "politically correct" projects often shot on alternative formats (8mm, 16mm, and then video). *Wind from the East,* for example, was co-scripted by German revolutionary Daniel Cohn-Bendit. The last film of this phase, *Vladimir and Rosa,* found Godard pleased with its negligible reception, for this made him confident that he had avoided the temptations of entertainment and pleasure in his quest to attack the system completely from the outside.

Future critics may be able to make fine distinctions in his career, but Godard's last phase has generally been treated as beginning in 1972 with *Tout va bien,* a film that, rather like *Contempt,* stands apart because it employs spectacle and a big budget. Starring Jane Fonda and Yves Montand, this political fable was made with all the cinematic resources at Godard's command, a heroic, though failed attempt to address and convince a mass audience. After this, without giving up the Maoism that dominated his thinking, he begin again to explore the medium that had been his first love. Paradoxically, this exploration took him to television. In Switzerland, Sweden, and France he was given an opportunity to experiment with video. This work, examples of which have recently traveled across the United States, is provocative and inventive. Its consequences are only beginning to be felt in the world of video.

As for the cinema, Godard reconquered his lost audience to a large extent with *Everyman for Himself, Prénom Carmen, Passion, Hail Mary,* and *Detective.* While his political concerns are evident in the iconoclasm of the scripts and in the way he oversteps every norm, none of these films can be described as a tract. Each is interested in exploring the limits of cinematic representation, reflecting en route on music, painting, and acting, as well as on color, space, and editing. His films continue to be troubling, exasperating, and yet eagerly anticipated by almost everyone interested in the cinema. If his need to overturn everything around him has made many suspicious of his politics, allowing them to describe it as whimsical, irresponsible, and self-serving, these same qualities have served him well in the cinema, at least to the extent of allowing him to remain a crucial figure throughout the full thirty years he has been making films. This past year *Cahiers du Cinéma* published his immense collected writings. Godard has begun to summarize his life. It is important to remember that throughout all his phases, adhesions, and doubts, he considers himself a man of the cinema, in fact a man whose life and memory span the century of cinema. The history of the cinema is in his head, he claims. He is now seeing the doubtful future of this medium wind down, like himself, with the century.

Breathless

Breathless

One of the liberating features of *Breathless* was the break it made with standard production routines. No complete script was prepared before shooting. Godard improvised on ideas provided him in the treatment that Truffaut had given him (reprinted in this volume). Consequently there exists no authoritative shooting script for the film.

The following continuity was prepared from American release prints of the film. Several prints were consulted to insure against an aberrant copy. While no French copy was available for inspection, two published continuities were employed for verification. The first appeared in *L'Avant-Scène Cinéma* in March 1968. The second was a volume published by Ballard in 1974 in their screenplay series. This version contains photographs from every scene.

The French versions agree closely with each other and with the English subtitled prints. Three small departures are marked in the notes. These have to do with the opening title credit, with a missing fragment in the English print, and with what appears to be an alternative bit of dialogue in one scene. But overall, I am confident that the continuity presented here derives from the complete film.

Breathless poses several complex problems to verbal transcription. First, the dialogue. I have completely ignored the subtitles on the English-language prints. Although they are frequently excellent, there are enough compromises and shortenings as to make them unreliable as a guide to a full rendering of the verbal portion of the film. Michel speaks a highly colloquial French that frequently gives the American Patricia trouble. I have tried to reproduce the tone of his vocabulary, much of which belongs to the 1959 period and would sound dated to a French speaker today. As for Patricia, it should be recalled that she has an extremely noticeable accent, that she employs a brand of French that is quite often peculiar and sometimes completely ungrammatical. I have not indicated her lapses, although in one scene Michel himself corrects the grammar of another character. Finally, an effort has been made to include all speeches heard in the film, including those coming from sources such as the radio or passersby. This proved impossible in the confusing scene of Parvulesco's interview, in the movie theater Patricia runs through when chased by the detective, and at a few other points.

As for the rest of the sound track, while few sound effects are noted (the film being shot on location provides a normal ambient density), most music cues are provided. Godard punctuated his film with major changes in music, some themes associated with individual characters, some with situations, such as suspense or relaxation.

The visual track of *Breathless* is renowned for its improvised camerawork and its staccato cutting, both of which complicate any attempt at shot breakdown. I have chosen to number the shots according to new camera placements, listing as JUMP CUTS

changes that editing makes within a single camera setup, often within a single take. These JUMP CUTS are frequently subliminal; at other times they are most apparent. The term QUICK CUT is reserved for those changes of camera setup (and therefore of shot number) that shock the viewer because they break the visual flow, either through an abrupt change of screen direction and size, or through a change from static to moving figures, and so on. Two dissolves, one iris, and a couple of fades complete Godard's armory of punctuation. Unless otherwise noted, straight cuts link the numbered shots.

The camera distance is signaled with the traditional abbreviations (ELS, LS, MLS, MS, MCU, CU, and ECU). POV indicates a shot obviously taking on the optical sightline of a character. Camera movements are described in the normal manner, though the reader should beware that a number of scenes involve movements that are incredibly intricate, lasting several minutes. Here camera movement really becomes the subject of the shot. I have pointed to a couple of these in the description, but more often leave it to the reader's memory or imagination to evoke the film's visual prowess.

An effort was made to divide the overall film into a number of sequences based on location and time of day. This should enable the reader to locate a given scene readily. It also allows us to avoid repeating this information with every shot. Finally, *Breathless,* among other things, is a toybox of cultural artifacts. Names, objects, locations, signs, and so forth are woven through it and give it much of its density and interest. I have addressed this issue somewhat in my Introduction. Notes are appended to the continuity to specify further the significance of details that might be throwaways on the screen. Following *L'Avant-Scène Cinéma*'s lead, I have sought to distinguish the various parts of the city that this quintessentially Parisian film uses. One could obviously go further in this, noting the precise location of most of the scenes.

One of the innovations of *Breathless* was the suppression of credits. Only the title of the film and its dedication precede the first shot. In prints subtitled into English, even the film's dedication has been omitted. The listing of Cast and Credits, then, is placed here before the continuity as a convenience only.

Credits

Director
Jean-Luc Godard

Producer
Georges de Beauregard

Production Companies
Impéria Films, Société de Vouvelle de
Cinéma

Screenplay
Jean-Luc Godard, based on an
original treatment by François
Truffaut

Director of Photography
Raoul Coutard

Camera Operator
Claude Beausoleil

Assistant Director
Pierre Rissient

Music
Martial Solal; Clarinet Concerto, in
the key of A, K. 622, by Wolfgang
Amadeus Mozart

Sound
Jacques Maumont

Editor
Cécile Decugis

Assistant Editor
Lila Herman

Technical Advisor
Claude Chabrol

Locations
Marseille
Paris

Shooting Schedule
August 17–September 15, 1959

Process
Black and White; 1 × 1.33

Release Date
March 16, 1960 (Paris)
February 1961 (New York)

Length
89 minutes

Cast

Patricia Franchini
Jean Seberg

**Michel Poiccard, alias
Laszlo Kovacs**
Jean-Paul Belmondo

Inspector Vital
Daniel Boulanger

Antonio Berruti
Henri-Jacques Huet

Carl Zumbach
Roger Hanin

Van Doude
Van Doude

Liliane
Liliane Robin

Other inspector
Michel Favre

Parvulesco
Jean-Pierre Melville

Used car dealer
Claude Mansard

Informer
Jean-Luc Godard

Tolmatchoff
Richard Balducci

with brief appearances by André S. Labarthe, Jean Domarchi, Philippe de Broca, Jean Douchet, Jacques Siclier (all filmmakers or film critics)

The Continuity Script[1]

The Port at Marseille, exterior, day

1. MCU: *a newspaper,* Paris Flirt. *Michel Poiccard is holding it up, so as to conceal completely his face. The front page of the paper features a woman in a swimsuit.*[2]

   MICHEL (*voice-over*): All in all, I'm a dumb bastard. . . . All in all, if you've got to, you've got to. *Michel lowers the paper, revealing his face. He wears a fedora tipped low on his forehead. Taking the cigarette out of his mouth and looking around, he rubs his lips slowly with the side of his thumb.*

2. *As a foghorn sounds, cut to* CU *of a dark-haired woman about the same age as Michel. She looks around and nods affirmatively to him.*

3. MCU: *Michel looking left, puffing on his cigarette. He turns and looks toward the woman.*

4. *As in 2, again at the sound of a foghorn. The woman nods emphatically.*

5. MLS: *a middle-aged couple getting out of their big American car. The man sports a military cap.*

6. MCU: *Michel glancing quickly and stealthily to the right.*

7. MLS: *the woman walking behind the couple. She stops, turns, and then signals while the couple walks on. She continues to follow them.*

8. MS: *Michel deliberately folding his paper. He nods in reply to the signal and begins to walk left.*

9. LS: *pan follows an old fishing boat chugging into the harbor. The pan ends on the woman standing on the quay. She glances anxiously left.*

10. QUICK CUT *to* MS *of Michel at the couple's car with the hood up. Track in as he begins to hotwire it. The car starts; Michel slams the hood.*

11. *As in 9.* MLS *of woman, still on the quay, running toward Michel.*

12. MLS: *pan of Michel from inside the car as he opens the door and slides into* MS *behind the wheel. He rolls down the driver's window as the woman approaches and leans in.*

> WOMAN (*placing her arm on his shoulder*): Michel, take me along.
> MICHEL: What time is it?
> WOMAN: Ten to eleven.
> MICHEL: No. Ciao! (*He turns his head around to look out the rear window as he backs the car up, looking just off the camera axis as he does so.*) Now I'm off [*je fonce*] . . . Alphonse![3] *Violin music and dissolve.*

National Highway, exterior, day

13. POV *shot of a tree-lined rural highway from the car.*

> MICHEL (*off, singing to himself*): La, la, la, la . . . Buenas noches mi amor.

14. MS: *Michel from the rear seat of the car. He turns to look at a car following him.*

> MICHEL: He'll never pass me in that boat. *He turns his head forward again.*

15. POV *of car ahead.*

> MICHEL (*off, singing to himself, across shots 15–18, cut in quick succession*): Pa . . . Pa . . . Papapa . . . Pa . . . tricia! Patricia!

16. POV *of a BP oil truck to his right as he passes it.*

17. POV *of a car as he passes.*

18. POV *of an old truck as he speeds past it.*

19. CU: *Michel's right profile. His theme, first heard over the main title, returns.*

20. POV *of the road ahead of him as he passes another car.*

> MICHEL: First I'll pick up the dough . . . (*A car horn sounds.*) . . . then I ask Patricia—yes or no . . . and then—buenas noches, mi amor! (*He begins to sing again.*) Milan, Genoa, Rome. (*He speeds past all traffic.*)

21. QUICK CUT *on blaring horn to* LS *pan of his car speeding down the left-hand side of a two-lane road. The camera follows from the roadside until the car disappears in the distance.*

22. MCU: *Michel from the back.*

> MICHEL: It's pretty, the country. *He looks around, reaches down, and turns on the radio.*
> RADIO VOICE (*singing*): His life . . .

23. POV *from the passenger's seat of the passing countryside.*

> MICHEL (*off*): I love France!

24. MCU: *Michel's profile. He turns to his right to look straight at the camera and says:*

> MICHEL: If you don't like the sea . . . (*Glances back at the road, then back to the camera.*) . . . and you don't care for the mountains . . . (*Glances at the road, then back again.*) . . . and don't like the big city either . . . (*Glances at road and then into the camera.*) . . . go fuck yourself!

> JUMP CUT *and pan to* POV *of the roadside.*

> MICHEL (*off*): Aha! A couple of dolls hitchhiking.

Pan back to Michel.

25. QUICK CUT *to a* CU *profile.*

    MICHEL: Right, I'll stop and charge a kiss a mile.

26. POV *shot of the two hitchhikers, looking at Michel and the camera as his car approaches and slows.*

    MICHEL: The short one looks okay. She has cute thighs. Yes, but the other one! Oh no!

    POV *pan continues, now out the side and back windows as the car accelerates past them.*

27. CU: *Michel, looking out the back window.*

    MICHEL: Oh! Really, shit! They're both too ugly.

    The music stops. He reaches down and changes the station on the radio.

    RADIO VOICE (*singing*): . . . talking of love . . .

28. JUMP CUT *and pan to* MS *of his hand going into the glove compartment where he finds a gun. Michel's theme music plays.*

    MICHEL (*picking up the gun*): Hey, hey, hey!

29. JUMP CUT *to his hand with the gun on the steering wheel. He mimes shooting out the windshield, then at a car coming toward him. He makes his own sound effects for the gun.*

    MICHEL: Pow! Pow! Pow!

30. JUMP CUT *to a closer shot of Michel with gun.*

    MICHEL: Lovely sunshine.

    Pan with the gun as he points it out the window on the passenger side. He pretends to shoot.

31. LS: *the tops of the trees going by with the sunshine coming through them. Three genuine gunshots are heard.*

32. MS: *Michel's back, and the road ahead visible over his shoulder. A slow-moving truck is in the way and Michel's impatience grows as the car in front of him is afraid to pass it.*

    MICHEL (*talking to himself*): Women drivers, completely gutless! Why doesn't she pass? Oh, yes! Shit, road repairs. (*He drives past men working, seen out the driver's side.*) Never use the brakes. And like old man Bugatti said, cars are made to go, not to stop!

33. MS: *the car head-on from the grille down to the road as it pulls out. Whistles can be heard.*

34. LS: *from the passenger's seat, starting to pass the truck.*

    MICHEL: Shit, the cops!

35. LS: *pan left of his car speeding by the truck.*

36. *Quick pan left (matched to 35) from inside the car to rear window, showing the motorcycle cops chasing Michel.*

37. JUMP CUT. *Still seen from the rear window, the cops are farther back but now clear of traffic. Pan right to the front seat and Michel.*

38. LS: *very quick pan right from the roadside following Michel's car as it passes another car screen left to right, matching pan in 37.*

39. QUICK CUT *to* LS: *the cops in pursuit, speeding from right to left across the screen.*

40. QUICK CUT *to* LS: *pan of Michel pulling into a somewhat hidden area off the road. He stops the car, tires squealing.*

    MICHEL: Oh! My clip's broken off![4] *He leans out of the window on the passenger side to look back at the road.*[5]

41. LS: *a motorcycle cop driving by on the road.*

42. LS: *Michel putting the hood of the car up. He hides behind it, then peeks out at the road.*

    MICHEL: What a booby trap!

43. *The other motorcycle cop rides by.*

44. *As in 42. Michel fiddles with the wires he used earlier to start the car. He looks up.*

45. *As in 41. The cop is pulling into the secluded area.*

46. MLS: *Michel walks over to the open window on the passenger's side. He reaches into the glove compartment for the gun.*

    COP (*off*): Don't move or I'll drill you.

47. ECU: *pan starting with Michel's hat, down to his elbow, with a* JUMP CUT *to a pan along his forearm, wrist, and hand as he pulls back the hammer. Another* JUMP CUT *to an even bigger* ECU *of the gun's chamber, panning along its barrel. The gun fires.*

48. MLS: *the cop falling backward into the bushes.*

49. QUICK CUT *to* ELS: *Michel running across a field. Pan left with him as dramatic music swells. He gets smaller and smaller in the distance. Fade out.*

Center of Paris, exterior, day

50. *Fade in on Patricia's theme.* ELS *tracking left to right along the streets of Paris. The cathedral of Notre Dame comes into view as the camera continues across the bridge toward Saint Michel. Michel's musical theme returns.*

51. MS: *a car pulling into frame from right to left. Michel can be seen through the side window biting his thumb in the back seat. The car comes to a stop and he moves to climb out.*

52. MLS: *short track left to right with Michel as he enters a phone booth. He deposits a coin and then doesn't place the call. Frustrated in trying to retrieve his coin, he slams the side of the telephone. The music changes back to Patricia's theme.*

53. LS: *Michel buying a newspaper from a man on a bicycle. He begins to read it while walking left. The music, which has restored his theme, now stops.*

54. MLS: *Michel coming out of a hotel doorway to address a man on the sidewalk. A policeman passes between them.*

MICHEL: Miss Franchini's, what number is it?
MAN: She's not in.
MICHEL: She does live here?
MAN (*angrily*): I said that she's no longer in!

Hotel Lobby and Room, interior, day

55. QUICK CUT *to* MS: *Michel at the deserted reception desk in the hotel lobby. He leans back to make sure the man on the sidewalk isn't looking and reaches across the desk to grab a key. Jazz trumpet tune sounds as he tosses the key in his hand and moves off right.*

56. MS: *Michel coming out of a bathroom wiping his face with a towel. The camera pans when he walks right across the bed to an end table and opens a drawer. Magazines are all he finds.*

MICHEL: Girls—never any dough around!

Café, interior, day

57. MLS: *an average café. Michel walks in and up to the counter.*

MICHEL (*to the waitress behind the counter*): A beer.

He turns his back, leans on the counter, puts his hands in his pants pocket, and pulls out some coins.

58. CU: *Michel's outstretched palm holding the coins. With his other hand he counts how much he has.*

MICHEL (*off, to the waitress*): How much is a plate of ham and eggs?
WAITRESS (*off*): A hundred and eighty.[6]

He closes his fist around the money.

59. QUICK CUT *to* MS: *Michel turns back to the counter.*

MICHEL: Okay, then, I'll take one.
WAITRESS: Okay.

Michel takes a sip of his beer and then backs away from the counter.

MICHEL: I'm going for a paper. I'll be right back. *He turns around and runs out the door. The camera pans from inside the restaurant as he runs down the street.*

Courtyard of Apartment Building, exterior, day

60. *Match cut to* LS: *Michel running into the courtyard. He is carrying a newspaper. Piano arpeggios play in the background. He slows and begins to walk, opening the paper. Putting his foot on a railing by a stairway, he buffs his shoes with the paper, then quickly tosses it to the ground and jumps down the stairs to enter the building. A very brief tilt from the doorway up the side of the building.*

Small Apartment, interior, day

61. CU: *a young woman's face as she opens the door.*

YOUNG WOMAN: Oh, là, là! Michel!
MICHEL (*off*): Can I come in?
YOUNG WOMAN (*nodding her head*): Yes. *She opens the door to let him in.*

62. MLS: *Michel shutting, then leaning against the door of the apartment.*

MICHEL: How's it going, baby?
YOUNG WOMAN (*off*): No coat? *She crosses in front of the camera.*
MICHEL (*crossing his arms*): It's in my Alfa Romeo Super Sprint.

63. MLS: *the young woman rolling on her bed, searching for something under it.*

MICHEL (*off*): You want to eat breakfast at the Royale?
YOUNG WOMAN: No, I'm late. I've got to be on TV at 9:10.

64. MLS: *Michel leaning on his elbow against a shelf in her closet. He rifles through her small purse. Glancing up at her, he quickly hides the purse under something on the shelf and shuts the closet door.*

65. MS: *the woman now sitting up on the bed.*

YOUNG WOMAN (*looking down at her pajama top*): Now I've torn it! (*She pulls a radio from under the covers and puts it to her ear.*) Here it is. *She switches on American rock and roll, gets off the bed, and puts the radio on her dressing table. Camera pans right with her and past Michel who twirls in the center of the room and goes to sit on the off-screen bed. She ends up by the closet and combs her hair, looking back at him.*

YOUNG WOMAN: What's become of you? No one sees you anymore.
RADIO VOICE (*very loud*): It's two minutes past seven o'clock.

66. MS: *Michel sitting on the edge of the bed playing with a small stuffed monkey.*

MICHEL: Me? Nothing! Just traveling.
RADIO VOICE: Radio Luxembourg . . . (*The DJ's voice continues in the background throughout the rest of their conversation.*)

67. MLS: *the woman at the mirror. Michel gets up and walks over to join her in a two-shot.*

MICHEL: What's new in the neighborhood?
YOUNG WOMAN: I don't know.
MICHEL: You don't go out anymore?

JUMP CUT. *Michel is closer to her.*

YOUNG WOMAN: Sometimes! Sometimes to the clubs; but there's nothing there but jerks.

MICHEL (*playing with the stuffed monkey*): Still in the movies?

YOUNG WOMAN (*sitting down at the dressing table*): No, you have to sleep with too many guys. . . . Enrico, recall him?

MICHEL: Do I recall . . . do I remember Enrico? Sure![7]

YOUNG WOMAN (*looking at herself in the dressing table mirror*): I work with him on TV . . . script girl.

MICHEL (*opening her closet door and going through her clothes*): In Rome, in December, I was broke. I was assistant director in a film . . . at Cineccità!

YOUNG WOMAN: You? *She stands up and looks at him.*

MICHEL: Yes, me.

JUMP CUT. *Michel is now sitting on the dressing table, the young woman on his right. She bends down a little to talk to him.*

YOUNG WOMAN: You've never been a gigolo, by chance?

68. MS: *over the shoulder of Michel sitting at the dressing table looking at himself in a hand mirror so that the camera catches his reflection in the small mirror as well as in the large dressing table mirror.*

MICHEL: Why? *The phone rings.*

YOUNG WOMAN (*off*): Just like that.

MICHEL (*looking discriminatingly at himself in the larger mirror and hesitating*): Me, I'd like to, yes. *He begins to make faces in the mirror, which look like an attempt to stretch his face muscles or to convey various emotional extremes.*

YOUNG WOMAN (*off, into the telephone*): Oh, yes, call me in a few minutes.

Michel rubs his lip with his thumb in his characteristic manner, then spins when her reflection passes by him in the mirror.

69. MS: *Michel and the young woman. She is standing next to the closet with her back to him.*

MICHEL: And Gaby, is he back from Spain? *He tosses the monkey and catches it, while she looks at, and then puts back, a skirt in the closet.*

YOUNG WOMAN: He bought the Pergola.[8]
MICHEL: Oh, ya? (*He stands up.*) That's great.

JUMP CUT. *She is now at the wall mirror and he is next to the closet.*

MICHEL (*referring to the walls of her apartment*): It's stupid to paint everything black.
YOUNG WOMAN: No. *She walks over toward him and then over to a table on the opposite side of the room. The camera follows her, revealing on the wall the first five letters of the word "Pourquoi" [Why] spelled out with Gauloises cigarette packs.*
MICHEL (*off*): What's written there?
YOUNG WOMAN: Pourquoi. (*She takes a cigarette and lights it.*) But I never finished it. And now I'm smoking Luckies.

70. CU: *Michel sitting on the edge of the bed with a cigarette in his mouth looking down at something.*

71. ECU: *Michel's hands holding an ashtray with a picture of a 1904 Rolls Royce on it.*

MICHEL (*off*): You haven't got 5,000 francs to lend me till noon?[9]

72. CU: *Michel and young woman facing each other in profile; he is on the left. Their faces barely fit on the screen.*

YOUNG WOMAN: I might have guessed.

Music from the radio can be heard in the background. She looks down and then back up at him endearingly. He puts a lighted cigarette in his mouth.

YOUNG WOMAN: You're disgusting, Michel.[10]
MICHEL: No, really, I'll give it back by noon.

73. LS: *young woman walking to the closet to get her purse. Michel goes over to the dressing table and sits on it. She opens her purse and looks in.*

YOUNG WOMAN: Besides, I haven't got that much.

He takes out a cigarette and lights it. She pulls some money out of her purse and offers it to him.

YOUNG WOMAN: I have 500 francs if you want.
MICHEL: No, keep it.

She puts her purse away, then gets a dress off a hanger. They exchange positions as she sits down at the dressing table while he has walked over to the closet. He turns around and looks at her. Her back is to him. When she has her dress over her head, he opens up the closet door, gets her purse out, takes some money, puts it in his pocket, and puts the purse back.

MICHEL: Well then, you're not coming to breakfast at the Royale?
YOUNG WOMAN: No, I'm really late.
MICHEL: Fine. Arrivederci! *He kisses his hand and touches the top of her head with it, as he walks out.*
YOUNG WOMAN (*softly, her back still to him*): Ciao, Michel.

Fade out.

Large Travel Agency, interior, day

74. *Fade in.* MLS: *Michel leaning on a counter, facing the receptionist. He is wearing his fedora, a sportcoat, and a different tie.*

MICHEL: Is Mr. Tolmatchoff in?
RECEPTIONIST (*looking up at him*): Yes, he's here, but he isn't "in."

Avenue Champs Elysées, exterior, day

75. MLS: *Michel walks up to a young girl wearing a* New York Herald Tribune *T-shirt and taps her on the shoulder. She is selling newspapers.*

MICHEL: Is Patricia with you?
PAPERGIRL (*in English*): Yes. She's over there.

76. *Patricia's theme swells.* LS: *the Champs Elysées.*[11] *Patricia is walking away from the camera. She is wearing the same* New York Herald Tribune

*T-shirt as the other girl and carrying a few newspapers under her
left arm.*

PATRICIA (*calling out with a definite American accent*): New York Herald Tribune! New York Herald Tribune!

*The camera follows her at a low angle as she walks down the boulevard.
From off-screen right Michel walks toward her into the shot.*

MICHEL: Are you coming to Rome with me? (*Patricia stops and turns
   around toward him.*) Yes, it's foolish . . . I love you. (*He is now next to
   her. She smiles at him and they start to walk together down the street
   with their backs to the camera.*) I wanted to see you again to know if
   seeing you again would make me happy.
PATRICIA: Where are you back from? Monte Carlo?
MICHEL: No, from Marseille. . . . I stayed Saturday and Sunday at
   Monte Carlo. I had to see some guy. Monday, I tried to call you from
   Marseille.
PATRICIA: Monday and Sunday, I wasn't in Paris. (*Calling out in En-
   glish.*) New York Herald Tribune!
MICHEL: I'll buy one.
PATRICIA: How nice.

*They pause. He takes some money from his pocket and gives it to her. She
gives him a paper. Then they saunter aimlessly on.*

PATRICIA: What are you doing here, since you hate Paris?
MICHEL: I didn't say I hated it. I said I have a lot of enemies.
PATRICIA: Then you're in danger?
MICHEL: Yes, I'm in danger. You don't want to come to Rome with me,
   Patricia?
PATRICIA: To do what there?
MICHEL: We'll see.
PATRICIA: No, I have a lot to do in Paris, Michel.

They have stopped walking and are facing each other, looking about.

MICHEL: And now, what are you doing? You're going up or down "les
   Champs"?

PATRICIA: What are "les Champs"?

MICHEL: The Champs Elysées. . . . Me, I've got to go to Avenue George V.

PATRICIA: Okay, I'll let you go.

MICHEL: Come on, walk with me.

PATRICIA: Only to the corner.

They now have turned around and are walking the other way down the boulevard, this time toward the camera. Someone briefly walks in front of the camera. Michel lights a cigarette and opens the paper he has bought.

PATRICIA (*calling out in English*): *New York Herald Tribune!*

MICHEL: I'm giving it back. There's no horoscope. *He folds the paper up and gives it back to her.*

PATRICIA: What is "l'horoscope"?

MICHEL: The future. I'm interested in it. I want to know the future. Don't you?

PATRICIA: Oh, yes. (*Calling out in English.*) *New York Herald Tribune!*

The camera begins to track more slowly than they are walking, so that they are now close to it in MLS.

PATRICIA: What's wrong?

MICHEL: Nothing, just looking at you.

PATRICIA: Angry because I left without saying goodbye?

MICHEL: No, but I was angry because I was sad. (*A man passes by them, stops and shows something to Patricia. Michel shakes his head and the man leaves.*) It's nice, not to fall asleep, but to wake up next to a girl.

PATRICIA: Are you staying in Paris?

MICHEL: Yes, I've got to see a guy who owes me money. After that, I've got to see you. *He puts his arm around her. They are now close enough to the camera so that they are shot only from the waist up.*

PATRICIA (*taking his arm off her shoulder*): No, better not.

MICHEL: Why?

PATRICIA: There are lots of girls in Paris prettier than me.

MICHEL: No, it's funny, I've slept with two other girls since I saw you. It just didn't click [*gazait*] with them.

PATRICIA (*confused by the French word*): Didn't click?

MICHEL: They were very pretty, but it didn't click, it didn't work out, it was sad! Well, then, you want to come to Rome? Me, I'm sick of France.

PATRICIA: But I can't, Michel. I've got to register at the Sorbonne. Otherwise, my parents wouldn't send me any more money.

MICHEL: I'll give you some.

PATRICIA: But we only spent three nights together!

MICHEL: No, five . . . (*Pointing to her chest.*) Why don't you ever wear a bra?

PATRICIA: Listen, don't talk to me like that.

They have finally slowed to a stop.

MICHEL: I apologize. . . . What time is it? (*Lifting up her arm to look at her watch.*) See you again in a little bit?

PATRICIA: (*as he leaves from the foreground of frame right*): Not in a bit. This evening, yes?

MICHEL (*off, in English*): Yes. (*In French again.*) Where?

PATRICIA: Oh, here. *She turns and begins to walk away from the camera, but then suddenly spins around and runs toward Michel.*

77. *Blaring music. High crane shot over the boulevard. Patricia runs to Michel who is standing at the newsstand where he has bought still another paper. Michel's theme swells dramatically. She kisses him and runs off. The music changes to Patricia's theme. He walks away in the opposite direction and the camera briefly pans with him.*

78. CU: *a portion of a movie poster that in French reads: "To live dangerously until the end!" In the lower right-hand corner of the shot the names Jack Palance and Jeff Chandler are visible.*[21] *Michel's theme music returns very loud and brassy as the camera tilts quickly down to catch him walking into the shot from screen left. He continues down the street while the camera pans behind him in* LS. *Once again he is skimming a paper. A young girl runs in from the left to meet him at the corner.*

79. CU: *the young girl looking up at Michel. She holds up a copy of* Cahiers du Cinéma.[13]

GIRL: Mister, pardon me. You haven't anything against youth?
MICHEL (*off*): Sure, I prefer old people.

She reacts as if she has been insulted.

80. QUICK CUT *to* LS: *a car squealing around a corner. The car speeds to the left as the camera pans right.*

81. QUICK CUT *to* MS: *Michel glancing left. He takes the cigarette out of his mouth. He is wearing sunglasses.*

82. LS: *the car, which has now stopped. The driver gets out and looks at a man lying on the ground next to the car. He has apparently just been run down.*

83. LS: *four passersby, including Michel, who quickly approach the accident. A man reaches down to feel the victim's heart. Michel's theme music starts as he bends down and looks at the victim. He then gets up, makes the sign of the cross, and walks away, retrieving the folded paper from his coat pocket.*

84. CU: *a newspaper page featuring a picture of a motorcycle cop.* JUMP CUT *to headline: "Police have identified the interstate killer."*

Large Travel Agency, interior, day

85. MS: *Michel walks into the travel agency with the camera tracking him frontally.*[14] *He goes straight to the receptionist behind the counter.*

MICHEL (*to the receptionist*): Is Mr. Tolmatchoff in?
RECEPTIONIST (*pointing left*): He's at the air travel counter.

In a continuous movement, the camera smoothly circles to his left, so that as he heads in that direction it stays with him in MS. *He casually makes his way over to Tolmatchoff who is behind another counter. The shot widens by tracking behind Michel to include both the men.*

TOLMATCHOFF: Hello, amigo!
MICHEL: Hello, kid!
TOLMATCHOFF: It was you who stopped by at ten o'clock?
MICHEL: I came for my money, yes.
TOLMATCHOFF: It's there. Come on.

During the conversation the camera tracks from Michel's left to his right, reversing the movement it had made earlier at the receptionist's desk. Neither hesitating nor slowing, it seems to lead Michel back in the direction he had come. He is in MS *again when he meets Tolmatchoff who has come from behind the counter to join him. Together they wander down the lobby. Tolmatchoff has his arm around Michel, who is still wearing his sunglasses.*

TOLMATCHOFF: How's it going?
MICHEL: Got bored on the Riviera. I came to see a girl. And you?
TOLMATCHOFF: Me, I'm going to hit bottom here. I'm beginning to get rusty.
MICHEL: Better rusty than dusty.

They laugh. Tolmatchoff removes his arm from Michel's shoulder. As they enter a large room, the camera tracks left and pulls back to a MLS, *revealing a large counter with several clerks behind it.*

TOLMATCHOFF: It's there. (*To clerk.*) Do you have the envelope that I gave you? (*The clerk hands him an envelope.*) Tolmatchoff takes the envelope, turns from the counter, and walks toward Michel. As he does this the camera circles around until it is in front of them once more as *they walk back. He hands the envelope to Michel as they leave the room. Michel looks at the envelope, opens it, and takes out a check.*

MICHEL (*slamming the back of his hand against the check*): The idiot! Why did he mark it for deposit only?

TOLMATCHOFF (*pointing to the check*): I don't know. Endorse it. But not to me. (*Tolmatchoff takes the envelope and crunches it up while Michel folds up the check and puts it in his breast pocket.*) I bet everything at the track on Sunday. I've nothing left.

MICHEL: And your friend Bob Montagné, he could cash it for me.

TOLMATCHOFF: He's in the cooler, the idiot! [15]

MICHEL: No joke? There's Berruti too, but I don't trust him.

TOLMATCHOFF: I thought he was your pal.

MICHEL: Has he returned from Tunis?

TOLMATCHOFF: Yes, I saw him yesterday. He was hanging around Montparnasse last night.

A voice from off-screen calls for Tolmatchoff. He turns and leaves to go back to his desk, indicating that Michel should meet him there. The camera stays with Michel as at the beginning of this lengthy shot.

MICHEL (*to the off-screen Tolmatchoff as he approaches the counter*): What's his number, now?

Once more the camera circles left to right at Tolmatchoff's desk so that Tolmatchoff slides into view.

TOLMATCHOFF: Elysée 99–84.

MICHEL: Can I call him from here?

TOLMATCHOFF: Go ahead. (*Michel dials.*) Who's the girl you came to see?

MICHEL: A New Yorker.

TOLMATCHOFF: Pretty?

The camera has circled 180 degrees around Michel, stopping on his right side as he faces Tolmatchoff in a medium two-shot.

MICHEL: She's cute. I like her. (*Into the phone.*) Hello? Elysée 99–84?[16] May I speak with Antonio? Oh, well. No, no, I'll call back later. (*He hangs up the phone and starts to leave. Then, to Tolmatchoff.*) He isn't there. I'll find someone else. See you later, kid.
TOLMATCHOFF: Ciao, amigo!

Michel's theme starts. The camera tracks left again with Michel as he goes out the door. Through the large window next to the door two detectives can be seen walking up the sidewalk. They pass by Michel as they enter the building.

86. MLS: *the two detectives at the receptionist's desk. The older detective shows the receptionist his badge, while the younger one stands behind him. The older detective is Inspector Vital.*

VITAL: Inter-America Agency?
RECEPTIONIST: Yes, that's right.
VITAL: You have clients who have their mail sent here?
RECEPTIONIST: Yes.
VITAL: Do you know a certain Michel Poiccard?
RECEPTIONIST (*shaking her head*): No.
VITAL (*pulling his notes from his pocket*): He also calls himself Laszlo Kovacs.[17]
RECEPTIONIST (*pointing toward Tolmatchoff's desk*): Ask the gentleman over there. He's in charge of that.
VITAL: Fine.

He puts the piece of paper back in his pocket and slowly walks toward Tolmatchoff, his assistant following him. The camera tracks them both, retracing its path toward Tolmatchoff who is now standing in front of his desk looking over a model of an airplane. As the detectives reach Tolmatchoff, the camera circles to include all three men in the shot.

VITAL (*touching Tolmatchoff on the shoulder*): Well, well, Tolmatchoff.
TOLMATCHOFF (*nervously*): Hello, Inspector.
VITAL: Organizing guided tours now?
TOLMATCHOFF: As you see.

VITAL: Remember when you tipped us off to your friend Bob?
TOLMATCHOFF: So?
VITAL: Well, you're going to repeat that performance. Michel Poiccard
. . . (*He takes out his piece of paper and reads from it.*) . . . six foot
one, brown hair, former steward for Air France. He gets his mail deliv-
ered to the Inter-America Agency.
TOLMATCHOFF: I know him.
VITAL (*putting the piece of paper back in his pocket*): Has he been here
lately?
TOLMATCHOFF: No.

*The receptionist passes by in front of the camera and the camera pans left
with her.*

VITAL (*to the receptionist*): Miss!

*She stops, turns, and walks over to Vital. The camera tracks back with
her, lining up finally behind Vital and facing her.*

VITAL: Has anyone come to see Mr. Tolmatchoff lately?
RECEPTIONIST: Five minutes ago, a rather tall man . . .

*The younger detective cries out "My God!" and races for the door. Vital
follows him. The camera pans on Vital. As he reaches the doorway, he
stops and turns to Tolmatchoff.*

VITAL: Accessory to a murder. Know what that means?

*He hurries outside, turns left, and runs down the sidewalk. The camera
pans back to Tolmatchoff and the receptionist. She sticks her tongue out
at him. Michel's theme music begins.*

Metro Exit on the Champs Elysées, exterior, day [18]

87. MLS: *low angle from the bottom of Metro stairs. Michel is once again
reading a newspaper while he casually descends the stairs.*

88. LS: *the two detectives running to the top of the stairway. As they descend out of view, the camera pans across the Champs Elysées, holds on the Arc de Triomphe, then pans to the other side of the street and zooms in to reveal Michel coming up a stairway, calmly reading his newspaper. The music stops.*

89. MLS: *a movie poster for* The Harder They Fall *with a large picture of Humphrey Bogart on it. Michel walks up to the poster from the left and looks at it.*[19]

     MICHEL (*mumbling to himself*): Bogey. *He moves left a bit to peruse a display of stills from the film, staring at one picture in particular. He takes his cigarette out of his mouth.*

90. C U *of a Humphrey Bogart still.*

91. C U *of Michel with cigarette in his mouth. Deliberately he takes off his sunglasses and puffs his cigarette.*

92. *As in 90. Smoke from Michel's cigarette flows in front of the still.*

93. *As in 91. Michel exhales more smoke, then takes his thumb and rubs it from left to right over his upper lip. He puts his sunglasses back on.*

94. M S: *match cut of Michel walking off-screen right. The camera pans and holds on the theater door as he passes. In the glass door of the theater we can barely make out the distant figures of the two detectives who appear confused and frustrated. Iris out on the detectives.*

A Paris Street, exterior, day

95. *Black screen. Music comes up.*

> MICHEL: I saw a guy die today.
> PATRICIA: Why did he die?
> MICHEL: In an accident.
> PATRICIA: Are you inviting me to dinner?

Iris in. CU: *Michel's outstretched palm with a few coins in it. He closes his fist around them.*

> MICHEL (*in English*): Evidently.

96. *Slight tilt up to a* MS: *Michel and Patricia face each other while leaning on two parked cars on the street. Many people are walking by in the background. Michel places the coins back in his pocket and straightens his hat.*

> MICHEL: I've got to phone again. You'll wait?
> PATRICIA: Call from the restaurant.
> MICHEL: No.

They circle each other and switch places.

> MICHEL: I'll be back in a second. *He places his hat on her head and leaves. The music changes to Patricia's theme.*
> PATRICIA: The French always say a second when they mean five minutes. *She smiles and takes a puff of her cigarette.*

Quick fade out.

Café Washroom, interior, day

97. *Jazz music.* LS: *Michel coming down a cramped stairway and through a door to the men's lavatory of a café. It is fairly dark, yet he still wears his sunglasses.* JUMP CUT *inside the lavatory. He washes his hands at the sink and as he is drying them an older, middle-class man comes out of the*

stall at the far end of the room. Michel glances at him but then turns away as the man approaches the sink. Michel walks over to a urinal next to the sink and stands there. As the man washes his hands Michel peeks out from behind the wall dividing the urinal from the sink. When the man is finished washing his hands, Michel quickly comes up behind him and knocks him out with a blow to the back of his neck. He catches the man as he falls back and drags him back into a stall.[20] Michel disappears for a moment behind the door, then reappears backing out, locks the door, and tosses the key on the ground. He then walks toward the camera while going through the money he has just filched. He places the money in his breast pocket and opens the door. The music stops.

Paris Street, exterior, day

98. MS: *Patricia walking down the crowded sidewalk toward the camera. She is carrying a white string purse in her left hand; her coat is over her left arm. The camera pulls back with her as she walks towards it. From behind Michel runs up and walks beside her on her right. He is carrying a newspaper, still wearing his sunglasses and smoking a cigarette.*

MICHEL: Where to?
PATRICIA (*giving him his hat back*): Anywhere. To Saint Michel.
MICHEL: Sleep with me tonight?
PATRICIA: I don't know.
MICHEL: Why, you don't feel good with me? *He puts the paper under his arm and plays with his hat.*
PATRICIA: Yes, I do.
MICHEL (*taking the paper out from under his arm*): Just now, in *France-Soir,* I read a news item. (*Pointing to the paper.*) Seems a bus driver stole 5 million francs to seduce a girl. . . . He made out like he was a tycoon. (*A Jean Seberg look-alike walks by, glances at Patricia, and goes on.*) They went down to the coast together. In three days, they dropped the 5 million. But there, the guy didn't back down. He said to the girl: "It was stolen money. I'm a poor slob, but I love you." (*Patricia takes her sunglasses off and a man whom they pass on the sidewalk stares into the camera.*) But the best part is that the girl didn't drop him. She said: "I love you too." They went back to Paris together,

and were picked up burglarizing villas at Passy. She was keeping watch. It was nice of her.

SOLDIER (*to Michel*): Pardon me, have you got a light?

MICHEL (*handing him some money*): Listen, here's 100 sous. Go get yourself a box of matches.

The soldier leaves.

PATRICIA (*anxious, looking at her watch*): Lord, I forgot. I've got to go. I've got a date.

MICHEL: With whom?

A man passes in front of them, stares, then walks off-screen.

PATRICIA: A journalist, at the Champs Elysées, is taking me to a press conference.

They have stopped, but the camera keeps tracking back to LS *range.*

MICHEL: Where? Now?

They begin walking again.

PATRICIA: None of your business. You're . . . you're really a nuisance.

They stop once more.

MICHEL: You're not staying with me then?

They begin to walk.

PATRICIA: I'll see you tomorrow, I will!

MICHEL: Not tomorrow, tonight, Patricia.

PATRICIA: I told you that it's impossible.

MICHEL (*putting his arm around her shoulder*): Why are you so cruel?

PATRICIA: Where are some taxis? *Irritated with him, she reaches up and brushes his arm off her shoulder.*

MICHEL: Right, fine, my car is at the Opéra. You want a lift?
PATRICIA: Okay.

They both walk off-screen left.

A Car Driving along Paris Streets, exterior, day

99. MCU: *brief shot of Michel taken from the back seat of the car he is driving. Jazz theme with trumpet begins.*

PATRICIA (*off*): And your Ford, you don't have it anymore?
MICHEL: It's in the garage.

100. MCU: *the other side of the back seat behind Patricia's left shoulder.*

MICHEL (*off*): Right, then! I'm staying with you.
PATRICIA (*turning toward him*): Anyway, I've got a headache.
MICHEL (*off*): We won't sleep together, but I want to stay by your side.
PATRICIA: No, it's not that, Michel. (JUMP CUT. *She fixes her hair, staring at a compact mirror, then turns to look at Michel. Another* JUMP CUT *to a closer shot of Patricia.*) Why are you sad?
MICHEL (*off*): Because! I'm sad.
PATRICIA: It's stupid. Why are you sad? Is it better when I say "vous" or "tu"?[21]
MICHEL(*off*): The same. I can't do without you.
PATRICIA: You can very well.
MICHEL (*off*): But I don't want to. (*The music stops.*) Look, a Talbot, it's beautiful. 2.5 liters.

JUMP CUT. *Patricia's face is suddenly blanched by light.*

PATRICIA: You are a boy . . .
MICHEL (*off*): What?
PATRICIA: I don't know.
MICHEL (*off*): Patricia, look at me. I forbid you to see this guy. (JUMP CUT *cues Michel's theme music, but the camera remains fixed on Patricia.*) Alas! Alas! Alas! (JUMP CUT *shifts the lighting.*) Here I

am in love with a girl . . . (JUMP CUT. *This and the following cuts punctuate Michel's speech like a litany. Patricia's head remains in precisely the same spot while the lighting and background keep shifting.*) . . . who has a very pretty neck . . . (JUMP CUT.) . . . very pretty breasts . . . (JUMP CUT.) . . . a very pretty voice, very pretty wrists, a very pretty forehead, very . . . (JUMP CUT.) . . . pretty knees . . . (JUMP CUT.) . . . but who's a coward.
PATRICIA (*not reacting at all to Michel*): Here it is! Stop!

101. MS: *high angle of Michel from behind his right shoulder.*

MICHEL: Wait, I'll park . . .
PATRICIA (*off*): No, it's useless. *She leans over, comes into the frame, kisses him on the cheek, and gets out of the car.*
MICHEL: Fine, beat it! I don't want to see you again! (*He looks down at the wheel, then left where Patricia has exited.*) Beat it. (*He hesitates a few seconds, then speaks emphatically.*) Beat it, you bitch!

Café-Restaurant on the Champs Elysées, interior, day

102. LS: *Patricia walking past tables, pulling on her coat as she steps on an escalator. Her theme music with trilling flutes accompanies her to the second floor. The camera glides up, facing her in MLS.*

103. LS: *the second-floor interior. It is full of empty tables. The camera continues the smooth tracking motion of the previous shot, though now laterally as it follows Patricia to a table where a man stands by a very large window that looks out on the Champs Elysées. A waiter converges on the table at the same moment, removes a bottle, and leaves screen left.*

VAN DOUDE (*in English*): Hello.
PATRICIA (*in English*): I'm sorry, I'm awfully late.
VAN DOUDE (*in English*): Ah! That's all right. Sit down.

Patricia takes the seat opposite him at the table. They both sit as the camera continues tracking until it establishes a MLS on a diagonal from them.

104. *As Van Doude speaks we switch to a* MS *perpendicular to the table so that the Champs Elysées is visible out the window.*

> VAN DOUDE (*setting a book on the table in front of her, speaking in English*): This is the book I promised you.
> PATRICIA: Thanks.

The waiter comes in and serves Van Doude coffee, then leaves.

> VAN DOUDE (*to the waiter, in French*): Thanks. (*Then continuing the conversation with Patricia in English.*) I hope that nothing happens to you like the woman in the book.

PATRICIA (*taking her coat off, speaking in English*): Oh! What?
VAN DOUDE (*in English*): Read it, you'll see. Well, she doesn't want a child, but the operation is unsuccessful and she dies.[22]

105. MCU: *Patricia with her finger in her mouth, striking a pensive pose.*

VAN DOUDE (*off, now speaking in French*): I'd be so sad if that happened to you, Patricia.
PATRICIA (*in French also*): We'll see.
VAN DOUDE: What's wrong?
PATRICIA: If I could dig a hole in the ground so that no one would see me, I'd do it.

106. MLS: *from the diagonal angle as at the end of shot 103.*

VAN DOUDE: No, you have to do like elephants. When they are sad, or the opposite, they leave. (*In English.*) They vanish. *He takes a sip of coffee.*
PATRICIA (*in English*): I don't know if I'm unhappy because I'm not free, or if I'm not free because I'm unhappy.
VAN DOUDE (*in French*): I got involved in a story. I'm going to tell you about it. It'll change your mind.

107. MCU: *Patricia, chin in hand.*

VAN DOUDE (*off*): It was this girl that I've known for two years.

108. MCU: *Van Doude.*

VAN DOUDE: All of a sudden three days ago, I said to myself: "I'm going to tell her we should sleep together." *While he speaks the image pulses with minute* JUMP CUTS, *barely noticeable.*

109. *As in 107. Patricia shakes her head in disbelief.*

VAN DOUDE (*off*): I had never thought of it before.

110. *As in 108. He picks up a cigar. The minute cuts continue to make his face pulse while he speaks.*

> VAN DOUDE: So I made a date, for lunch together. (*He lights the cigar.*) I wanted to tell her "Look here, we're good friends. I think we should sleep together." Just to see, that's all. And I don't know, it flew right out of my head. *He laughs.*

111. *As in 107. She looks off into space, then smiles to herself.*

> VAN DOUDE (*off*): Suddenly, I thought again and, right away, I sent her a line saying that I had completely forgotten to tell her that we should sleep together!

112. *As in 108.*

> VAN DOUDE: Three hours later, I get a note from her saying: "What an amazing coincidence. I had exactly the same idea on my way to lunch." *He puffs and exhales, staring at Patricia.*
> PATRICIA (*off, in English*): What's happening to your projects for me to write?
> VAN DOUDE (*in English*): You go to Orly tomorrow to interview Parvulesco, you know, the novelist.[23]

113. *As in 104.*

> PATRICIA (*in English*): Marvelous! What time?
> VAN DOUDE (*in English*): Just come to the office early tomorrow afternoon. (*He gathers up his books and she puts on her coat while they both stand up. He helps her with her coat.*) Well, I'm going. . . . You're coming with me, of course.
> PATRICIA (*in English*): Of course. . . . (*Tries out a more tender intonation.*) Of course! . . . (*Then brightly.*) Of course!

114. MLS: *the two coming down a spiral staircase. The camera pans around from below the stairs. The couple heads left out the door, Van Doude putting his arm around Patricia. The camera tracks back smoothly away*

from them as they exit. From off-screen, coming up the spiral stairs from the basement, Michel enters wearing his hat and sunglasses. He casually glances toward Patricia and Van Doude and without expression continues around the stairs in the other direction. From his coat pocket he pulls out a cigarette and uses the one he is already smoking to light it. Nonchalantly he tosses the old one away, and walks, always in MS, *through the restaurant puffing on his cigarette. The sound of dishes and banging pans gives way to Michel's theme.*

Champs Elysées, exterior, late afternoon

115. LS: *pan of Patricia and Van Doude walking left to right down the busy sidewalk. He has his arm around her. The music continues from the previous scene.*

116. LS: *pan right to left of Patricia and Van Doude walking quickly across the street toward his white convertible.*

117. MLS: *Michel at a newsstand.*

> MICHEL: *France-Soir*—is this the latest edition?
> VENDOR (*off*): Yes, Mister! Eighth and latest.

Michel steps back, looks at the paper, then glances up toward the camera.

118. MCU: *Michel's* POV *of Van Doude and Patricia kissing in his car. His back is toward the camera but we see Patricia's face; her eyes are closed.*

119. *Reverse angle, a bit tighter, of them kissing. They stop.*

120. MCU: *Michel, almost head-on. He mutters something to himself, obviously jealous and irritated.*

121. LS: *pan of Patricia and Van Doude driving off-screen from left to right.*

122. LS: *the avenue des Champs Elysées. Many cars are driving from left to right. Van Doude's is not especially visible. Streetlights come on as dusk falls.*

123. ELS: *high-angle pan of the white convertible driving up the Champs Elysées toward the Arc de Triomphe. The place de l'Etoile sparkles with streetlights. Music ends with a fadeout to black.*

Paris, exterior, day

124. ELS: *the Eiffel Tower. Michel's theme accompanies a tracking shot from a car window. It becomes obscured by a row of trees.*

125. LS: *Patricia alighting from the back of a bus onto a busy street.*

126. MLS: *Patricia crossing the street, hopping playfully along the white markers of the crosswalk. The music stops.*

127. CU: *Patricia looking slightly off-camera to the left. She is looking at herself in a store window. She takes a deep breath and with a slight smile*

on her face adjusts her coat. A woman holding an infant walks behind her, out of focus. Patricia turns sideways.

128. MLS: *showing Patricia from behind, looking at herself in a mirror placed in the store window display. She pats her abdomen and pulls it in.* QUICK CUT.

Patricia's Hotel, interior, day

129. MLS: *Patricia enters her hotel through its French doors and walks behind the desk to get her key from her letterbox. When she doesn't find it, she checks the other pigeonholes with no luck. She turns to the clerk behind the desk.*

PATRICIA: My key isn't there?

The desk clerk looks up from the register and glances back at the letterboxes.

DESK CLERK: You must have left it in the door, I suppose.

Patricia crosses in front of the desk clerk and walks right to climb the stairs. The camera pans with her.

130. *Black screen for an instant. Then with the sound of a switch the light reveals a* MS *of Michel lying in bed. He flips over on his side, reaching under the pillow, perhaps for his gun. He is covered to the waist by the sheets but is nude from the waist up.*

PATRICIA (*off*): Oh, darn it!

Michel relaxes upon hearing her voice and turns over on his back. He smiles and rubs his hand over his hair.

MICHEL: Buongiorno!

Jazz piano music comes up.

131. LS: *Michel in bed and Patricia walking past him to her desk. This side view of the bed looks out past the open drapes to a bright sky, despite the darkness suggested by the opening of the scene.*

> PATRICIA: What are you doing here?
> MICHEL: There were no vacancies at the Claridge.[24] (*Patricia takes her coat off.*) So, then, I came here. I grabbed your key downstairs.

Patricia walks over and hangs her coat on a chair by the window.

> PATRICIA: You could have gone somewhere else, there's not just the Claridge.
> MICHEL: I always stay at the Claridge.
> PATRICIA: Oh, you! You're completely nuts.
> MICHEL: Go on! What's wrong? Don't make such a face.

The music stops. She walks around the bed toward the camera and out of frame. Michel grabs the bathrobe on the bed, puts it on, and gets up.

> PATRICIA (*as she is walking to the bathroom, in English*): Let me be alone. I can't ever be alone when I want to.
> MICHEL (*at the same time Patricia is talking*): Besides, that look doesn't suit you at all.

132. MCU: *Patricia in the bathroom looking in the mirror. The camera looks over her shoulder at her reflection. She is brushing her eyebrows, then her hair with a brush.*

> PATRICIA (*turning to look off-screen left at Michel*): What do you mean, "make a face"?

133. MCU: *Michel, leaning against the bathroom door.*

> MICHEL: It's like this. *He makes faces at her: opening his mouth wide, forming "ah"; then baring his teeth for "eeh"; and, last, scowling and circling his lips for "ooh."*

134. *As in 132. She repeats his faces, staring in the mirror; then turns back to him.*

PATRICIA: I think it suits me just fine.

135. QUICK CUT *to* MS: *pan left of Patricia. She walks by Michel to get a towel.*

MICHEL: You're nuttier than I am.

136. MCU: *Michel looking in the mirror. He rubs his thumb over his upper lip.*

MICHEL (*speaking to his image in the mirror while jazz music comes up again*): That pisses me off. I always go for girls who aren't made for me.[25] (*He turns quickly to yell at her.*) Patricia!

137. MLS: *Patricia is standing at the opposite end of the bedroom by the window. Michel walks across the bed instead of around it toward her. She appears sad.*

MICHEL: You saw me following you last night? Come on, answer. Answer! What's wrong with you?

They sit together on the edge of the bed with their backs to the camera. The music stops.

PATRICIA: Let me alone. I'm thinking.
MICHEL: What about?
PATRICIA: The thing is that I don't even know! *She stretches her arms up.*
MICHEL (*gently rubbing the back of her head*): I do.
PATRICIA (*pulling away*): No, nobody knows.
MICHEL (*leaning back on the bed*): You're thinking about last night. Why, yes, you are!
PATRICIA (*leaning toward him*): Last night, I was furious. Now, I don't know, it doesn't matter. (*As she falls flat on her side on the bed.*) No, I'm thinking about nothing.

138. CU: *Patricia lying on her stomach with her face buried in the bed.*

PATRICIA (*leaning up and supporting her chin with her hand*): I'd like to think of something . . . (*She looks back at Michel.*) . . . but I can't.

139. MS: *Michel from the foot of the bed.*

MICHEL (*sitting up*): Well, me, I'm tired. Very tired, and I'm going back to bed.

Patricia crosses over to the other side of Michel as he is getting under the covers. She sits on the bed, leans on a teddy bear, and looks at him.

MICHEL: Why are you looking at me?

PATRICIA: Because I'm looking at you.

MICHEL: You should have stayed with me yesterday.

PATRICIA: I couldn't.

MICHEL: Yes, you could have. You just had to tell the guy you couldn't see him.

PATRICIA: But I had to see him. He's going to have me writing articles. It's very important for me, Michel.

MICHEL: No, what's important is going to Rome with me.

PATRICIA (*staring out the window, screen right*): Maybe, I don't know.

MICHEL: You sleep with him?

PATRICIA: No.

MICHEL (*pulling the covers over his head as the music comes in*): Bet you did!

PATRICIA: No, Michel. You know, he's very nice . . . (*Leaning on her bear.*) . . . He says one day we'll make love, but not right now.

MICHEL (*pulling the covers down from his head*): What does he know about it! He doesn't even know me.

PATRICIA: Not you. Him and me. (*Michel covers his head up again.*) We went to Montparnasse. For a drink.

MICHEL (*pulling the covers down*): To Montparnasse? I was there too! What time?

The music stops.

PATRICIA: I don't know. We didn't stay long. . . . Why did you come here, Michel?

MICHEL (*pulling the covers back over his head*): Me? Because I feel like sleeping with you again.

PATRICIA: I don't find that a reason.

MICHEL: Evidently it is. It means that I love you.

PATRICIA (*lifting her head off the bear*): And me, I don't know yet if I love you.

MICHEL (*flinging the sheet off, he sits up and moves closer to her*): When will you know?

PATRICIA: Soon.

MICHEL: What does that mean: soon? In a month, in a year?[26] *Michel grabs a magazine from the bed and flips through it.*

PATRICIA: Soon means soon.

140. CU: *the pages of the magazine Michel is looking at. It contains pictures of nude women in various poses.*

MICHEL (*off, declaiming*): Women never want to do in eight seconds . . . (JUMP CUT *as the pages of the magazine flip by.*) . . . what they are willing to do eight days later. . . . (*Another* JUMP CUT.) It's all the same . . . (JUMP CUT.) . . . eight seconds or eight days, or why not then eight centuries?

141. MS: *the two on the bed. Patricia is kneeling.*

PATRICIA: No, eight days is plenty.

MICHEL (*throwing the magazine down on the bed*): "Yes." "No." With women it's always halfway. You know, it really wears me out. (*Michel grabs Patricia's drawstring purse from the desk and starts to go through it.*) Why don't you want to sleep with me again?

PATRICIA: Because I'd like to know. There's something about you . . . (*Michel snaps the purse shut and throws it back on the desk.*) . . . that I like but I don't know what. I wish we were Romeo and Juliet.

142. *Cut away to a* CU *of a small reproduction of a Picasso on the wall.*[27]

MICHEL (*off*): Oh, là, là. What a girlish idea.

143. *As in 141.*

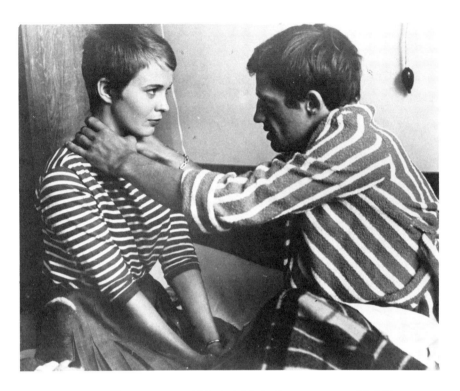

PATRICIA: You see, you said last night, in the car, you couldn't live
without me. But you can. (*Michel looks annoyed with her. He rubs and
pats his stomach.*) Romeo couldn't live without Juliet, but you can,
you can.
MICHEL (*closing his bathrobe around him*): No, I can't live without you.
PATRICIA (*imitating Michel's previous tone*): Oh, là, là! Now that's just
a boyish idea.
MICHEL: Smile at me!

Patricia shakes her head no.

MICHEL (*pointing his finger at her*): Fine, I'll count to eight . . . if by
eight you haven't smiled at me, I'll strangle you.

144. CU: *Patricia with Michel's hands around her neck. She straightens her hair and prepares herself for the countdown. Michel's theme comes in.*

MICHEL: . . . two . . . three . . . four-five-six . . . seven . . . seven and a half . . . seven and three-fourths . . . (*Patricia looks determined not to smile and not at all frightened.*) You're such a coward, I'll bet you smile.

Patricia smiles at him and laughs.

145. MS: *the couple from the foot of the bed, their hands entwined. Patricia extricates herself.*

PATRICIA: I don't feel like playing anymore today.

She gets up and, walking on the bed, crosses in front of Michel. As she hops off, Michel reaches up and flips her skirt up. She slaps him in the face and walks off, leaving him alone in MS.

MICHEL (*rubbing his face where she slapped him*): You're a coward. It's too bad.
PATRICIA (*off*): Why do you say that to me?
MICHEL (*taking his bathrobe off*): You bother me. I don't know.
PATRICIA (*off*): You, too.
MICHEL: No, me, I'm not a coward.
PATRICIA (*off*): How can you know that I'm afraid?

146. MCU: *Patricia standing by the window in silhouette. She is trying to strike a match to light the cigarette in her mouth.*

MICHEL (*suddenly off-screen, his voice cues the cut to 146*): As soon as a girl says everything is just fine and she can't manage to light her cigarette, well, it's that she's scared of something. I don't know what, but she's afraid.

Patricia lights the cigarette.

147. MLS: *a higher angle on Michel and Patricia. He is leaning against the headboard as before, she is sitting facing him. Behind her is the window, putting them both slightly in silhouette.*

PATRICIA (*offering a box to Michel*): Have a cigarette.
MICHEL: No, shit, not Chesterfields! Get my coat. Mine are in the pocket. *He points to his coat which is lying at the foot of the bed. She goes over to get it and holds it up for him to see.*
PATRICIA: This one?
MICHEL (*impatiently*): Give!

She tosses the coat over him. Michel goes through his pockets looking for his cigarettes. Patricia walks over to the side of the bed, kneels down, and picks his passport off of the floor.

PATRICIA (*opening the passport*): Is this your passport?
MICHEL: No, it's my brother's. Mine's in the car.
PATRICIA: But the name Kovacs is written on it.
MICHEL: Oh, yes, it's not my real brother. When he was born, Mama was already divorced. (*He reaches over and grabs the passport from her.*) Come on, give! (*He lights his cigarette.*) You see, I'm not afraid.
PATRICIA: I never said you were.
MICHEL: You did so, Joe! [*Tu parles, Charles!*]
PATRICIA: No.
MICHEL: You wanted to say it, and now you're sore and can't anymore.
PATRICIA: Now, I'm not talking to you anymore. *She gets up off the bed, walks to the window, and stands looking out to the street below with her back to Michel.*
MICHEL (*picking up the teddy bear and looking at it*): Do you think about death sometimes? Me, I never stop thinking about it. *He tosses the teddy bear away.*
PATRICIA (*turning around from the window to face him*): Michel?
MICHEL: What?
PATRICIA: Say something nice to me.
MICHEL: What?
PATRICIA: I don't know.
MICHEL: Well, neither do I.

PATRICIA (*picking up the ashtray with the Rolls Royce embossed on it that he took from the young woman's apartment in shot 71*): I like your ashtray. *She walks over to the side of the bed and hands it to him.*

MICHEL (*taking it from her*): A BM6. My grandfather had a Rolls. Great car! We never lifted the hood in fifteen years.

Michel grabs Patricia by the waist and pulls her toward him. She frees herself and walks over to the wall facing the bed, the camera panning with her. She reaches beside her for a loosely rolled up poster and holds it flat against the wall to see what it looks like.

PATRICIA: Have you seen my new poster?

MICHEL (*off*): Patricia, come here!

PATRICIA (*to herself in English*): No.

MICHEL: But yes, God! What!

PATRICIA: Here, it doesn't go well at all. Where can I put it? *Patricia takes the poster to the opposite wall, above the desk. The camera pans left with her.*

MICHEL: Why did you slap me when I looked at your legs? *He rubs his hands on her legs as she is putting the poster on the wall.*

PATRICIA: It wasn't my legs.

MICHEL: It's exactly the same.

Patricia rolls the poster up while Michel flips through a newspaper.

PATRICIA: The French always say that things are the same when they aren't at all.

MICHEL: I've found something nice to say, Patricia. *He puts down the paper.*

PATRICIA (*turning toward Michel*): What?

MICHEL: I want to sleep with you because you're beautiful.

PATRICIA (*shyly*): No, I'm not.

MICHEL: Then, because you're ugly.

PATRICIA: It's the same?

Going around the bed, she walks off-screen in MLS. He follows her with his eyes. She reenters the frame brushing past and blocking the camera

*lens. She disappears to the left of the camera, which is stable throughout
the shot.*

MICHEL (*taking the cigarette out of his mouth*): Sure, my little girl, it's
the same.

148. MCU: *Patricia turning to answer him. She stands by the bathroom door
with the poster rolled up in her hands.*

PATRICIA: You're a liar, Michel.

149. CU: *Michel's face, then tilting quickly up the wall as he replies.*

MICHEL: It would be stupid to lie. (*The tilt rests on a Picasso print directly above Michel.*[28] *He continues, off.*) It's like poker, might as well
tell the truth. The others still think you're bluffing. (*Tilt back down to
Michel.*) And that way you win. (*Looking at Patricia.*) What is it?

150. *As in 148. Patricia's theme comes in. She is rubbing her eyes and nose
as if she has been crying.*

PATRICIA: I'm going to look at you until you stop looking at me.
MICHEL (*off*): Me, too.

151. CU: *Michel from Patricia's* POV. *He rubs his upper lip with his thumb.*

152. *As in 150. She rolls the poster tighter, holds it to her eye and looks
through it at Michel.*

153. POV *from Patricia's eye, looking through the rolled-up poster. Michel
poses with his hand clutching a cigarette resting under his chin. Zoom in
to an intense* ECU *as Patricia's theme on the piano is transformed into
Michel's.*[29]

154. *Reverse zoom out of their lips parting after a tender kiss. The zoom continues to a* MCU *showing them together framed by the bathroom doorway.
The piano music trills softly to a halt.*

155. JUMP CUT *to* MS: *Michel leans back on one edge of the doorway while putting his hand on the other edge. Patricia is almost under his arm.*

PATRICIA: I'm going to put my poster in the bathroom.

Camera pans as she walks over to a bathroom wall. Michel shifts position to stand on her right. Now he leans with his right hand on the wall.

MICHEL: Can I use the phone?
PATRICIA: Yes. (*As she tacks up the poster, he rubs her derrière. The camera tilts down to catch him at it.*) There. Not bad, eh?
MICHEL (*ambiguous as to his referent*): Yes, very nice!

The camera tilts back up to the poster reproduction of a young girl in profile.[30]

PATRICIA: You like this poster?
MICHEL (*taking the cigarette out of his mouth*): Not bad.
PATRICIA: Renoir was a very great painter.
MICHEL (*irritated*): I said: not bad!

Patricia suddenly stops looking at the picture and turns to put her head against it, facing out toward Michel. She is whimsically posing to the left of the painted girl, who seems to be looking at her.

PATRICIA: Do you think she is prettier than I am?

156. MCU: *Patricia and the painted girl, carefully matching profiles, facing each other. She holds this pose briefly, then pulls away from the poster to look off-screen at Michel.*

MICHEL (*off*): As soon as you're afraid or you're surprised, both at the same time, you have a funny reflection in your eyes.
PATRICIA (*turning her head left where Michel has presumably moved*): And then?
MICHEL (*off*): I'd like to sleep with you again . . .

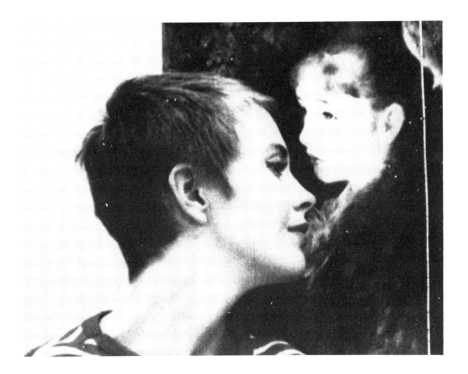

157. MCU: *reverse angle of Michel washing his face at the sink, while Patricia enters from behind the camera.*

   MICHEL: . . . because of that reflection.

   She leaves the frame screen right while he keeps rubbing his face with a washcloth. When she is off-screen, she addresses him.

   PATRICIA (*off*): Michel.

158. MS: *Patricia washing her feet at the bidet, which is just under the Renoir poster.*

159. *As in 157. Michel continues washing. They speak at the same moment.*

PATRICIA (*quietly repeats, off*): Michel.
MICHEL: Can I piss in the sink?

160. *As in 158.*

PATRICIA: Guess what I'm going to tell you.
MICHEL (*off*): No idea.
PATRICIA: I'm pregnant, Michel.
MICHEL: Eh?
PATRICIA: You heard very well.
MICHEL (*off*): Go on! By who? By me?
PATRICIA: Yes, I think so.
MICHEL (*off*): You saw a doctor?
PATRICIA: I went yesterday morning. (*She begins to dry her feet.*) He
   told me to come back on Thursday for the results.
MICHEL (*angrily, off*): You could have been more careful.

Patricia looks at him, shocked and hurt.

161. MLS: *high angle on Michel coming out of the bathroom. He is wearing
   only his shorts. He steps off-screen right, starting to climb across the
   bed. Patricia follows him out of the bathroom a second later. She stops,
   puts her foot on the bed, and continues drying it with a towel. Then she
   walks across the bed to the window, the camera panning with her. She
   passes in front of Michel who is sitting on the bed with the telephone.*

MICHEL (*into the telephone*): Hello, I want Elysée 99–84 . . . 99–84.

*The camera pans back with Patricia as she leaves the window and walks
back across the bed. The camera now holds on Michel sitting on the bed
and talking into the phone.*[31]

MICHEL: Is Antonio there? You don't know if he's coming back? I'll call
   back later. Michel Poiccard. (*He hangs up the phone, then picks it up
   again.*) Elysée 25–32. (*To Patricia, who has walked into the shot from
   the left, crossing the bed to stand in front of her desk. She fishes for*

a record album.) I phoned the guy who owes me money. (*Into the phone.*) Mr. Tolmatchoff, please.

Patricia, with her back to the camera, picks a record out and walks screen left over the bed once more to the record player atop the closet.

MICHEL (*into the phone, off*): Hey, kid! Tell me, I can't manage to find Berruti. . . . He wasn't there. . . . I wandered Montparnasse all night. (*Patricia puts on an album of piano music—Chopin. The camera pans quickly to the right over to Michel.*) The police?! Thanks. Ciao, kid! (*Michel hangs up the phone, stands up on the bed, and walks on it toward the bathroom. The camera pans with him. When he reaches the edge of the bed he slips off.*) Oh shit!

162. MCU: *Patricia in the bathroom in front of the mirror. She is wearing a different top.*

PATRICIA (*turning to her left toward Michel*): What is it?
MICHEL (*coming into the shot from the left*): I slipped. (*He takes his cigarette out of his mouth.*) Reminds me of the one about the condemned man. You know it?
PATRICIA (*putting on perfume*): No.
MICHEL: A man condemned to death is mounting the scaffold. He slips on a step and says, "Well, I am unlucky!" [32] (*JUMP CUT as Michel cups her face in his hands and brings it close to him. He stares at her for a moment, then lets go. Slight pan right follows her. Michel's face slips out of frame.*) At times, you have the face of a Martian.
PATRICIA (*brushing her hair*): Yes, that's because I'm on the moon.

JUMP CUT minutely reframes so that Michel is in the shot again with Patricia.

MICHEL: What an idea, my God . . . having a baby!
PATRICIA: But it's not certain, Michel. I only want to know what you'll say.

JUMP CUT. Michel's hand pulls at her shoulder strap.

MICHEL: Why don't you get naked?
PATRICIA: What's the use?
MICHEL: You Americans are dumb.
PATRICIA: I don't see why.

In the background, besides the Chopin, there is the sound of a siren that almost drowns Michel out.

MICHEL: Yes. The proof is that you admire Lafayette and Maurice Chevalier, when they're the dumbest of all Frenchmen. I'm going to the phone. (*He leaves Patricia, who is clipping a few strands of hair, and speaks into the phone, off.*) Belle-Epine 35–26. Patricia, come here.

Patricia utterly ignores him. She brushes her hair, then counts to nine on her fingers, covers her eyes with her hands for a moment, uncovers them, and stares at herself in the mirror. While she is doing this, Michel talks on the phone.

MICHEL (*into the phone*): Hello! Mr. Loursat? He'll be there this afternoon? Tell him I'll come to see him. I'm calling on behalf of Toni . . . from Marseille. . . . Laszlo Kovacs. . . . I'm bringing him an American.
PATRICIA (*saluting to herself in the mirror. In English*): Dismissed. (*She turns left, military fashion, then speaks to Michel.*) An American?

163. MS *of Michel on the bed talking on the telephone.*

MICHEL (*into the phone*): Laszlo Kovacs . . . (*He hangs up and crawls into bed. To Patricia.*) No, not you! An American one. An American car!

164. MCU: *Patricia looking down at Michel. She is at the record player and has just taken the record off.*

165. JUMP CUT *to* MS: *Patricia kneeling beside Michel who lies in bed smoking. She looks at the record album.*

MICHEL: I can't find the guy who owes me the dough. It's the shits!

Patricia is more interested in her record and ignores Michel.

PATRICIA: Do you like records or the radio better?
MICHEL: Shut up! I'm thinking!

Patricia gets up from the bed and walks across Michel's body, jumping off the bed and out of frame. As she does so, Michel pulls at her shorts. Patricia leans back into the shot and slaps him across the face. Michel takes a puff of his cigarette, turns his head away, then looks toward her once more.

166. MCU: *Patricia standing by the window. She looks at a record and flips it over.*

PATRICIA (*to herself*): Bach! I know them all by heart. *She puts the record albums down.*
MICHEL (*off*): How old are you?
PATRICIA (*turning as if she doesn't hear him; to herself*): I'm going to turn on the radio. (*Answering Michel and cueing the next cut.*) Twenty.

167. QUICK CUT *to* CU: *Patricia leaning down toward Michel. Pan down Patricia's arm to a* CU *of Michel lying in bed smoking. She is out of frame. Jazz piano music starts up.*

MICHEL (*to Patricia, who is now sitting on the bed near his head*): You don't look it.
PATRICIA (*off*): Why don't you like music?
MICHEL: That depends, yes! (*As he answers her the camera pans up to* MCU *of Patricia, leaving him just out of frame. His hand can be seen tugging at her shirt.*) Come on, Patricia! Come to Italy. (*With an Italian accent.*) Italia! (*Patricia smiles down at him.*) Where do they get you, your classes at the Sorbonne? Really!
PATRICIA: You, didn't you ever take exams?

The camera pans down again to a CU *of Michel and the music stops.*

MICHEL: Yes. Only the first "bac." [33] After that, I dropped out [*plaqué*].
PATRICIA (*not comprehending the French term, off*): What is "plaqué"?

MICHEL: I did something else.
PATRICIA (*off*): What?
MICHEL: I sold cars.
PATRICIA (*reaching down to rub something from under his eye, off*):
   Here? In Paris?
MICHEL: No. (*The camera pans up to Patricia.*) In New York, did you
   sleep with guys often?
PATRICIA: Not that often.
MICHEL (*off*): How many times?

*She thinks about it for a moment, then holds up seven fingers. The piano
music starts again.*

PATRICIA: And you?
MICHEL: Me? (*The camera pans down to Michel as he gestures five
   times with his open hand.*) Not that many either.
PATRICIA (*off*): You know where I'd like to live? In Mexico. Everyone

told me it's beautiful. When I was little, my father always told me, "We're going next Saturday." But he always forgot.

During her speech the camera pans back up to Patricia. The music stops. Michel sits up and gets closer to Patricia so that he is in the shot.

MICHEL: No, Mexico, I'm wary. I'm sure that it's not so beautiful. (*The camera pans slightly to a* CU *of Michel.*) People are such liars. (*He takes the cigarette out of his mouth.*) It's like Stockholm. Everyone who comes back says: "Swedish girls are great. I had three of them every day. You should go!" Me, I went, and it's a lie. (*Piano music.*) First, Swedish girls are . . . (*He puts the cigarette back in his mouth.*) . . . very different from what they are in Paris . . . and then, they are, in general, just as ugly as Parisian girls.

PATRICIA (*off*): But no, Swedish girls are very pretty.

Slight pan right to frame Patricia in MCU *just after her speech.*

MICHEL (*off*): No, no, a legend! One or two, yes, right.

The music stops and Patricia looks down at Michel.

MICHEL (*off*): Exactly like in Paris or London, but not all of them. No, the only towns where the girls one meets in the street are good-looking, not sublime, okay, but like you, charming, girls you can rate . . . I don't know . . . fifteen out of twenty, because they've all got something . . . (*Patricia looks at him and carefully listens, off-screen.*) . . . it's not Rome, not Paris, not Rio. (*The camera pans over to Michel as a very loud siren drowns him out.*) It's Lausanne and Geneva.[34] (*He leans over to her and kisses her shoulder. The jazz piano comes in.*) You too, tell me something nice.

PATRICIA: And me too, I don't know what. *She turns away from him and leans back on the headboard. He slides out of frame right. Patricia's theme comes in. His hand enters the frame touching her shoulder. He begins to slide it down her arm, which is encircling her bent legs.*

MICHEL (*off*): If you were with another guy, would you let him caress you? *His hand is touching her knees now.*

The camera pans back up to Patricia's face.

PATRICIA: You know, you said I was afraid, Michel. . . . (*Staring off toward the window.*) It's true: I'm afraid because I want you to love me. . . . And then, I don't know, at the same time, I want you not to love me anymore. I'm very independent, you know.

Michel moves into this CU, *and turns her head toward him by the chin.*

MICHEL: And so what? Me, I love you, and not like you believe.
PATRICIA (*freeing her chin by turning her head away*): How?
MICHEL: Not like you believe.
PATRICIA: You don't know what I believe.
MICHEL: Yes, I do.
PATRICIA: You don't know what I think.

Michel sits back, moving out of the shot, except for his hand which continues to touch her hair and neck.

MICHEL: Yes, I do.
PATRICIA (*sadly, looking down*): No, it's impossible. (*She glances up with a new thought.*) I want to know what's behind your face. (*The camera pans over to Michel, who has a surprised look on his face. She goes on, off.*) I've watched it for ten minutes and I see nothing . . . nothing . . . nothing! (*Michel rubs his upper lip with his thumb as his theme music comes in.*) I'm not sad, but I'm afraid.
MICHEL (*as the camera pans over to Patricia and he strokes her face*): Sweet, gentle Patricia.
PATRICIA: Oh, no.

168. ECU: *Patricia looking at Michel. The music stops. She lights a cigarette and smiles at Michel.*

MICHEL (*off*): All right. Cruel, stupid . . . heartless, pitiful, cowardly, hateful . . .
PATRICIA (*smiling in a sly manner and puffing on a cigarette*): Yes, yes.
MICHEL (*off*): You don't even know how to put on lipstick. It's amazing. Suddenly, I find you ugly.

Patricia turns away from him.

169. QUICK CUT *to* CU: *Patricia from the front.*

PATRICIA (*turning left toward Michel, then defiantly away*): Say what
  you want, it's all the same to me. I'm putting it all in my book.
MICHEL (*coming in closer so that both of their faces are contained in
  the* CU *shot*): What book?
PATRICIA: I'm writing a novel.
MICHEL: You?
PATRICIA: Why not me?

*He tosses his cigarette out, and begins to rub her shoulder then tries to
slide the shoulder of her sleeveless top down.*

PATRICIA: What are you doing?
MICHEL: Taking off your shirt.

The camera pans to Patricia so that Michel is out of the shot.

PATRICIA: Not now, Michel.
MICHEL (*off*): Oh, you're annoying. Why not, anyway?
PATRICIA (*picking up a book and looking at the cover*): Do you know
  William Faulkner?

*Michel leans in closer to her so that he is in the shot. He puts his head
just over her right shoulder.*

MICHEL: No, who is it? You've slept with him?
PATRICIA (*looking up at him*): Of course not, darling.
MICHEL: Then to hell with him. Take off your shirt.
PATRICIA (*pulling away from him*): He's a novelist that I like. . . .
  You've read *The Wild Palms*?[35] *She holds the book up to him so that he
  can see the cover.*
MICHEL: Take your jersey off.
PATRICIA: Listen, the last sentence is beautiful. (*She reads in English.
  Michel looks at her as she reads.*) "Between grief and nothing I will
  take grief." (*She turns to him and repeats the line in French.*) "Be-

tween grief and nothingness, I choose grief." And you, what would you choose?

The music stops. Michel leans back on the bed, away from her. The camera pans with him so that Patricia is off-screen.

MICHEL: Show me your toes. (*He leans on his elbow.*) A woman's toes are most important. Don't laugh.
PATRICIA (*off*): What would you choose?
MICHEL: Grief is idiotic; I'd choose nothingness. (*Patricia leans in front of Michel to put the book back on the desk.*) It's not any better, but grief, it's a compromise. You've got to have all or nothing. So, now, I know it, there it is. (*Patricia's theme begins.*) Why do you shut your eyes?

The camera pans to Patricia. She has her eyes shut, Michel's hat on, and her chin resting on her hands, one of which has a cigarette between the fingers.

PATRICIA: I'm trying to shut them very hard so that everything goes black. But I can't manage to. It's never completely black.

Michel's theme starts. Patricia looks at him and the camera pans minutely to include him.

MICHEL: Your smile . . . in profile . . . it's the best thing you've got. It's you. *Michel pushes himself up so that his head starts to cross left behind her. The music stops.*

170. QUICK CUT *to a slightly closer* CU: *Patricia now looking left at Michel who is off-screen.*

PATRICIA: It's me. *She laughs.*

171. MLS: *Michel and Patricia next to each other on the bed, leaning against the headboard. Michel's legs are under the sheet. Patricia tosses the hat and cigarette off-screen right. Patricia turns to face Michel. They stare at each other, motionless.*

PATRICIA: We're looking into each other's eyes and it's useless.

Jazz piano music quietly fades in.

MICHEL (*in an Italian accent*): Patricia Franchini.
PATRICIA (*looking down as if embarrassed*): I hate that name. I'd like to be called Ingrid.
MICHEL: Kneel down.

She kneels a bit further down the bed, closer to the camera. The music stops and the sounds of a radio broadcast can be heard.

PATRICIA: What's the matter?
RADIO VOICE: . . . This broadcast, ladies, gentlemen, ends . . .
MICHEL: I'm looking at you.
RADIO VOICE: . . . a broadcast of Nadia Tagrine, featuring the artist.[36]
PATRICIA: The French are idiots too.

Michel pulls the sheet over his head. Trumpets blare over the radio. His head comes out from behind the sheet.

MICHEL: I want you to stay with me.

The music stops.

PATRICIA: Yes. *She looks at him and gets under the sheet. He ducks his head back under the sheet so they are both completely covered.*
RADIO VOICE: We momentarily interrupt our broadcast in order to syn-chronize our transmitter.
PATRICIA (*from under the sheet*): It's strange.
MICHEL: What?
PATRICIA: I see my reflection in your eyes.

JUMP CUT *to a slightly wider angle. They are rolling around under the covers.*

MICHEL: I'm laughing because this is truly a Franco-American encounter.

JUMP CUT. *Patricia's head alone is outside the sheets.*

PATRICIA: We'll hide like elephants when they're happy.

JUMP CUT. *The sheet covers both of them completely again.*

MICHEL: A woman's hips . . . this really gets me.
PATRICIA: I'm too hot.

Michel gets out from under the covers and throws off the top blankets covering their legs. Then he carefully replaces the sheet over her head. JUMP CUT *so that he too is fully under the sheet.*

MICHEL: If it was another man than me that caressed you, would you care, or not?
PATRICIA (*gently*): You already asked me.

172. MS: *on a sudden sound, the radio.*

RADIO VOICE: Our broadcast, "Work in Music," is starting. For you, "Work in Music."

A light military tune played by a dance band begins to play on the radio. The camera pans over to the bed. Patricia and Michel are rustling under the covers. The camera then pans back over to the radio. Patricia's arm reaches into the frame and turns it off.

PATRICIA: And there we are!

173. MCU: *Michel sits up. Patricia gets out of bed and crosses in front of him. His eyes follow her.*

174. MS: *Patricia, now wearing Michel's longsleeved white shirt, standing next to a photograph of herself. She walks away. The camera holds on the photograph.*

PATRICIA (*off*): Do you know a book by Dylan Thomas . . .

175. MCU: *Michel.*

  PATRICIA (*off*): . . . *Portrait of the Artist as a Young Dog?*[37]

176. MCU: *from behind, Patricia drinking a glass of water.*

  MICHEL (*singing, off*): Sunday morning, it's the perfect time to stay in bed all day.

177. MS: *an angle off to the right of Michel in bed. The camera pans left to Patricia at her closet.*

  PATRICIA (*as she sits on the end of the bed*): I'm getting dressed.
  MICHEL (*rubbing her back*): What time is it?
  PATRICIA: Noon.
  MICHEL (*pulling her toward him to try to kiss her*): It was good?

PATRICIA (*in English with her teeth clenched*): Yes, sir! *She pulls away.*

MICHEL: We'll sleep until tonight.

PATRICIA: No! I've got to buy a dress. (*She gets up and walks toward the closet, the camera following her.*) You have your car?

MICHEL (*off*): My car. Yes, yes.

PATRICIA (*going over to him and kissing him*): Good morning, Michel.

The camera holds on Michel as she walks to the closet. From off-screen she throws him his hat and his white shirt. Michel gets on the telephone and asks for a number.

MICHEL (*putting on his hat*): Elysée 99–84. Hello. Good day, Madame. Has Antonio been in yet? (*He begins to put his shirt on with one hand while the other is holding the phone.*) Oh, boy! This is terrible. You don't know where he is? No, oh well . . . Still Michel Poiccard. *He has his shirt on and starts buttoning it. Patricia passes in front of him to pick up her purse from the desk. He hangs up the phone.*

PATRICIA (*off*): Do you want me to wear my brassiere, Michel?

MICHEL (*in English*): As you like it, Baby.

178. QUICK CUT *to* MLS: *Patricia standing in the doorway of the bathroom putting on a shoe. She turns around to look at herself in the mirror.*

PATRICIA: Do you like most my eyes, my mouth, or my shoulders? *She turns right, waiting to hear Michel's answer.*

179. QUICK CUT *to* MLS: *Michel, head-on, with his hat, shirt, and tie on, putting on his pants.*

PATRICIA (*off*): If you had to choose . . .

180. JUMP CUT. MS: *pan as Michel approaches Patricia at the closet, where she stands before the mirror. He touches her derrière, then moves right off-screen.* JUMP CUT *pans to reframe him before another mirror adjusting his hat.*

MICHEL: Your press conference, it was a gag, right?

PATRICIA (*off, while he adjusts his tie*): No, it's in just a bit at Orly.

MICHEL (*shadowboxing with his image in the mirror*): I'm not especially handsome, but I'm a great boxer.[38] (*He turns left facing her as he stops boxing.*) Where are you going? To this press conference?

Pan to Patricia adjusting her dress in front of her mirror.

PATRICIA: I've got to stop by the office first.

MICHEL (*off*): I'll accompany you.

PATRICIA (*in English*): All right.

RADIO VOICE: This afternoon, then, President Eisenhower is to accompany General de Gaulle to the Arc de Triomphe, where they will place a wreath on the tomb of the unknown soldier. Then they will go down the Champs Elysées . . .

PATRICIA: Did you go to war? *The camera pans as she takes her purse, walks over to the bed, and sits down with her back to the camera.*

MICHEL (*off*): Yes.

PATRICIA: And, what did you do?

MICHEL (*off*): Cut [*zigouillais*] the sentries' throats.

PATRICIA: What is "zigouiller"?

181. MS: *high angle looking down on Michel and Patricia. They are lying on the bed with their heads toward the camera. Both wear sunglasses, Michel is leaning over her.*

MICHEL: I laid them down like this . . .

PATRICIA: Oh, Michel.

MICHEL: I'm tired. I'm going to die. *He lays his head on her chest and Patricia's theme comes in.*

PATRICIA: You're crazy.

MICHEL: I'm completely nuts [*dingue*].

PATRICIA: What is "dingue"?

MICHEL: (*pointing to himself*): It's me. *They start to kiss.*

182. ECU: *match cut of Michel and Patricia kissing. They both take their sunglasses off and kiss again.*

Center of Paris, exterior, day

183. ELS: *aerial view of the Louvre. The violin music from the previous shot carries over and soars.*

184. *Match cut on motion to similar aerial view of Notre Dame.*

185. MS: *Patricia and Michel sitting in chairs at a sidewalk café. They are facing out onto the street.*

> PATRICIA: It's not here . . . your car?
> MICHEL (*pointing*): Yes . . . No . . . Yes. . . . It's in the garage. I'll go get it and then we're off. *He gets up and leaves.*

186. MLS: *Michel running across the street away from the camera.*

187. MS: *Patricia, sitting in the chair, looking through a book.*

188. LS: *Michel kicking tires of cars parked along a narrow street. He crosses the street toward the camera.*

189. QUICK CUT to MLS: *looking up the street. Michel is leaning into a convertible, evidently searching for the keys. A man comes walking out of a building behind Michel. He stops and regards Michel suspiciously.*

190. MLS: *a different street. Michel walks into the shot from frame left. Camera pans slightly right with him. A man in a white T-shirt is just getting out of a white convertible. He heads left out of frame against the pan. The camera slows with Michel as he goes by the car, then turns to watch the man off-screen.*

191. MCU: *over Patricia's right shoulder. She puts down a drink and looks at her wristwatch.*

192. *As in 190. Michel is on the sidewalk now, looking the car over.*

> MICHEL (*to himself*): Neat, a Ford. *He runs around the back of the car and off-screen left to follow the driver.*

193. ELS: *Michel running right. When he gets close behind the man, he slows to follow him quietly around a corner.*

Apartment Building Lobby and Elevator, interior, day

194. LS: *lobby of an apartment building. The camera faces a very large mirror. The driver walks in and turns right off-screen. Michel then enters.*

195. *Black screen.*

MICHEL: What floor?
DRIVER: Fifth.

Michel strikes a match to light his cigarette, revealing a MS of the two men facing the camera. Through the ironwork of the elevator in the background, the various floors can be seen going by, and it gets brighter as they go up. Michel looks anxiously around while the driver, in a T-shirt, mainly stares at him. The elevator stops. The driver hurries out.

MICHEL: I picked the wrong floor.

He turns and punches the ground floor button. The elevator begins to descend.

196. QUICK CUT *to shot 194 with Michel running full speed out of the building.*

Paris Streets, exterior, day

197. QUICK CUT *to LS: through a car window, Michel getting into the Ford.*

198. QUICK CUT *to LS: Michel driving down the street.*

199. CU: *Patricia looking out into the street. She lifts her sunglasses up on her forehead. She takes the glasses off and has a puzzled look on her face.*

200. MLS: *from behind Patricia onto the street. Michel drives up in the white convertible. He stops in front of the café. Patricia stands, gets her things, and walks to the car.*

201. QUICK CUT *to* MS: *Patricia and Michel from the back seat.*

   PATRICIA (*looking at herself in her compact mirror*): Are you afraid to
      get old? I am.
   MICHEL: You're stupid. I already told you that the worst fault is
      cowardice.

   They kiss.

202. *Tracking shots of the buildings along the street.*

   PATRICIA (*off*): Are you going to buy me the dress at Dior's?
   MICHEL (*off*): Not on your life. They have dresses ten times more beau-
      tiful at Prisunic.³⁹ No, at Dior's you don't buy dresses, you use the
      telephone. (*The camera pans up a floor on a building and then back
      down, outlining the entrance as they pass. It then continues panning
      buildings till the end of the block.*) You know, it's the only place in Paris
      where you can phone for free. There are twelve booths with outside
      lines.

203. LS: *looking down a street at a slight angle. A man slowly walks down the
   sidewalk repeatedly but laconically calling out, "France-Soir." Michel
   pulls the car into center frame. Slight pan effaces the newspaper hawker
   as Michel parks in* MLS. *Behind, on the other side of the street, is the
   New York Herald Tribune office. The music stops. Patricia gets out of the
   car and runs off-screen right. Michel gestures to the man selling papers.*

   MICHEL: Hey! *France-Soir.*
   PATRICIA: I'll get dressed and be right back.

   *Michel takes a paper, reaches into his pocket, and hands the man, who
   has come back into the frame, some money. Another man, who has just
   crossed the street, calls out impatiently for a paper. The vendor walks in
   front of the camera to sell him one.*

   NEWSMAN: Yes, Mister.
   MICHEL: *France-Soir.*

A MAN (*off*): *France-Soir.*
NEWSMAN: Thank you, Mister.

204. MS: *high angle over the front of the car. Michel is reading the paper.*

A MAN (*off*): Come on! *France-Soir,* please.

205. MS: *a man buying a newspaper.*[40]

NEWSMAN: Here, here you are.

206. *As in 204. Michel looks up from his paper and glances around.*

207. ECU: *the newspaper. Pan up the paper reveals a large photo of Michel with the heading, "Route 7 Road Killer still at large."* [41]

208. MS: *the man who has just bought a paper. He looks deliberately up from his paper and over at Michel.*

209. *As in 204. Michel barely glances up, then pulls his sunglasses down a bit and looks over the top of them at the man.*

210. *As in 208. The man looks back down at his paper. He seems to have recognized Michel from his picture in the paper.*

211. *As in 209. Michel, still looking at the man, pushes up his sunglasses.*

212. MLS: *Michel in the car on the street in front of the* New York Herald Tribune *office. Patricia runs out the door. Michel turns around to look at her and puts the paper in the back seat.* JUMP CUT *so that Patricia, wearing a new dress, is in the middle of the street twirling around in front of Michel. A pan keeps her in frame when she runs around the front of the car to the passenger side. Michel reaches over to open the door for her. Slight* JUMP CUT *as she gets into the car. The man who is suspicious of Michel walks by the driver's side of the car, takes a quick glance at Michel, and walks over to the* New York Herald Tribune *office as the convertible drives off. He stops two policemen on the street and shows*

them the paper. Iris out on the three men with dramatic music as punctuation.

Orly Airport Terrace, exterior, day

213. *Iris in.* MLS: *Michel and Patricia as she puts a token in a turnstile at Orly airport. No music but a great deal of airplane noise in the background.*

> MICHEL: How long will it take?
> PATRICIA: Half an hour, I don't know.
> MICHEL: Fine, I'll go find my man and come back.
> PATRICIA: Okay!

214. QUICK CUT *to* MLS: *Patricia heading away from the camera and up some stairs.*

> MICHEL (*off, as she runs up the stairs*): Patricia . . .

215. MCU: *Michel.*

> MICHEL: . . . Patricia!

216. CU: *Patricia from a low angle. She has turned around and stopped on the stairs. She laughs.*

217. MLS: *Michel shadowboxing. A man opens the glass door next to Michel, pushing him back a bit. After the man walks off-screen toward the steps, Michel resumes boxing.*

218. MS: *low angle of Patricia going up the steps. The man who has just walked out the glass door now walks past Patricia. She glances at him, then back at Michel, laughs, and waves him off.*

219. MCU: *Michel rubbing his lip with his thumb. He starts to exit through the glass door.*

220. QUICK CUT *to* MLS: *high angle pan of Patricia walking onto a rooftop terrace.*

221. MCU: *a man with a Bell & Howell movie camera.*

A VOICE (*off*): Mr. Parvulesco, why have you chosen *Candida* as the title of your novel?[42]
SECOND VOICE (*off*): Mr. Parvulesco, if you please . . .
THIRD VOICE (*off*): Ah, wait a moment . . .

The cameraman begins to film.

222. MS: *Parvulesco looking up to the left at the off-screen interviewer. He is the man who came through the door in shot 217, and is wearing sunglasses and a hat like Michel's.*[43]

SECOND VOICE (*off*): Fine, I'll let my colleague speak, and then . . .
PARVULESCO: I'm persuaded that the book, in France, will receive, because of French Puritanism, a rather cool reception.

223. MCU: *a still photographer.*

PHOTOGRAPHER (*motioning toward his subject, then raising his camera to snap a shot*): Mr. Parvulesco.
A VOICE (*off*): Mr. Parvulesco, I wanted to ask you, in the . . .

224. MCU: *a seated reporter looking left at the author.*

REPORTER: Do you think that one can still believe in love in our age?

225. *As in 222.*

PARVULESCO (*looking screen right this time*): Certainly. One can no longer believe in anything but love, especially in our era.

226. *As he finishes his reply off-screen,* MCU *of a very serious Patricia with a pen to her mouth. She begins to write some notes.*

A VOICE: Mr. Parvulesco.

227. MLS: *another reporter.*

REPORTER: What do you think of that sentence where Rainer Maria Rilke claims that modern life will drive men and women further apart?[44]

228. CU: *Parvulesco looking to his right and listening. Patricia's voice amidst all the other voices, calls his name to ask a question, but he answers the previous question.*

PARVULESCO: Rilke was a great poet. Therefore, he must be right.

229. MCU: *Patricia bending down to write.*

230. MCU: *Parvulesco. There are many people trying to get his attention by calling his name. He looks to his left and then to his right.*

A VOICE (*off*): Mr. Parvulesco.
ANOTHER VOICE (*off*): Back off a little.

231. MCU: *the cameraman filming while voices compete off-screen.*

FIRST VOICE: Oh, fine, *Paris-Match,* fine, fine, eh?
SECOND VOICE: Oh, you, Pathé-Journal, eh, go on![45]

232. CU: *Parvulesco.*

233. MCU: *profile of a woman in a scarf. The background noise from the airplanes is very loud.*

WOMAN REPORTER (*as she speaks there are many voices calling out his name*): Do you think that there's a difference in the way French and American women go about love?

234. MCU: *Parvulesco, turning to face the woman.*

PARVULESCO: There's no comparison between French and American women. The American woman dominates man. The French woman doesn't . . . yet.

A man calls out his name and he looks. Now Patricia calls out and he responds by looking screen right toward her.

235. MCU: *Patricia as in 227.*

A VOICE (*off*): Mr. Parvulesco.
PATRICIA: What is your great ambition in life?

236. MCU: *Parvulesco. He looks at Patricia but does not answer her. A man's voice calls his name. He looks right.*

MAN'S VOICE (*off*): In your opinion who is the more moral: a woman who betrays or a man who abandons?
PARVULESCO: The woman who betrays.
A VOICE (*off*): Mr. Parvulesco.

He looks around, reacting to questions.

A VOICE (*off*): Are women more sentimental than men?

237. MCU: *Patricia, writing, as in 227.*

PARVULESCO (*off*): Sentiments are a luxury few women can afford.

Patricia looks up from her notepad in reaction to his answer.

238. MCU: *another reporter.*

REPORTER:[46] Mr. Parvulesco, do you believe that there's a difference between eroticism and love?

239. MS: *Parvulesco. A man is holding a microphone near his face. An airplane taxis past behind his head.*

PARVULESCO: No, not really. I don't think so, I think nothing of it, because eroticism is a form of love and love a form of eroticism.

240. MCU: *profile of Patricia with pen in mouth, looking down at her notebook. A tape recorder slung over a man's shoulder is in the background. She looks up.*

WOMAN'S VOICE (*off, her question bridging the cut*): Mr. Parvulesco, do you believe in the existence of the soul in the modern world?
PARVULESCO: I believe in graciousness [*gentillesse*].
A VOICE (*off, translating into English*): I believe in gentleness.
SECOND VOICE (*off*): Don't ask stupid questions!
THE WOMAN (*off*): Oh, go on, you!
PATRICIA: Do you believe that woman has a role to play in modern society?

241. CU: *Parvulesco looking almost on camera axis. He takes the pipe out of his mouth.*

PARVULESCO (*pulling down his sunglasses to make eye contact*): Yes, if she is charming, if she has a striped dress, and smoked sunglasses. *He puts his sunglasses back on.*
A VOICE (*off*): Mr. Parvulesco!

Another man begins to ask a question.

242. MCU: *Patricia smiling at Parvulesco while holding her pen to her mouth.*

A VOICE (*off, bridging the cut*): What do you think of Casanova's assertion that there is no woman who can't be seduced by making her grateful enough?
PARVULESCO (*off*): Cocteau, through *The Testament of Orpheus*, will answer . . .[47]

243. MCU: *a young reporter. He is nervous and does not look up when he asks his question, but speaks it into the microphone.*

YOUNG REPORTER: How many men, in your opinion, can a woman love in her lifetime? I . . . I mean physically.

244. MCU: *Parvulesco looking off-screen left. He flashes open the fingers of one, then both hands, numerous times, just as Michel had in shot 167.*

A VOICE (*off*): Excuse me, please, Mr. Parvulesco!
PARVULESCO: More than that.

245. *As in 242.*

A VOICE (*off*): There's no way to work here!
SECOND VOICE (*off*): Miss, not in the picture.
THIRD VOICE (*off*): But, Miss, you're in the picture!

Patricia smiles at Parvulesco.

PARVULESCO (*off*): There are two things important to people. For men it's women. And for women it's money.

246. MCU: *low angle of the man with the movie camera. He is not filming.*

A VOICE (*off*): Ah, you see then, you're a pessimist.

247. MCU: *high angle of Parvulesco looking straight up into the camera.*

PARVULESCO: As soon as you see a pretty girl with a rich man, you can say automatically that she's a nice girl and he's a rat.

248. MCU: *the photographer fiddling with his camera.*

A VOICE (*off*): In your opinion, is it better to love to live or . . .

JUMP CUT *as the photographer snaps a shot.*

249. MCU: *Parvulesco looking left, then turning right. There are many questions being hurled at him.*

MAN'S VOICE (*off*): What is the most intelligent country on Earth?
PARVULESCO: France.

250. MCU: *profile of a young woman.*

YOUNG WOMAN: Do you like Brahms?[48]

251. CU: *a portable tape recorder with its reels turning.*

PARVULESCO (*off*): Like everyone: not at all!
YOUNG WOMAN (*off*): Chopin?
PARVULESCO (*off*): Disgusting!

252. MCU: *Patricia looking up from her notebook.* JUMP CUT *on the same angle.*

PATRICIA: What is your greatest ambition in life?

253. CU: *Parvulesco, staring at Patricia and ignoring all the other questions.*

254. MCU: *the photographer shooting pictures.*

255. *As in 253. Parvulesco takes off his sunglasses.*

PARVULESCO (*very deliberately*): To become immortal and then to die.

256. CU: *Patricia. Michel's theme music comes in. She takes off her sunglasses, puts the end of the earpiece in her mouth, and slowly turns to stare straight at the camera. Slow dissolve.*[49]

Garage and Junkyard, exterior, day

257. *Crane shot of Michel in the stolen car driving down a road toward a garage and used car lot. He turns into the lot, pulls in near the office, and stops. The music from the previous scene carries over.*

258. MLS: *Michel in the car. Mansard walks into the shot. He is an older man wearing an old rumpled shirt, tie, and suspenders. He walks up to the driver's side of the car. The music stops.*

   MICHEL: Mr. Laszlo Kovacs. Claudius Mansard, that's you?
   MANSARD: Yes, Mr. Kovacs. *He begins to circle the car, going off-screen while Michel turns his head to keep him in view.*
   MICHEL: I called you this morning. They said you'd be here.

259. MCU: *Mansard lighting a cigarette.*

   MANSARD: Yes, Mr. Kovacs.
   MICHEL (*off*): Tony sent me.
   MANSARD: Yes, Mr. Kovacs.

260. MLS: *across the top of the car taken from the driver's side. Mansard is standing by the passenger's door, while Michel hops out to meet him dead on.*

   MICHEL: We met in Nice already, through him, I think.
   MANSARD: No, Mr. Kovacs.
   MICHEL (*taking out a cigarette and putting it in his mouth*): Nobody phoned?
   MANSARD: Yes, Mr. Kovacs. They called and said it would be an Oldsmobile.
   MICHEL: Yes, but at the last moment, the deal fell through.
   MANSARD (*leaning back on the car*): And now?
   MICHEL: So there you are.

261. MLS: *high angle from the rear left-hand side of the car. Mansard gets in the car and revs it up a few times.*

MANSARD (*turning and looking at Michel*): 800,000.[50]
MICHEL: Okay. *He jumps in over the door on the passenger's side.*

262. MCU: *Michel, now suddenly in the driver's seat, looking at the camera.*

MANSARD (*off*): The only problem is that I'll give you the money next week.
MICHEL: Ah, no, you're a real bastard.

263. MS: *the car from the front. Michel slides over to the passenger side. The camera tracks with him. Mansard immediately walks up to the car and shows him the newspaper. The noise from the highway almost drowns him out.*

MANSARD: And you, Mr. Kovacs, who are you? . . . So, I'm not giving you the money now.
MICHEL: Too bad. Is it 3:00 yet?
MANSARD: 3:15.
MICHEL (*standing up in the car*): Can I use your phone?

Mansard nods toward his office. Michel walks off-screen left and Mansard leans back on the car.

264. MS: *doorway to the office. Michel goes through and starts to use the phone.*

265. MS: *from behind Mansard. He has the hood of Michel's car open and is tinkering with the engine. He takes something out and puts it in his pocket. Then he quietly shuts the hood and waits for Michel.*

266. MS: *Michel on the telephone.*

MICHEL (*into phone*): Is Antonio there?
VOICE ON THE PHONE: No, he just left.
MICHEL: Ah! Shit!
VOICE ON THE PHONE: He told me to tell you he'd be at the Réamur or at L'Escale at four o'clock.

MICHEL: Four o'clock at L'Escale. Fine, thanks. *He hangs up the phone and starts looking through a drawer in the desk on which the telephone is sitting.*

267. QUICK CUT *to* MCU: *high angle of Michel as he rummages through the desk drawer.* JUMP CUT *shows him at another drawer.*

MANSARD (*off*): You're wasting your time.

Michel looks up at him.

268. MCU: *Mansard standing in the doorway looking at Michel.*

MANSARD: I keep my money on me.
MICHEL (*walking over to him to form a two-shot*): Advance me 10,000 francs.
MANSARD (*shaking his head*): No.

Michel lights a new cigarette from his old one.

MICHEL: 5,000!
MANSARD: No.
MICHEL: 2,500!

Mansard smiles and looks at Michel, who then roughly pushes him out the doorway.

269. MLS: *the car. Michel walks over to it and looks in on the driver's side.*

MICHEL: It won't start anymore! (*He lifts the hood. Mansard is pacing in the background. A young boy walks by.*) Hey! You there! (*He walks quickly around the front of the car to the boy and speaks to him. On the way over he slams the hood shut. The camera cranes up over the car so as to frame Michel, the boy, and, in the background, Mansard.*) Was it you who disconnected the distributor wire? (*The boy points to Mansard who begins to walk away from Michel. Michel runs after him.*) Give me my machine, jerk!

270. QUICK CUT *to* LS: *the interior of a dark garage. Michel shoves Mansard against a wall. The camera pans with them.* JUMP CUT *to the far left corner of the garage. Michel, with his back toward the camera, is punching Mansard in the stomach.*

MANSARD: You owe me for the phone call.

JUMP CUT. *Michel punches him again.*

271. QUICK CUT *to* MS: *a different angle on Michel leaving the garage. He turns to Mansard, who lies just off-screen.*

MICHEL: It's for my taxi.

Intense piano and bongo music. Michel shoves the money he took from Mansard into his pocket as he hurries out. The camera pans with him, then fades out to black.

Taxi, interior, day

272. *Fade in.* MS: *from the back seat of a taxi. The driver's head is in clearest focus. The intense music carries over from the previous scene.*

> MICHEL (*off*): Go on, step on it! Step on it! Don't worry about pedestrians. Hurry, that's all I ask you. Go on, step on it! In the name of God, you're dragging!

273. MS: *from the front passenger seat of Michel and Patricia sitting in the back seat. Michel takes a cigarette out of his mouth, and exhales.*

> MICHEL: Bang! (*This interjection cues the cut. He throws both arms up in the air as he continues speaking now to Patricia.*) All of the front left fender of the Thunderbird ripped off. Me, nothing! (*Pointing out of Patricia's window, he changes the subject.*) Look at the house where I was born.

274. LS: POV *of the old apartment buildings along the street.*

> MICHEL (*off*): Across the street, they put up a horrible house.

> *As the car moves along, the camera reveals a newer 1950s building on the corner across the street. Its façade is plain and it is built so that it curves with the street corner.*

275. *A different angle of the building seen from the car window.*

> MICHEL (*off*): Houses like that really depress me. All the beauty of the intersection is ruined now.
> PATRICIA: Yes.

276. *As in 273.*

> MICHEL (*touching Patricia's face and gently turning it toward him*): Yes, me, I've got a feeling for beauty . . . beauty!

277. *As in 272.*

MICHEL (*off*): But no, go by way of Châtelet. (*To Patricia.*) If I'm late it's your fault.
PATRICIA (*off*): Absolutely not.
MICHEL (*to the driver after a* JUMP CUT, *off*): Get going, my man, pass that 403. (JUMP CUT.) Don't touch your gear shift. What do you mean dragging yourself behind a 4-CV? (JUMP CUT.) Hang on, look, you're being passed by a Manurhin. (JUMP CUT.) Put on your turn signal, we're turning left.[51]

278. MS: *from the passenger seat of Michel leaning over Patricia to get out of the car.*

MICHEL: Stop. I'll be back.
CAB DRIVER: Yes, Mister.

Patricia slides to the other side and out of the shot. Through the driver's window, Michel can be seen walking down the sidewalk at least a hundred feet. While pedestrians continually cross in front of the camera, we still see him through the driver's window as he stops to talk with a man, turns around, and saunters back to the car. He opens the door and begins to get in. The frenetic piano music continues. JUMP CUT. *He is now sitting next to Patricia.*

MICHEL: He left five minutes ago.

JUMP CUT. *The car is already moving.*

PATRICIA: The one who owes you money?
MICHEL: Antonio Berruti, yes! Your fault! Now it's double or nothing.
PATRICIA: Why?
MICHEL: I'll explain later.

279. *As in 277. Michel's* POV *of the driver and the traffic he is racing through.*

MICHEL (*to the driver, off*): Come on, big daddy, don't stay behind the 2-CV.[52] (*To Patricia.*) Where are you going now?

JUMP CUT, *barely changing the road seen through the window.*

PATRICIA (*off*): To the *New York Herald*.

JUMP CUT *as above*.

MICHEL (*to the driver, off*): Don't turn your head. Look ahead of you.

JUMP CUT *as above*.

MICHEL (*to Patricia, off*): What good does it do you to write articles?
PATRICIA (*off*): It does me the good of having money and of being free from men.

280. *As in 278.*

PATRICIA (*looking out her window*): I think Parisian women wear dresses that are too short; it makes them look like whores.
MICHEL: Come on, are you kidding? It makes you feel like running up behind them and doing like this. JUMP CUT *as he makes the motion of flipping a skirt up.*
PATRICIA: Don't be so shy.
MICHEL (*to the driver, slight* JUMP CUT *as he points ahead*): Stop here!

281. MLS: *the front of the taxi. Michel gets out. The camera pans with him as he runs across the street to the sidewalk, follows a woman for a few feet, and flips her skirt up. She immediately turns around, while he is already in retreat toward the cab.*

282. QUICK CUT *to* MLS: *the taxi parked on a street. Michel hurries out, runs around the front, and meets Patricia as she gets out of the car.*

MICHEL (*to the driver*): We'll be back.
CAB DRIVER: Okay.
PATRICIA: You're not paying?
MICHEL: Come on, hurry up!

Paris Passageway, exterior, day

283. LS: *an old building. The camera tilts down to the courtyard as Patricia and Michel walk together through it. They turn left and disappear through a doorway.*

284. *A very dark passageway. They are walking slowly to an exit at the end of the walkway. The camera tracks from behind. Their figures can be barely discerned at first because of the small amount of light, but as they approach the exit, they become more visible in* LS *silhouette.*

PATRICIA: Where are we going?

MICHEL: To the Champs Elysées. All Paris knows this corridor. It'll serve him right. I hate taxi drivers who are scared to scratch their paint. You see, here, during the war, the Gestapo . . . built a wall to keep people from slipping out between their legs.

PATRICIA: You know, I was thinking about the girl in *France-Soir.*

MICHEL: Which girl in *France-Soir*?

PATRICIA: You know, the one who stayed with her friend on the Côte d'Azur. You spoke well of her yourself.

MICHEL: Yes, a girl who's normal, that's rare.

PATRICIA (*as they near the exit*): Are you staying with me? I'm going to the paper.

MICHEL: No, me, I'm going to telephone. I'll stop by to say hello to my tailor and then I'll come back to get you.

PATRICIA: Okay.

MICHEL: Ciao, little girl.

Michel exits from the glass door to the right; Patricia goes to the left.

New York Herald Tribune Office, interior, day

285. MLS: *Patricia's friend Van Doude is facing a large window which has printed across it the masthead of the* New York Herald Tribune. *He is talking to a shorter, older journalist who has his back to the window. Immediately the camera begins panning right. During this lengthy shot it will in fact make two complete 360-degree circles, scanning the sidewalk,*

following subjects into the office, watching them pass by the reception desk, and around until it winds up by these two men at the window.

VAN DOUDE (*in English*): Hey, there she is! I'll introduce you to her.
JOURNALIST (*in English*): Wonderful.

The camera pans over to the window to reveal Patricia walking down the sidewalk from the left. Van Doude waves at her and she excitedly waves back. Camera pans to the door as Patricia walks in. She is in front of the camera, which tracks her as she walks through the office. She takes off her sunglasses, nods and smiles in the direction of the two men. Turning screen right, she stops at a receptionist's desk. The woman sitting behind the desk is wearing a T-shirt with the paper's name imprinted on the front. The room is very noisy with the sounds of typewriters.

PATRICIA (*to the receptionist*): Hello, Hélène.
HÉLÈNE: Hello, Patricia. You're late. They're waiting for you.
PATRICIA: Oh, that's right. *She turns and walks toward the men.*
VAN DOUDE (*as Patricia approaches, in English*): Hello, Patricia. How is the work?
PATRICIA (*taking off her gloves, in English*): Oh! Not so bad. I have to type up my notes now.

The camera slows momentarily and even stops when she reaches the two men, framing the group in a three-shot. Van Doude introduces Patricia to the older journalist.

VAN DOUDE (*in English*): This is our new star reporter!
JOURNALIST (*shaking her hand, then, in English*): Great pleasure.
PATRICIA (*in English*): How do you do, sir?

On its own the pan continues to the sidewalk, revealing Inspector Vital and his assistant walking by the window and to the door just as Patricia had done earlier in the shot. Vital says something to his assistant, who waits outside while the camera keeps panning with Vital as he walks in the door. He takes a newspaper out of his pocket and approaches the receptionist's desk. He stops but the camera keeps circling to reveal the receptionist.

VITAL (*showing his badge*): Miss Patricia Franchini?
HÉLÈNE: She's over there, I think.

He walks slowly over to Patricia. The camera circles right as Vital moves through the office, taking everything in with his eyes. Ultimately he stalks forward on the group three-shot by the window and, with his rolled-up newspaper, he taps the shoulder of Patricia who is still engaged in her English conversation with the two journalists. She turns around.

VITAL: Miss Franchini?
PATRICIA (*in English*): Yes?

Vital shows her his badge and leads her away from the two men and toward the camera. In the background they take their leave of one another, ignoring Patricia and Vital.

VAN DOUDE (*to the journalist, in English*): I'll see you later.

Vital puts his badge back into his pocket and turns so that his back is toward the window. Patricia faces him, and in between them, through the window, the other detective can be seen waiting.

VITAL: Do you speak French?

PATRICIA (*in English*): Yes.

286. MCU: *Vital holds up a copy of* France-Soir *so that it covers all of his face but his eyes. On the front page is a very large picture of Michel with the headline: "The Murderer of Motorcycle Cop Thibault Still on the Run."*

VITAL: Do you know this guy?

Dramatic music starts.

287. CU: *reverse angle of Patricia. She reluctantly takes the paper and looks at the picture.*

PATRICIA (*shaking her head*): No. *She looks up for a moment, then peers down trying to read the story. She looks up again, a bit frightened, at Vital, but shakes her head "no" once more.*

288. MCU: *Vital.*

VITAL: Careful, my young lady, one doesn't joke with the Paris police.

289. MS: *the two facing each other. Vital is holding the paper up for her. She has her sunglasses on.*

PATRICIA (*taking the paper*): Why yes, it's Michel.
VITAL: Michel Poiccard?
PATRICIA: Yes, I hadn't recognized him. It's old, this photo.

290. MS: *Patricia and Vital with the window behind them so we can occasionally see the other detective pacing outside. Music fades out.*

> VITAL (*angrily, as he takes the paper from her*): This morning, in front of this building, you were seen in the company of Michel Poiccard.
> PATRICIA: Who saw me?
> VITAL: He was driving a Thunderbird 3382 GF-75.
> PATRICIA: Yes.
> VITAL: Where is he?
> PATRICIA: I don't know.
> VITAL: Careful, careful, my young lady.
> PATRICIA: No, really, he's a guy I've seen only five or six times. He seemed nice. I don't know where he lives or what he does.
> VITAL (*irritated*): Have you known him for a long time?

291. CU: *Patricia, from a 30-degree angle. Her sunglasses conspicuously act as mirrors. The music fades back in.*

> PATRICIA: No, I met him in Nice, three weeks ago. I was on vacation. He told me he came to Paris to see a man who owes him money.
> VITAL (*angrily, off*): Who?
> PATRICIA (*taking off her glasses*): I don't know. An Italian man. *She smiles.*

292. *As in 290, slightly further back. The music stops.*

> VITAL (*taking a small notebook out of his pocket*): This Michel Poiccard, do you think you'll see him again?
> PATRICIA: Perhaps. Sometimes he phones me to go out, like this morning. I don't know.
> VITAL (*beginning to write in his notebook*): Yes, yes . . . yes, yes. You have a work permit?
> PATRICIA: Yes.
> VITAL: You don't want to have any trouble with your passport?
> PATRICIA: No, I don't want to.
> VITAL: Yes, then if you see him, here's my number. *He hands her the piece of paper from his small notebook and walks off-screen right.*

PATRICIA (*to herself*): Danton 01–00. *She looks around the room, then out the window, leaning up against the window to get a better view. Music cues the cut.*

Paris Streets, exterior, day

293. MLS: *Michel coming out of a newsstand reading a paper. He is wearing a different hat, a casquette. He flips open the paper and walks down the sidewalk. He stops and holds the paper so that it hides his face, peeks out from behind it, and looks across the street.*

294. ELS: *the two detectives standing in front of the* New York Herald Tribune *office. They scurry inside a doorway next to the office as Patricia comes out. She turns to the left and walks down the sidewalk past the detectives and does not seem to notice them. The detectives come out of the building to follow her.*

295. CU: *Michel drawing the paper down from his face. He looks out, then brings it back up.*

296. *As in 294. The detectives split up. Vital walks screen right and his assistant follows Patricia.*

297. *As in 295. Michel draws the paper down and looks off-screen right.*

298. MCU: *tracking shot of Patricia walking slowly down the sidewalk. She turns and looks across the street, and points surreptitiously back at the detective.*

299. *As in 297. Michel, with cigarette in mouth, looks screen right, then screen left, then back screen right again while he nods.*

300. *As in 298. Patricia, evidently having seen Michel nod, walks away from the camera, which is panning left to follow her.*

301. *As in 297. Michel looks left.*

302. MCU: *the detective following left intently.*

303. *As in 297. Michel pulls the paper down from in front of his face and walks off-screen right.*

304. MLS: *the sidewalk through a shop window. Patricia walks by in front of the window. Just as she passes out of view on the right,* JUMP CUT *so that the detective following her enters from the left. When he too passes out of view to the right,* JUMP CUT *as Michel, reading a newspaper, enters in identical fashion from the left. The camera is stationary as the three characters pass by.*

305. LS: *a crowded sidewalk taken slightly off its axis. Patricia walks toward the camera but off-screen right, followed by the detective, followed by Michel who is still reading the newspaper. Michel's theme is replaced by pedestrian noises.*

306. LS: *from the opposite angle of another sidewalk. The three are closer together as they continue walking. The camera pans from right to left, following them as they move past a group of policemen who are standing on the sidewalk in the foreground. Sounds of a crowd applauding off-screen.*

307. ELS: *from a high balcony. Patricia, followed by the detective, followed by Michel, walk closer to the street where a parade is in progress. Many people are lined up along the curb watching. When she gets closer to the huge crowd Patricia begins to run. The camera pans away from her toward the street to reveal the parade. It is a government procession. A group of motorcycles in the outline of an upside-down V go by. Another V group goes by.* JUMP CUT *as a dignitary's car comes into view surrounded by a motorcycle escort. The camera pans right on the car.* JUMP CUT *as the camera continues panning.* JUMP CUT *as it pans back toward the crowd and finds Patricia further up the boulevard, pursued by the detective, and followed by Michel.*[53]

308. LS: *down the sidewalk of Patricia walking toward the camera and screen left, trying to dodge the people in the crowd and lose the detective. Michel follows, reading the newspaper.*

309. LS: *reverse angle. The camera pans right as Patricia runs across the street toward a movie theater. "La Marseillaise" is playing in the background. The camera now stops in a* LS *of the theater entrance with the booth in the background. Patricia hides behind a pillar in front of the theater. The detective spies her and runs up to the pillar. She dodges him and desperately races to the ticket booth, buys a ticket, and slips inside. The detective rushes toward the booth.*

Movie Theater, interior, day

310. LS: *Patricia from the bottom of a stairway leading into the theater. She turns on her descent to look back to the door at the top of the stairs. Then she continues down.*

311. LS: *the dark theater, taken from next to the screen toward the audience. Above the audience, the light from the projector shines out. Patricia enters, followed by an usher with a flashlight. Patricia sits down. The dialogue of an American film can be heard.*[54] *The detective enters soon after Patricia and sits one row behind her, forcing a surprised spectator to move over one place. Patricia turns, sees him, and hurries out with the detective in close pursuit.*

312. MLS: *match cut of Patricia walking away from the camera to the rear of the women's lavatory. The English dialogue of the film continues without interruption. When she reaches the washbasin at the back of the lavatory she turns and looks back out the door, listening for the detective. The camera pans right and discovers him entering the adjoining men's room. He walks toward the urinal, then turns back, watching for Patricia to leave. A quick pan to the left reveals her still in the lavatory, testing a door to one of the stalls to her right. When the door opens, she leans back out to see if anyone is looking and then rushes through it. Pan back over to the detective facing the wall away from us. Evidently suspecting something, he suddenly turns around, buttons his coat, and hurries out of the men's and over into the women's lavatory. He opens the door to one stall, looks in, and shuts it. Then he goes to the farthest door, the one Patricia had just entered, and opens it.*

Paris Streets, exterior, day

313. MLS: *Patricia jumping out of a ground-floor window. She is carrying her shoes. After landing on the sidewalk she runs off to the left and hides in a small doorway while she puts her shoes back on. A loudspeaker announcement can be heard in the background describing the procession still in progress on the Champs Elysées.*

314. MLS: *Patricia crossing a street lined with parked cars. She runs toward the camera, which pans slightly. A* JUMP CUT *finds her with Michel in a two-shot in the center of the street. He cups his hands around her face and looks at her, then releases her face.*

PATRICIA: That's why you said it's double or nothing a little bit ago?
MICHEL (*lighting a cigarette*): Yes, a bit for that.
PATRICIA: Let's go see a western at the Napoléon.
MICHEL: Yes, it's better to wait till nightfall.

Trumpet music fades in as they walk screen left down the center of the street. Michel puts his arm around Patricia's shoulder. The camera pans with them until it frames the front of a movie theater, where it holds. Passersby on the sidewalk are conscious of the camera or of the actors. The music becomes dramatic. The detective appears, running out the theater door, then stopping on the sidewalk to look both ways. Above the music gunshots are heard as the detective takes off the wrong way screen right.

Movie Theater, the Napoléon, interior, day

315. ECU: *Patricia and Michel in profile, facing each other. The background is completely black and the lighting on their faces flickers, as it is coming from the movie screen. The music and gunshots carry over to become diegetic. They are accompanied by sounds and dialogue of the film in progress off-screen. The dialogue is in French and is recited in an incantatory manner.*[55] *Michel and Patricia gaze at each other, then kiss long and gently, then pull back slightly to gaze once more in each other's eyes.*

MAN'S VOICE (*off*):
> Beware, Jessica,
> The bevelled edge of kisses.
> The years pass by too swiftly.
> Shun, shun the memories that hurt.

WOMAN'S VOICE (*off*):
> You're wrong, sheriff . . .
> Our story is noble and tragic
> Like the mask of a tyrant.
> A drama neither perilous nor magic.
> No cold detail
> Can turn our love pathetic.

Fade out.

Paris Streets, exterior, night

316. *Fade in.* LS: *Michel and Patricia coming out of a movie theater. Over the door is a huge sign with the name of the movie, "Westbound" and a picture of Virginia Mayo underneath it.*[56] *The camera tilts down from the marquee to pan with the couple as they walk briskly down the sidewalk. Michel tosses a coin in the air, tries to catch it, but misses. When he leans down to pick it up, two passersby speak flippantly to Patricia.*

    FIRST PASSERBY: Oh, what a pretty girl!
    SECOND PASSERBY: Hi, cutie.

317. LS: *a white car pulling up at the curb of a busy, brightly lit street.*

318. QUICK CUT *to* LS: *Patricia jumps out of the car. The camera pans with her until she enters a drugstore.*

319. LS: *the storefront, and above it a tele-news marquee displaying the latest headline: "Dragnet Being Drawn about Michel Poiccard." Dramatic piano music.*

320. MS: *Patricia from the back seat of the car. She is sitting in the front reading* France-Soir. *A picture of Michel is featured on the front page.*

MICHEL (*off*): What do they say?

PATRICIA: I'm still reading.

MICHEL (*off*): The cops are looking for me. They're dumb. I'm one of the rare few, in France, who likes them well enough. . . . Patricia, I'd like to hold you. Speak to me, eh!

321. MCU: *Michel also from the back seat. He is wearing his sunglasses even though it is dark out.*

PATRICIA (*off-screen, cueing the cut*): Oh, come on!

MICHEL (*lighting a cigarette*): What?

PATRICIA (*off*): You are married.

MICHEL (*taking the paper from her*): Show me. (*He looks at the paper, then folds it up.*) Yeah, a long time ago with a crazy girl. *He gives the paper back to Patricia.*

322. *As in 320 but slightly closer.*

MICHEL: She dumped me. Or me, I dumped her. I don't remember anymore.

PATRICIA: I love you very much . . . enormously, Michel.

MICHEL (*off*): How do you feel, Patricia, riding in a stolen car?

PATRICIA: And you, when you killed the policeman?

MICHEL (*off*): I was scared.

323. *As in 321. The car has stopped.*

PATRICIA (*off*): How did the police find out I knew you?

MICHEL: Some jerk must have seen us together and squealed on us.

PATRICIA: That's really bad.

MICHEL: What?

PATRICIA: Informing. I think it's really bad.

324. *As in 320, but the angle is now less oblique so that we see fully out the windshield. The lighting is darker, too, making Patricia barely visible in silhouette. Outside the window, as they drive, all the buildings and the Place de la Concorde are lit up.*

MICHEL (*as if reciting a poem, off*): No, it's normal. Informers inform. Burglars burgle. Lovers love. Look, the Concorde is beautiful.
PATRICIA: Yes, it's mysterious with all those lights.
MICHEL (*off*): It's stupid to keep this car. We'll change.
PATRICIA: What?
MICHEL (*off*): We're going to change cars.

325. *The music stops.* LS: *the car squealing to stop in front of a parking ramp. Michel waits for the gate to rise, then drives in, away from the camera and up the ramp.*

326. MLS: *inside the parking garage. Michel is getting out of the driver's seat. Patricia is standing near the trunk. Lighter music now.*

PATRICIA (*already starting toward the car directly opposite the place they parked*): We'll steal the Cadillac?
MICHEL (*off*): Ah, sure! Cadillac Eldorado?

327. MLS: *the Cadillac from the reverse angle.*

PATRICIA (*getting into the driver's seat of the convertible*): The keys?
MICHEL (*jumping in the right rear seat*): You, you drive, I'll hide. In this garage, they always leave the keys in the cars.

Patricia accidently turns on the wipers and then manages to start the car. They drive off-screen.

328. MS: *Michel's* POV *as Patricia drives down to the exit.*

PATRICIA: What do I say to the guy down below?
MICHEL (*off*): You say good night. Say it in English. That way, he won't dare to say anything. The French are cowards [*trouillards*].

They approach the exit.

PATRICIA: What is "trouillard"?
MICHEL (*off*): Scared. Are you scared?
PATRICIA: It's too late now to be scared.

PATRICIA (*to the guard off-screen, in English*): Good night!
GUARD (*off*): Good night, madame.

The gate rises and they drive out.

329. LS: *large tele-news marquee that reads: "Paris: Arrest of Michel Poic-card Is Certain. . . ." The camera then pans down to the street. Michel and Patricia drive into the shot from the right and the camera pans with them for a slight distance.*

330. MS: *from the rear left-hand seat of Michel, who is now sitting in the passenger seat. The shot is framed so that he is off-center to the right; Patricia is off-screen.*

MICHEL: I've absolutely got to find Antonio. What's annoying, here, is that as soon as you look for someone, you don't find him.

Xylophone music enters. They are driving along the boulevard Saint Germain. As they continue slowly, the camera reveals many people walk-ing and standing on the sidewalk. Just below the Royale Café, Michel suddenly recognizes a woman on the corner and starts to duck down in his seat.

MICHEL (*as he ducks*): Oh, oh!

331. MS: *a woman on the corner reading the issue of* France-Soir *with Michel's picture and story on the front page. She is the woman from whom he had taken the money in the earlier scene (shots 61–73). She glances up and is shocked to see him.*

WOMAN: Michel?

332. *As in 330.*

PATRICIA (*off*): Michel, who's that?
MICHEL (*to Patricia after he has sat upright again*): Step on it, sweetie [*Minouche*]!
PATRICIA (*off*): What's "Minouche"?

333. ELS: *the car approaching a big intersection. It swings screen right and pulls up by the curb, stopping right in the crosswalk. While cruising to a halt, its convertible top has mechanically come up, sticking staight in the air before dropping to cover them.* JUMP CUT. *Patricia gets out and runs around the front of the car toward the Pergola. Michel has gotten out on the passenger's side.*

A Parisian Café, the Pergola, interior, night

334. *Extreme high angle* LS *of the interior of the crowded Pergola. Music is playing. Michel walks in, followed by Patricia.*

335. CU: *the bartender, taken straight on. He is a slightly older, balding man.*

MICHEL (*off, to the bartender*): Have you seen Antonio?
BARTENDER (*glancing at Patricia, enthusiastically*): I'll tell you if I can kiss the doll.

336. CU: *Patricia turns her head screen left to look at Michel and then turns back to the bartender.*

MICHEL (*off*): That doesn't depend on me, that depends on her.

Patricia, looking back toward the bartender, smiles.

337. MS: *bartender from behind Michel and Patricia. Patricia has given her hand to him. He kisses it gently, then looks up.*

BARTENDER (*to Michel*): He's gone to Montparnasse with Zumbach.

Montparnasse, exterior, night

338. MLS: *the car pulling up directly under the camera and coming to a stop at a curb along the boulevard Montparnasse.*

339. MLS: *a sidewalk café. Carl sits with his back to the camera.*

MICHEL (*off, cueing the cut*): Carl!

Carl gets up, puts on his sunglasses, and walks screen right. Pan with him till he stands in front of the passenger door of the car. Patricia is still sitting in the car, but Michel is standing on the driver's side.

CARL: How are you?
MICHEL: The same! Antonio isn't with you? Gaby told me that you would be at the Pergola.
CARL: Yes, he's at the Select. Wait, here he is.

340. LS: *Berruti and his girlfriend on the other side of the street. Berruti waves as they cross the busy street, dodging traffic.*

341. MS: *Patricia just shutting the passenger door she has exited from.*

PATRICIA: Who's he?
MICHEL (*walking into the frame opposite her*): Who? Antonio?
PATRICIA: No, that one!

JUMP CUT *as they move.*

MICHEL: Patricia Franchini, Carl Zumbach.

Carl walks on-screen, forming a three-shot, takes Patricia's hand and kisses it.

342. QUICK CUT *to the same shot from the angle in front of the car. Carl lets go of her hand. Patricia, lit by a streetlight, stands between and slightly behind Carl and Michel.*

CARL (*pointing at Michel*): Show your socks. (*Michel lifts up his leg, looks at it, and puts it down.*) You're wearing silk socks with a tweed jacket.
MICHEL: Yes, I like silk.
CARL: Fine, but then no tweed.

Minute JUMP CUT as Michel breaks into a warm smile and waves at Berruti. Berruti walks in from screen left.

MICHEL: Berruti!
BERRUTI (*slapping Michel on the arm*): Hello, amigo!
MICHEL: Hello, kid!
CARL: I'll leave you.
BERRUTI (*to Carl as he is leaving*): See you later!

Berruti's girlfriend walks over and stands next to Patricia in the background.

343. CU: *Patricia looking at Berruti.*

BERRUTI (*off*): Well, you wanted to see me. They told me you phoned several times.

Patricia looks right at Michel.

MICHEL (*off*): Yes, I'm in trouble.
BERRUTI (*off*): Eh?
MICHEL (*off*): Oh God! Oh God!

344. *Tight* MS *of the four. Michel and Berruti face each other. Patricia stands slightly behind Michel, while the other woman hovers in the background. Michel shows Berruti a newspaper. Berruti looks quickly at it, and hands it back to Michel.*

BERRUTI: Shit! . . . Do you have a minute?
MICHEL: Yes.

Berruti turns to his girlfriend and steps a bit out of the shot.

BERRUTI (*to girlfriend*): Here, you see, it's that guy.

A man walks in front of the camera.

GIRLFRIEND: What do I say to him?
BERRUTI: Whatever you want, anything . . . I need two minutes.

She leaves. Michel lights a cigarette as Berruti follows her. Only Patricia and Michel remain.

PATRICIA (*to Michel*): What are they doing?
MICHEL (*turns to Patricia*): Antonio's going to take a picture when she kisses the guy.
PATRICIA: What for?
MICHEL: For blackmail.

345. CU: *Berruti's girlfriend kissing an older man.*

346. MS: *Berruti from the side looking down into his camera. He has an Italian newspaper under his left arm. He looks up from the camera, then takes another picutre.*

347. MCU: *Patricia looks left toward the sidewalk tables and smiles.*

348. MCU: *Van Doude with a cigar in his mouth and sunglasses on. He pulls down his glasses, smiles back at Patricia, and beckons with his finger.*

349. MS: *Michel and Berruti facing each other. Patricia is between and behind them.*

BERRUTI: There we are!
PATRICIA (*to Michel*): I'll be right back.

They both turn and watch her as she leaves.

BERRUTI (*to Michel*): Who's the mouse?
MICHEL: I'm even more in trouble because I'm in love.
BERRUTI: Oh, crap!

350. MLS: *Patricia sitting at a café table with Van Doude and an older couple who can be seen between them. He takes both of Patricia's hands and kisses them together. Patricia then turns and blows a kiss toward Michel who is off-screen.*

351. CU: *Patricia leaning with her chin in her hand and looking pensive, as if posing for a picture.*

VAN DOUDE (*off, in English*): Why don't you smile, Patricia? (*Patricia*

smiles.) I just left McGregor. He was at Chez Adrien with me and . . .
Monique.[57]

*A siren sounds in the distance. Patricia turns again toward Michel and
blows him another kiss. She does not seem to be very interested in what
Van Doude is saying to her.*

352. CU: *Michel without his sunglasses or hat. He is rubbing his thumb over
his lip in that familiar gesture while staring in the direction of Patricia.
He then puts a cigarette in his mouth, takes a puff, and exhales.*

PATRICIA (*off, in English*): It's just possible he'll say it's fantastic, but it
would certainly surprise me.

Michel takes the cigarette out of his mouth and rubs his lip again.

353. *As in 350. A man comes up from behind the group and without a word
tries to sell a portrait of someone to them. Van Doude waves him off.
Patricia is still looking off-screen right toward Michel.*

BERRUTI (*off*): A million three, I can do it. Perhaps tomorrow. It's drawn
on which bank, your check?

354. MS: *Michel, glasses and hat back on, facing Berruti.*

MICHEL: B.N.C.I.
BERRUTI: Show me.

*Michel reaches in his breast pocket for the check he got earlier from
Tolmatchoff. He hands it to Berruti who opens and reads it. Patricia walks on
screen and stands between the two men. Berruti glances at her, then down
at the check.*

PATRICIA (*to Michel*): What now?
MICHEL: I don't know.
BERRUTI (*looking up*): I can call you where tomorrow?
MICHEL (*shrugging his shoulders*): I don't know. The hotels are full of
these fucking tourists. We don't know where to go. Patricia's being
watched.

355. MCU: *Patricia turns toward Michel.*

> PATRICIA (*excitedly*): But in Montmartre! I've got a friend. She has a
> big apartment. JUMP CUT *as she looks toward Berruti.*
> BERRUTI (*off*): No, not Montmartre.

> JUMP CUT *as she looks toward Michel.*

> MICHEL (*off*): But no, not Montmartre, I tell you!

356. QUICK CUT *back to 354.*

> PATRICIA: Why?
> BERRUTI: We have too many enemies in Montmartre, little girl. No, but
> go to Zumbach's Swedish girlfriend's place.
> MICHEL: She still lives on rue Campagne Première?[58]
> BERRUTI: Yes!
> MICHEL: Call me at her place tomorrow. Go on, goodbye, amigo!
> BERRUTI: Ciao.
>
> *Michel and Berruti slap their hands together in the air. Berruti leaves.*
> *Michel walks over to the passenger side of the car, opens the door and*
> *gets in. Patricia follows him in. Michel's theme cues the next shot.*

357. ELS: *high angle on the car driving down the boulevard Montparnasse.*
   The camera pans slowly while the car gets lost in traffic and in the night.

Studio, interior, night

358. LS: *high angle taken from behind Zumbach's girlfriend, a model, who is*
   dressed in a white T-shirt and shorts. She opens the front door, revealing
   Michel and Patricia.

> MICHEL: Antonio sent us. He said we could spend the night here.
> MODEL (*shutting the door*): Yes, very well. (*Motioning.*) Sit down in
> there; I'll be through in five minutes.

359. QUICK CUT *to* LS: *high angle of the apartment. Lights and cameras are*
   set up. A photographer stands with his camera facing the model, who is

posing, almost dancing, under the lights. Michel and Patricia walk over to a couch situated in the rear of the studio.

PHOTOGRAPHER: Okay!

360. MCU: *the model posing with her hands clasped behind her head.*

PHOTOGRAPHER: Smile!

She smiles.

361. MCU: *the photographer from behind the camera.*

PHOTOGRAPHER (*peeking out from behind the drape, angrily*): Smile!

362. MS: *Patricia and Michel head-on, sitting on the couch looking at a magazine together. Michel is wearing his sunglasses. He holds his hat on his knee.*

MICHEL: You could do photography; it pays a lot.

363. MLS: *from behind the model, who is looking at herself in a hand mirror. Six photographer's lights behind her are pointing straight into the camera.*

PATRICIA (*off*): Oh no! You have to sleep with everyone.
MICHEL (*off*): Ah!

364. MCU: *Patricia and Michel on the couch. He has his arm around her shoulder.*

PATRICIA: I'm thinking of something.
MICHEL: What?
PATRICIA: I can't decide.
MICHEL: What about?
PATRICIA: If I knew, I wouldn't be undecided.

She looks at Michel. The music changes to Michel's theme. Michel does not respond to her but just continues to read the magazine, still wearing his sunglasses.

365. *As in 363, except that the model is now wearing a bikini.*

MICHEL (*off*): And your journalist, then, you've dumped him.
PATRICIA (*off*): Yes!

366. CU: *Patricia looking screen right at Michel. She smiles.*

MICHEL (*off*): Why did you speak to him?

367. CU: *Michel turning from profile to face the camera before looking down at the magazine. The right lens of his sunglasses has fallen out.*

PATRICIA (*off*): I wanted to be sure that I wasn't in love with him.

368. CU: *Patricia looking screen right as in 364.*

MICHEL: You do complicate your life, my girl.

Patricia looks screen left toward the model. The photographer's lights go out, causing the scene to darken noticeably.

MODEL: It's over . . .

369. LS: *high angle of the room. The shot is split down the middle by a column on which hangs a cubist painting. To the left, in front of the couch, stand Michel and Patricia. To the right stand the model and the photographer who have just finished their work.*

MODEL (*to the photographer*): You'll take me to the Champs Elysées?
PHOTOGRAPHER: Okay! (*The photographer crosses left to the other side of the room and grabs his coat. He retraces his steps to the right side and leaves with the model.*) Goodbye.
MICHEL: Goodbye.
PATRICIA: Goodbye.

Pan with Michel and Patricia who walk to the other side of the room to a table on which there is a phonograph and some records. Patricia picks up a record. Michel turns and leans against the table.

MICHEL: What record are you putting on?

370. CU: *the phonograph with a record on it. Patricia's hand places the needle on the record.*

PATRICIA (*off*): It's Mozart's Clarinet Concerto. Do you mind?
MICHEL (*as the music begins, off*): No, that one I like.
PATRICIA (*off*): I thought you didn't like music.
MICHEL (*off*): Only this record. My father played clarinet.
PATRICIA (*off*): Ah, yes?

371. ECU: *the cover of a book. The camera shakily pans down, revealing the name of the author, Maurice Sachs, and the title* Abracadabra.[59]

MICHEL (*off*): Sure, my father, he was a genius on the clarinet.

The camera continues to pan down the book. Michel's thumb holds the cover next to a quote: "Nous sommes des morts en permission" ["We're all dead men on leave"]. Below those words, the name "Lenine."

PATRICIA (*off*): We're going to sleep?
MICHEL (*off*): Yes.

372. MCU: *Patricia looking screen right at Michel.*

PATRICIA: It's sad to fall asleep. You have to . . . separ . . .
MICHEL (*helping her with her grammar, finishing the word*): . . . ate.
PATRICIA (*continuing sadly*): . . . to separate. They say, "sleep together," but it's not true. *She turns, looks down sadly, then back at Michel, and directly into the camera. Fade out.*

373. *Fade in.* MLS: *low angle on an interior balcony with a curtain pulled shut across the opening.*

MICHEL (*singing*): Patricia.

Patricia opens the curtains, looks out, and flips her dress over the edge of the balcony.

PATRICIA (*singing back*): What is it?

374. MS: *Michel sitting in a chair, with his back to the camera, wearing only a shirt and undershorts. He props his stockinged feet up onto a table, flips his hat on, and dials the phone.*

MICHEL (*looking up from the phone to Patricia*): Nothing.

375. *This long take begins on the second floor with* MLS *of Patricia in front of a huge mural on the wall. Pan with her as she walks left to a table. She picks up a belt and an earring; then, she moves toward the camera into* MS *before descending the stairs to the left. The camera pans with her.*

MICHEL (*off*): Patricia.
PATRICIA (*walking down the stairs and putting on her earring*): What?
MICHEL (*off*): Come here. (*The camera swirls to keep her in view as she descends. Then it frames her and Michel in* LS *from up on the balcony. The angle on the studio is similar to that in 368. Michel is on the phone, wearing his sunglasses. He reaches in his coat pockets and hands her some money.*) You're going to buy *France-Soir* and a bottle of milk.
PATRICIA: Okay. *The camera pans with her as she skips to the left of the pillar dividing the studio, to get her purse. The radio is tuned to a news program.*
RADIO VOICE: The Soviet delegation made a sensation with what is being called a completely categoric position. They don't have the right . . .

Patricia takes out a piece of paper, looks at it thoughtfully, glances toward Michel, and sets her purse down.

MICHEL (*off*): What time is it?
PATRICIA (*picking up her sweater to leave*): Five o'clock. *Patricia crosses back in front of the pillar and passes Michel on her way to the hall. Pan with her as she starts to exit the front door.*
MICHEL (*to himself and referring to the phone*): Always busy.

Patricia changes her mind and returns to the studio. The camera again pans with her, revealing Michel sitting at the table in the same position as before.

PATRICIA: Michel?

MICHEL (*irritated*): What! *He picks up the phone again.*

PATRICIA: Nothing.

MICHEL (*irritated*): *France-Soir!*

PATRICIA: I'm just looking at you. *She walks back through the hall and exits. The camera pans with her.*

Rue Campagne Première, exterior, day

376. LS: *pan with Patricia walking down a busy sidewalk from left to right and reading the newspaper.*

377. QUICK CUT *to* MS: *Patricia walking and reading* France-Soir, *but this time her screen direction is from right to left. She slows to read in front of a woman in a ticket booth who is selling lottery tickets.*

WOMAN (*calling out*): Lucky day! Try your luck! Take a ticket!

Café, interior, day

378. QUICK CUT *to* MLS: *Patricia sitting at a bar. The bartender faces her in profile.*

PATRICIA: A Scotch.

BARTENDER: I don't have any.

PATRICIA: A coffee then.

The bartender immediately turns to get her coffee. Patricia wearily puts her head down on the bar.

379. MCU: *profile of Patricia talking into a phone, apparently from her same position at the bar. Dramatic music swells.*

PATRICIA: Hello! Danton 01–00? Inspector Vital, please. *Waiting for Vital to come to the phone, she drops the phone from her ear to her mouth and takes a deep breath.*

380. QUICK CUT. *As in 378. Patricia is sitting at the bar alone, phone to her ear.*

> PATRICIA: Hello . . . Patricia Franchini. . . . You know, the guy you're looking for, I just saw him. He's at 11, rue Première Campagne. Yes, 11, rue Campagne Première. Hello . . . Hello . . . Hello?

> *Vital has evidently already hung up. The music has stopped. Patricia stares blankly for a moment, returns the phone to its place, grabs her paper, turns away from the bar, and runs out. The camera pans with her through the window of the bar as she hurries down the sidewalk.*

Studio, interior, day

381. MS: *high angle of Michel resting his head on the desk. He turns his head right, then left. The record player by his head is playing Mozart.*

382. LS: *high angle of Patricia entering the apartment. It is framed so that a pillar divides the shot in half, with Michel far over to one side and Patricia on the right. She walks over to Michel, wakes him up, and gives him the paper. The camera then pans with her as she moves to a closet in the foreground, directly below the camera. She takes off her sweater and walks back over to Michel, the camera once again panning with her. When she reaches the desk, she sets the bottle of milk down next to him. He is now sitting on the table. He puts on his sunglasses, picks up the bottle of milk, and drinks from it. Patricia turns and leans up against the edge of the table right next to him.*

> MICHEL: Are you thirsty?
> PATRICIA: No.
> MICHEL: Antonio's coming in a quarter of an hour. He just called. We're leaving for Italy, my little girl! *He starts to walk toward the camera while drinking milk from the bottle. He circles around the pillar in the foreground; her question makes him turn back toward Patricia who still leans against the desk in the far plane.*
> PATRICIA: Me, I can't go.

> JUMP CUT *so that Michel is on the other side of the pillar approaching Patricia.*

MICHEL: Oh, yes you can! I'm taking you. Berruti is lending me his Simca Sport with an Amedeo Gordini motor.

JUMP CUT *as Patricia sits down in the desk chair.*

PATRICIA: Michel, I called the police. I told them that you were here.

383. MLS: *low angle of Michel and Patricia.*

MICHEL (*putting his hands around her throat*): You're crazy. Isn't everything okay?

PATRICIA (*walking away*): Yes, things are going great! (*As she moves toward some photographer's lights, the camera tracks with her. She turns one on and off in her face.*) No, things aren't going well. (*Patricia turns to look at Michel behind her.*) I no longer feel like leaving with you.

MICHEL (*putting down his milk*): I knew it. *He turns his back to her.*

PATRICIA (*walking farther away*): I don't know.

MICHEL (*off*): When we talked, I talked about myself, and you about yourself . . .

The camera tracks with Patricia in MS *as she strolls around the room, ultimately making two complete circles. At this point Michel is no longer in the shot. They are speaking to themselves and simultaneously.*

PATRICIA: I feel stupid.

MICHEL (*off*): . . . while you should have talked about me, and me about you.

PATRICIA (*speaking as she continues to walk slowly around the room. The camera never stops tracking with her.*): I don't want to be in love with you. That is why I called the police. I stayed with you because I wanted to be certain that I was in love with you . . . or that I wasn't in love with you. And because I am mean to you . . . (*Michel turns the record player off.*) . . . it proves that I am not in love with you.[60] *She is now back at the table with Michel.*

MICHEL: Say that again!

PATRICIA: And because I am mean to you, . . . (*The camera pulls back as she turns to walk away again.*) . . . it proves that I don't love you.

MICHEL (*in the background*): They say there is no happy love, but the opposite's true.

PATRICIA (*talking to herself over his speech*): If I loved you . . . *She is walking in* MS *in the same path as before around the room. His speeches are all off-screen to himself interlaced with hers to herself.*

MICHEL (*off*): You thought so?

PATRICIA: Oh! It's too complicated!

MICHEL (*off*): On the contrary. There is no unhappy love.

PATRICIA (*angrily*): I wish people would just leave me alone!

MICHEL (*off*): I don't believe in independence, but I am independent.

PATRICIA: Maybe you love me?

MICHEL (*softly, off*): You, you believe it, and you aren't.

PATRICIA: That's why I turned you in.

MICHEL (*softer, off*): I am superior to you.

PATRICIA: Now you're forced to leave. *Patricia has returned to the table for the third time now so that Michel is now once again in the shot.*

MICHEL: You're crazy. (*Flicking the back of her neck in disgust, he goes on.*) That's a lamentable argument! *Michel now walks away screen right retracing Patricia's circular path but backwards. He lights a cigarette, and tosses the match away.*

PATRICIA (*off*): You are an idiot.

MICHEL (*interrupting her*): It's like girls who sleep with everybody and won't sleep with the only guy who's really in love with them . . . (*He tucks in and then buttons his shirt as he walks.*) . . . under the pretext that they have slept with everybody.

PATRICIA (*off*): Why don't you leave? (*Michel throws his arms up in frustration.*) I've slept with many men. You mustn't count on me. But leave, Michel, what are you waiting for?

Michel has changed direction. He pats his own head as he moves more quickly back toward Patricia.

384. CU: *profile of Patricia looking screen right at Michel.*

MICHEL (*off*): No, I'm staying! I'm all messed up. Anyway, I feel like going to prison.

PATRICIA: You're crazy.

Pan over to a CU *of Michel looking screen left.*

MICHEL: Yes. No one will talk to me. I'll look at the walls.
PATRICIA: You see, you said that . . .

385. QUICK CUT *on his interjection to* MLS *of Michel and Patricia by the table. Michel is already on his way out the door.*

MICHEL: Oh, shit! . . . Berruti!

Rue Campagne Première, exterior, day

386. QUICK CUT *to* LS: *Michel flags down Berruti just outside the studio apartment as he drives up in a convertible.*

MICHEL: Berruti!
BERRUTI: Hello, amigo. Wait, wait, wait, I'll go park.

Berruti drives right past Michel who runs after the car. Pan right to a LS *down the street.*

387. QUICK CUT *to* MS: *Berruti's car coming into the frame, this time from screen right. Michel runs up just after it, to stand next to Berruti, the driver.*

MICHEL: Beat it, the cops are coming in five minutes!
BERRUTI (*handing a briefcase to Michel*): But I brought you your money!?
MICHEL (*taking the briefcase*): Beat it, that little American squealed on me.
BERRUTI (*grabbing Michel's arm*): Shit . . . get going then, come on!
MICHEL: No, I'm staying! You, buzz off!
BERRUTI (*opening the door*): Don't be stupid. Climb in here.

388. QUICK CUT *to* MCU: *Michel, with his sunglasses on.*

MICHEL (*looking down*): No, I'm staying. (*He looks up.*) Yes, I'm beat, I'm tired, I feel like sleeping. *He looks down again at Berruti and laughs.*

BERRUTI (*off*): You're completely crazy. Come on, get in!

389. MLS: *Berruti and Michel from the sidewalk. Michel has the briefcase under his arm.*

MICHEL: No. The police, I don't care, I'd save my life. What bothers me, right now, is that I shouldn't think about her and I can't manage not to.

BERRUTI (*reaching into the glove compartment*): Do you want my automatic? *He tries to hand the gun to Michel, then forces it on him.*

MICHEL (*throwing it in the back seat*): No.

BERRUTI: I told you not to be stupid.

MICHEL: Beat it!

390. LS: *a black sedan driving up the street toward the camera.*

*At the intersection he falls flat on his stomach in the crosswalk. The camera
continues to move in closer on him as the music peaks and drops off.*

401. MS: *Patricia desperately running down the middle of the street toward
Michel.*

402. MCU: *looking down on Michel, now lying on his back. He still has on his
sunglasses. His hand wipes across his face, knocking the cigarette away.
Smoke rises from his mouth. The legs of three detectives enter to surround
Michel's body. A second later, Patricia's legs follow to stand to the right of
Michel. The trumpet music stops.*

403. CU: *Patricia holding her hand over her mouth and looking down at Michel.
Slowly she pulls her hand away and gazes without expression down at
Michel.*

404. CU: *Michel lying on the ground looking up at Patricia. He is no longer wearing his sunglasses. He begins to make the faces he made at her earlier in the film (shot 133): first opening his mouth wide forming "ah," then baring his clenched teeth as much as possible for "eeh," and finally putting his mouth in the form of "ooh."*

405. *As in 403. Patricia looks solemnly down at him, absently touching her hair.*

406. *As in 404.*

    MICHEL: That's really disgusting [*c'est vraiment dégueulasse*]. *He puts his left hand over his eyes. The hand then slowly slides off his face. His eyes are now shut.*
    PATRICIA (*as his head falls limply to the right and as his theme plays a final time, off*): What did he say?

407. CU: *Patricia.*

    VITAL (*off*): He said, "You are really a bitch [*une dégueulasse*]."
    PATRICIA (*turning to look straight into the camera and rubbing her thumb over her lip as Michel used to*): What is "dégueulasse"? *Her theme plays as she stares straight ahead, then Patricia finally turns away from the camera so that the back of her head fills the screen. Fade out.*

Notes on Continuity Script

1. The French version of the film bears a title shot that includes the censorship visa number, the title *A bout de souffle,* and the following phrase: "Ce film est dédié à la Monogram Films" [This film is dedicated to Monogram Pictures]. No other credits appear.

2. The film takes place in summer, presumably in the very moments during which it was shot, August-September 1959. A calendar appearing in the background in shot 266 would verify this. The first sequence in Marseille is set alongside the Vieux Port. Many of the boats that one sees and hears in the background are doubtless headed for the Château d'If. Indeed, we can assume this is the destination of the American couple whose car Michel steals. Truffaut's treatment, appended to these notes, would tend to substantiate this.

3. This is a colloquial construction not unlike "See you later, alligator."

4. The English subtitles translate "Le crocodile est sauté" as "My goose is cooked," but in fact it refers to the apparatus, "alligator clips," used to hot-wire cars.

5. Michel is seen here in his shirtsleeves, his coat having inexplicably come off. One can assume a continuity error.

6. Equal to 1 franc, 80 centimes today, or only about $0.40.

7. Michel here corrects her grammar. The troublesome word in French is "rappeler" (remember).

8. The Pergola is a café near the Métro Mabillon by the Boulevard Saint Germain, not too far from the Royale mentioned in shot 63, which stood at the intersection of the Boulevard Saint Germain and the rue de Rennes until it was transformed into a drugstore.

9. Equal to 50 francs today, or about $10.

10. This is the first use of the term "dégueulasse," which will recur frequently. Its meaning varies from "disgusting" (as an adjective) to "bitch" or "heel" as a substantive.

11. The cinematographer Raoul Coutard took this shot from within a post office mail cart. Hidden by canvas, he was pushed along the street by Godard. Small holes were cut out from the canvas for the camera lens.

12. The poster advertises a film then playing in Paris, *10 Seconds to Hell*, directed by Robert Aldrich (1959).

13. Godard was at this time a member of the editorial board of *Cahiers du Cinéma*.

14. This and two other extended tracking shots (in the *Herald Tribune* office and in the Swedish model's studio) were purportedly shot handheld by Coutard while he was pushed around in a wheelchair.

15. Bob Montagné is a reference to the character "Bob," the gangster hero in Jean-Pierre Melville's 1956 *Bob le flambeur*. Melville will appear later in *Breathless* as Parvulesco, the writer.

16. "Elysées 99–84." Michel uses the Swiss convention in speaking these numbers: "nonante-neuf, huitante-quatre." Later he will employ the standard French formula for speaking numerals.

17. Laszlo Kovacs, a young cinéphile, was in Paris during the shooting of *Breathless*. Godard liked and adopted his name for the movie. He later became a well-known cinematographer in America.

18. The Metro stop is George V, right at the Champs Elysées.

19. *The Harder They Fall* is a boxing film made by Mark Robson in 1956. Belmondo was a former boxer and will, in fact, demonstrate the sport in two later scenes.

20. This scene recalls a similar incident in *The Enforcer,* a 1951 Warner Brothers film directed by Bretaigne Windust, starring Humphrey Bogart.

21. "Vous" and "tu" are respectively the formal and the informal second-person pronouns in French.

22. The book he gives her is undoubtedly *The Wild Palms* by William Faulkner, for it is indeed about a woman who dies after an abortion, and it is the book Patricia later quotes from (shot 169).

23. In 1959 Orly was the principle international airport serving Paris.

24. The Claridge is a luxury hotel.

25. This line could be translated "I always fall for the wrong dames," making explicit the reference to Bogart in *The Maltese Falcon* (1941).

26. *In a Month, in a Year* is the title of a 1957 novel by Françoise Sagan, an author whose works will be referred to in the scene with Parvulesco as well.

27. The Picasso painting in question is *The Lovers,* 1923.

28. The Picasso reproduced here is an engraving from the 1933–1935 period.

29. While many compositions in *Breathless* purportedly mimic shots from films Godard loved, this one is unmistakable; it comes from Samuel Fuller's *Forty Guns,* 1957. Godard in fact described the quoted scene in detail in his review of *Forty Guns.* See *Godard on Godard,* p. 62.

30. The Renoir painting is *Head of a Young Girl,* 1894.

31. A postcard-sized reproduction of a Paul Klee painting (*The Timid Brute,* 1938) is centered on the wall in this and several later shots. Godard's taste for Klee may stem from their shared Swiss origins. Underneath the Klee, and visible in many of the subsequent shots, is a copy of *Silver Screen* that appears to have Dean Martin on the cover.

32. Michel here gives only the first word of the catch phrase in French, "Décidément, je n'ai pas de chance."

33. The "bac" refers to the "baccalauréate," the degree conferred after examination at the end of high school. It is usually awarded at nineteen years of age and permits entrance into higher education.

34. Lausanne and Geneva are the two principle French-speaking cities in Switzerland. Once again Godard alludes to his native country.

35. *The Wild Palms* was published by Faulkner in 1939. This novel is surely the one Van Doude handed Patricia earlier (shot 104) since it concerns a woman who dies after an abortion. Patricia may be imagining what life would be like, living on the run with Michel in the manner of the doomed protagonists of *The Wild Palms.*

36. Nadia Tagrine is a moderately well known French pianist.

37. *Portrait of the Artist as a Young Dog* was Dylan Thomas's posthumously published autobiography, 1955. Thomas lived from 1914 to 1953.

38. Belmondo was himself a boxer before turning to acting.

39. This discussion of shopping does occur in fact in front of the elegant Christian Dior store on the avenue Montaigne. An antique Citroën is parked in front of it. Prisunic is a chain store featuring inexpensive items.

40. The man who informs on Michel is played by none other than Godard, here literally stepping in to direct the plot of his film.

41. On the left side of the page a second story can be read. Its headline says: "Money given to prostitutes belongs to them. No one can reclaim it."

42. "Candida" is a variant of the French term for ingenuous or innocent. Voltaire's *Candide* (1759) depicts the adventures of just such an innocent in "the best of all possible worlds."

43. Parvulesco is played by the director Jean-Pierre Melville, a precursor of the New Wave, famous for his love of American film noir.

44. Rainer Maria Rilke, 1875–1926, the German poet and mystic.

45. *Paris-Match* is a popular glossy magazine. Pathé-Journal is the newsreel company increasingly responsible in this period for supplying footage to television.

46. This journalist is played by André S. Labarthe, a young critic who began making films and TV programs about this time. He would play a major role in Godard's later film, *Vivre sa vie* (*My Life to Live,* 1961).

47. Jean Cocteau was at this time in the midst of his final film, *Le Testament d'Orphée.* Godard had dedicated his own first short film to Cocteau.

48. *Aimez-vous Brahms?* was the title of the most recent Françoise Sagan novel. It appeared in 1959. It should be recalled that Godard discovered Jean Seberg in Otto Preminger's *Bonjour Tristesse* (1958), an adaptation of another Sagan novel.

49. This is the film's second and last dissolve. The first occurred at the end of shot 12.

50. Equal to 8,000 francs today, or about $1,700.

51. A "403" is a type of Peugeot, while a "4-CV" is a model made by Renault. A "Manurhin" is a brand of motor scooter.

52. A "2-CV" is a small Citroën.

53. The occasion of the parade on the Champs-Elysées was in fact a joint visit by De Gaulle and Eisenhower to the tomb of the unknown soldier at the Arc de Triomphe. It took place on September 2, 1959. One long shot showing DeGaulle and Eisenhower in the same shot as Michel and Patricia was removed by the censors.

54. The dialogue is from *Whirlpool,* a 1949 film noir directed by Otto Preminger, starring Gene Tierney and Richard Conte.

55. The dialogue presumably coming from the screen is actually the recitation of two poems. The first is by Louis Aragon and the second by Guillaume Apollinaire. Godard was fascinated by the Aragon poem, quoting it as early as 1950 in a review of Max Ophuls's *La Ronde,* then again in 1959 in a review of Jacques Rozier's *Blue Jeans.* (See *Godard on Godard,* pp. 20 and 115.)

56. The film playing at the Napoléon was purportedly *Westbound,* a 1958 film by Budd Boetticher, one of the favored directors of Bazin and the critics at *Cahiers du Cinéma.*

57. The dialogue as reported by *L'Avant-Scène Cinéma* is quite different. According to their script, Van Doude and Patricia argue about her love or lack of it for him. Since this dialogue is all off-screen (no lip-sync) it is possible that two versions of the film circulated. I have not encountered a version substantiating the *Avant-Scène* script. Theirs may simply be in error, for the Ballard script agrees with the prints I have studied.

58. Rue Campagne Première is in the fourteenth arrondissement, near Montparnasse. Those who hang out in the Montparnasse area have traditionally been at odds with those at Montmartre, on the other side of Paris.

59. Maurice Sachs (1906–1944) was a literary figure of the period between the wars who caused a number of scandals. Michel's attitudes recall Sachs's often childish anarchy.

60. Marcel Martin (in *Cinéma,* no. 46, May 1960) feels that Patricia's dialogue forms a parody of Jacques Prévert's style, though a parody that adopts at the same time Prévert's iconoclasm and love of youth.

The Original Treatment

François Truffaut

François Truffaut composed this treatment in 1956. After the success of his *400 Blows,* when he had other projects to pursue, he handed the idea to Godard who submitted it, along with three other treatments, to Georges de Beauregard. Doubtless Truffaut's name, recently made famous, impressed the producer enough for him to accept it.

Part of the mythology surrounding *Breathless* has it that Godard took nothing from the treatment save Truffaut's name, which he parlayed into backing for the film. Enlarging on some of Godard's own statements, virtually all the initial reviews of the film mention that Truffaut lent his name but little more. Some suggest that he handed Godard not a treatment but a snippet from the newspaper. We will now be able to see just how faithful Godard was to Truffaut's rather detailed idea. Even small "throwaway" moments, such as the motorcyclist being knocked down as Michel meanders toward the Inter-America Travel Agency (shots 81–83), are foreseen in the treatment. Godard's major addition to the script, it is quickly apparent, is the tremendous enlargement of the scene in Patricia's bedroom, which Truffaut renders in a single paragraph.

This treatment was published in *L'Avant-Scène Cinéma,* no. 79 (March 1968). The translation, the first in English, and long overdue, is by Dory O'Brien.

"We're going to talk about very nasty things . . ."
—Stendhal

Marseille, a Tuesday morning.
Lucien is pretending to read *Paris Flirt* at a sidewalk café at the bottom of the Cannebière. In reality, he is watching the traffic in front of the Vieux Port.

Near the boats that take tourists to view the Château d'If, a girl signals to Lucien. She indicates a convertible with the insignia "U.S. Army" that is at that moment pulling into a parking spot. The occupants, an American officer, his wife, and their children, go to buy tickets for the Château d'If tour. They are watched by Lucien and the girl, who are nonetheless pretending not to know each other.

As soon as the boat has departed, Lucien approaches the car—a DeSoto convertible. He inspects the car as if he were the owner, checking the tires and oil.

The girl asks Lucien to take her with him but he refuses. Getting behind the wheel, he drives off after hotwiring the car.

Some Hours Later, we see Lucien on the highway. Driving a stolen car is apparently nothing special to him, for he seems quite at ease. Alone at the wheel, he bellows snatches of songs at the top of his lungs.

He catches up with and drives alongside an Alfa Romeo driven by a pretty young woman. He asks her if she is not, by chance, Mrs. Lucien Poiccard. She shakes her head no. Lucien quips that this is a shame since *he* is Lucien Poiccard.

A little farther on, we see Lucien slow down to pick up two girls who are hitchhiking. As he passes them, however, he finds them too ugly and speeds up again.

From time to time he talks aloud to himself. Through these fragmentary remarks we learn about Lucien's current projects.

1. To get hold of some money in Paris from a more or less shady business deal. (As the film progresses, we will, from time to time, learn details of Lucien's activities from the brief conversations he has with people he runs into. Basically Lucien engages in some kind of "trafficking." But what kind of traffic? He is secretive about this even with Patricia.)

2. In Paris, Lucien wants to get back in touch with a woman named Patricia whom he hopes to persuade to go abroad with him.

But a third problem is about to complicate Lucien's plans. As the sun sets, he is driving north toward Paris, in the vicinity of Sens. Annoyed by a "Deux Chevaux" that won't dare pass a slow truck, Lucien overtakes both vehicles on a curve *and* on a hill.

The wheels of his car slide far over the center line. A whistle blasts. A motorcycle cop lurking at the top of the hill signals to him to pull over, but Lucien, in his stolen car, instead rushes wildly away.

There is a pursuit of Lucien by the motorcycle cop ending in a small village. Lucien has taken a short cut. It's a cul-de-sac. His motor dies. Lucien pulls from the glove compartment the revolver which he had found there just minutes before, stashed underneath some car wax. The motorcycle cop pulls out his gun. Everything happens at once. Lucien shoots at the cop almost before realizing it. He is furious with himself. The last thing he needed was an incident like this on his record.

We Find Lucien Again in Paris, early in the morning. He must have been hitchhiking, because a small Danish car drops him off at Saint Michel.

Lucien goes into a telephone booth, then changes his mind and hangs up without making a call. He leaves and starts to walk toward the Seine. He is wearing only a shirt, having left his jacket in the car after shooting the cop.

He buys a morning paper. There is no news yet of the murder. Lucien goes into a small residential hotel on the Seine. He asks if Miss Patricia Franchini is there. The doorman, in the process of washing the steps, says no. Lucien insists. But Patricia is not there—the key hanging on the board is proof. Lucien says he is going to leave a message, but when the doorman is not watching, he grabs the key. He enters Patricia's room. The bed has not been slept in. Lucien searches all around the room. He tries on a jacket. Too small. He finds some change in a drawer, but they are American coins. He leaves the room after washing his face.

We watch him enter the Royale Saint-Germaine and ask the price of eggs. He counts his money. He doesn't have enough. He orders two eggs with ham, saying that he'll be back in a minute.

Lucien crosses the boulevard Saint-Germain, passes in front of the Café Hune and enters the courtyard of an apartment building next to the Café Flore. We then see him in the corridor outside the maids' rooms.

Behind a door Lucien hears a woman's voice singing one of the melodies from *La Belle Hélène*. Lucien enters quietly without knocking.

A girl in pajama bottoms is in the process of drying her hair. She turns around, but does not seem surprised. We learn that she and Lucien lived together seven or eight months ago. She now makes public relations films, works in TV, and has abandoned the Latin Quarter. Lucien is less explicit about himself. He has not been doing so badly. He should be picking up two and a half million at noon. In the meantime, could she loan him two or three thousand francs? She replies that she doesn't have enough. Lucien invites her to breakfast, hoping that she will pay.

She can't; she is in a hurry. As she pulls her jersey over her head, Lucien takes the opportunity to extract some bills from her bag. He then tells her that he will see her soon and takes off. It is eight o'clock in the morning, Wednesday.

Around Ten o'Clock, Lucien enters a travel agency on the Champs Elysées. He has bought a second-hand jacket and dark glasses. Lucien asks one of the employees if Michel is there. The employee tells him that Michel will not arrive until eleven. Lucien replies that he will drop in again and asks the address of an American newspaper, the *New York Herald Tribune.*

Fade in on Lucien on his way to the *New York Herald.* He goes into the lobby, addresses a girl in a yellow jersey behind the information desk, and asks if a Miss Patricia Franchini doesn't work there. The girl tells him that she should be on the Champ Elysées selling papers. Lucien leaves again and walks down the Champs Elysées.

He spots a girl in a yellow jersey. She tells him that Patricia is on the opposite sidewalk, near the Pam-Pam.

Lucien crosses the Champs Elysées. He pushes aside a student selling pamphlets who asks him, "Do you have something against youth?" Lucien snubs her, saying that in fact he does hate young people and loves old people instead.

Lucien sees Patricia walking ten yards ahead of him. He follows her for a bit. Sensing that she is being followed, she turns around. She is wearing a yellow jersey with the initials of the *New York Herald* on the front. She also wears an American sailor hat pulled low on her forehead.

She is in blue jeans. Lucien buys a paper from her. She stares wide-eyed at him: What brings him to Paris? She had thought he was in Nice.

Lucien replies that he has come to Paris to do business. He suggests that Patricia go with him to Italy (when he is finished). We understand that they lived together some weeks ago on the Côte d'Azur, where Patricia was spending her holiday. She won't say "yes" or "no" to Lucien. She'll have to see. She must register at the Sorbonne and will perhaps be writing some articles for the *New York Herald.*

They arrange to meet that evening, in a café on the Boulevards, where she will be.

We stay with Lucien, who returns to the travel agency. On a small street in front of the Biarritz, he witnesses a fatal accident: a man on a motor scooter is hit by a car. The bloody face of the man makes Lucien recall the motorcycle cop. He buys *France-Soir* where, on the second page, he finds an account of his murder. The cop is in the hospital, between life and death. The police have a number of leads, the article states: some fingerprints, the jacket, although they had found only several ten-thousand franc bills in it.

With the newspaper under his arm, Lucien enters the same travel agency he had visited just before. Michel, the man he is looking for, has arrived. He hands an envelope to Lucien. Everything seems to be settled. But Lucien is fuming. He had been expecting cash but Michel has given him a check; worse yet, it is for deposit only. Michel insists that he knows nothing about the deal, that he is only making the transfer. He tells Lucien to see Berruti, who should be in Paris now, because he'd seen him the day before yesterday. Berruti will surely get his check cashed, perhaps even without a commission because a couple of years ago Lucien saved his life.

Lucien is annoyed but he will have to go see him. He certainly doesn't dare present his check at the bank after the mishap with the cop. He uses Michel's telephone to call Berruti, who is not in. He is in Paris but the cleaning lady doesn't know where.

Lucien leaves the agency. As he goes out, he passes two men. The camera stays with them. They are on their way to ask at the counter if anyone has seen Lucien Poiccard, who has his mail sent there, having once worked for the agency. Michel is forced to tell them that Lucien had come in five minutes before. The detectives run out and look around them. No Lucien.

It doesn't matter, one of them says, since they will have his photo and his fingerprints that afternoon from the Interpol. The other says that perhaps Lucien, having gotten away so quickly, has disappeared into the Metro.

They drop down into the Metro George V. We follow them. One goes to the Vincennes [eastbound] platform, the other to the Neuilly [westbound]. We leave them to focus again on Lucien, who climbs back out of the Metro exit onto the Champs Elysées in front of the Normandy. He enters the cinema next door, which advertises a Humphrey Bogart film. Lucien lingers in front of a photo of Bogart.

Wednesday Evening. The light falls obliquely on the Boulevards. Lucien has rejoined Patricia in a milk bar. They are going to eat in a snack shop. Because the service is slow, they go elsewhere. Lucien wants to spend the whole night with Patricia. She agrees. Suddenly she remembers that she has a call to make.

She returns from it. She kisses Lucien deliberately and very sweetly. "Now we go to bed," says Lucien. But Patricia replies that it is not possible. She cannot stay with him tonight. It is absolutely necessary that she see one of the editors at the *New York Herald* who has promised to have some articles assigned to her.

Tomorrow there is a novelist to interview and, as the woman who usually does such interviews is not there, Patricia might be able to replace her. This is very important to Patricia, and it is absolutely necessary that she see this editor.

Lucien asks her if she sleeps with him. Patricia says that it is none of his business. She asks Lucien to escort her to the appointment she has made on the telephone. If Lucien doesn't want to, she will go by taxi. But Lucien says that he will accompany her.

They get into a 403. Patricia asks Lucien if he has sold his big Ford. Lucien says that it is in the garage. The garage has loaned him the 403 until his is ready.

Lucien leaves Patricia off in front of the Pergola café at the top of the Champs Elysées. The camera stays with Patricia. She meets the journalist on the second floor. They talk while she eats a dessert and he drinks a coffee. We learn that Patricia is quite willing to sleep with him, partly out of friendship, but more importantly for personal gain. She hopes to get to write articles for the "Spectacles" page he oversees. He tells her that there is a novelist to interview tomorrow morning. He is giving a press conference at his hotel. Did Patricia want to go in place of Clara, a girl at the newspaper? Patricia says yes. The journalist asks if she will stay with him that night. Patricia agrees to this as well.

They walk down the Champs Elysées where the journalist's car is parked. Night has fallen. Patricia figures that Lucien has been watching them from the bar where he was having a drink. He follows them at a distance.

The camera stays with Lucien who buys the latest edition of the *France-Soir* while watching Patricia and the journalist get into an English car. The article in the *France-Soir* says that the police are back on Lucien's track, but that they don't know what name he is currently going under because he has several passports. He has no record in France but there have been incidents in New York and Italy.

Still reading, Lucien has returned to his 403 and he follows the English car.

He pulls up next to them at a red light. He exchanges looks with Patricia, which allows the camera to focus on her again. She seems sad. Then she makes a small gesture of indifference.

Thursday Morning. The camera follows Patricia's crossing the Pont du Louvre as she returns home on foot. Her key is not behind the desk. She goes up to her room. The key is in the door. Patricia enters and finds Lucien listening to the radio, stretched out on her bed. He explains that all the hotels are full because of the tourists.

She gets in bed next to him. They set up the day's agenda. He will take her to her press conference and then come to pick her up. In the meantime he will forge ahead with his own affairs which, we know, consist of following the progress of the police investigation and getting in touch with Berruti as soon as possible in order to get his check cashed. Because Patricia knows nothing about his identity, with her Lucien always plays the role of a guy who has plenty of money and a beautiful car.

They go to eat breakfast at an outdoor spot. While she eats, he says that he is going to get his car at the garage and will be back in five minutes. Now he has precisely this amount of time to find a car to steal. He locates one, a white Thunderbird convertible. The driver gets out and enters an apartment building. Lucien follows him, getting in the elevator with him without saying a word. He watches him go into an office.

Immediately, Lucien dashes back down, hotwires the car, and takes off to pick up Patricia at the sidewalk café.

While Patricia attends the press conference, Lucien goes to sell the Thunderbird in the suburbs. He has trouble with the used car dealer. The latter shows him the latest *France-Soir,* which Lucien has neglected to buy: there is his photo with the caption, "Traffic cop murderer still at large." The used car dealer is quite willing to buy the car but won't give him the money for it for several days.

Lucien tries to filch some money from a drawer. A scuffle ensues between him and the car dealer. Lucien clearly has the upper hand.

When he is gone, the car dealer calls the police and tells them that he has just heard Lucien ask if a Patricia was there, at the *New York Herald.*

This explains why the detectives whom we have seen at the travel agency are waiting for Patricia when she brings her article to the editorial department.

They show her the photo of Lucien. Patricia says that, in fact, she has gone out with him two or three times but that she does not know where he is.

The detectives give her their telephone number. If she sees him again, she is to inform them. "Okay," says Patricia.

She leaves. Now she's aware that one of the detectives is following her. She goes into a movie theater, having seen Lucien following both her and the cop. She comes out again from the back door; then she goes with Lucien into a cinema on the other side of the Champs Elysées while the detective, completely confused, emerges from the first theater.

Thursday Evening. When they leave the cinema after watching a western, Patricia and Lucien look for a hotel where they can spend the night since Patricia's room looks like it is being watched. But all the hotels are full, because of the tourists.

Lucien searches even more desperately for Berruti, to have him cash his check. He runs into various people in various quarters (a girl at Strasbourg-Saint Denis, a bar owner near the Opera and one at Saint Germain).

They are driving around in an obviously stolen car. Lucien tells Patricia that now he has nothing to lose, so that even if it does mean trouble, they might as well travel by car as on foot.

Just the same, in order to avoid unnecessary risks, he shows her the "garage scam." That is, he drives his car into a parking garage that only has a single, aged attendant. He leaves it on the third level and takes another. He has Patricia, whom he had told to hide when they drove in, take the wheel of this car. The old man, seeing a pretty woman driving an impressive car, says nothing when they leave.

Finally, Lucien does get in touch with Berruti who has been hanging around Montparnasse; Berruti promises to help him. Perhaps as soon as tomorrow he will be able to cash his check.

In the meantime, Lucien explains his problems to Berruti who gives him the address of a model who is never home, saying Patricia and Lucien can spend the night there.

The Next Morning, when Lucien is preparing to take off with the money that Berruti brings him, Patricia announces that she has changed her mind. She has just reported him to the police who will be there in ten minutes.

Lucien is furious. But he must flee. He starts off in the car in which Berruti has come looking for him. Out of the car door he hurls insults at Patricia.

The last shot shows Patricia watching Lucien leave and not understanding him because her French is still not very good.

Interviews, Reviews, and Commentaries

Interviews

In the late fifties, interviewing film-makers was an important activity for film critics. As a practicing journalist, Godard was himself a deft and clever interviewer. As soon as he began filming *Breathless* he found himself on the other side of the encounter. At first he responded to these sessions with verve and directness. Later, his interviews would become notorious games of hide and seek, of ludicrous overstatement and calculated lie. Always interesting, his interviews must be read symptomatically and indirectly, in the very manner one must learn to watch his films.

Included here are excerpts from some of the first interviews. The 1962 interview is of particular interest, not just because it is in its full version the most comprehensive, but because Godard is opening himself to his former collaborators at *Cahiers du Cinéma*. The article he wrote about himself for *Arts* appeared in his usual column for that journal, a column for which he frequently interviewed other filmmakers. Here we find him very aware of the fact that he is in effect interviewing himself. The result is disarming.

A section of statements about Godard and his film made by associates rounds out these interviews by giving us a glimpse of things from both the inside and outside. Truffaut's remarks are particularly endearing, especially in light of the rancor that developed between the two directors later in the decade.

Interview with Yvonne Baby

Godard: *Breathless* is my film but it's not me. It is only a variation on a theme of Truffaut who had the idea for the scenario. On this theme of Truffaut I told the story of an American girl and a Frenchman. Things couldn't go well between them because he thinks about death all the time, while she never gives it a thought. I told myself that if I didn't add this idea to the scenario the film wouldn't be interesting at all. The guy is obsessed with death, even has presentiments of it. This is why I shot the scene of the accident where he sees a man die on the street. I quoted the phrase of Lenin's: "We're all dead men on leave," and I chose the Clarinet Concerto by Mozart since he wrote it just before he died.

Int.: How do you see the relationship of the couple in the film?

Godard: The American, Patricia, is on a psychological level, whereas the guy, Michel, is on a poetic level. They use words—the same words—but they don't have the same meaning.

When she betrays her lover to the police, Patricia goes right to the end of herself, and it is in this sense that I find her very moving. You don't see in the film the night preceding this betrayal. I prefer showing the moment when she acts. All in all, from one work to another, for example from a film by [Robert] Bresson to one by [Jean] Delannoy, characters resemble each other. But the difference— and it's fundamental—comes from the fact that the first shows only his characters in interesting moments, whereas with the second it's the opposite.

Int.: Does Belmondo play a character very near you?

Godard: I was inspired by a friend who traveled a lot and was always suspected of smuggling. He also thought constantly about death. Socially I am quite distant from the character of Belmondo. Morally he resembles me a lot. He's a bit of an anarchist.

Int.: What was your working method? Did you improvise?

Godard: I improvised nothing. I took a great many unorganized notes and then wrote the scenes and the dialogue. Before beginning the film I sorted these notes and came up with a general plan. This framework allowed me later to rework every morning the eight pages corresponding to the sequence I was supposed to shoot that afternoon. Except for certain scenes that were already thoroughly worked out, I stuck with this working method and wrote my few minutes of film

From *Le Monde,* March 18, 1960. Translated by Dudley Andrew.

every day. The cameraman, Raoul Coutard, shot without artificial light in natural settings, and with the camera on his shoulder. Shooting took four weeks. How do I direct actors? I give lots of little instructions and I try to find just the essential gestures. This film is really a documentary on Jean Seberg and Jean-Paul Belmondo.

I'm Not Out of Breath

I'm afraid of all the furor around my film. I don't want to discourage my admirers who find it sublime and cry "genius," but really they do exaggerate. While I can't say that I'm not satisfied with the result, it still feels very small next to *The Testament of Orpheus* (Cocteau, 1960), or *Pickpocket* (Bresson, 1959), or *Picnic on the Grass* (Renoir, 1959), or *Two Men in Manhattan* (Melville, 1960), or *Hiroshima* (Resnais, 1959).

The danger for me would be that I might fall victim to my acolytes and lose a sense of my means. You can't promise a masterpiece without chancing disappointment.

The great cinéastes always confine themselves within the rules of genre, the rules of the game. I didn't do this because I am only a little cinéaste. Look at the films of Hawks, and particularly *Rio Bravo*. It's a film of extraordinary subtlety psychologically and aesthetically, but Hawks worked it out so that this subtlety slides by imperceptibly, not shocking the spectator who came just to see a standard western. Hawks is all the stronger for having succeeded in integrating naturally that which is important to him—his personal universe—into a banal subject. I prefer films like this because I would have the hardest time making them. Since I couldn't make this, I tell myself, "This is superior to what I do." I believe every real filmmaker ought to admire films of others while despising his own because they bring him nothing new. No doubt this is why I have doubts about *Breathless,* and I know I might be wrong. In sum, like all normal people, I love that which isn't like me at all and so I look to make films that don't resemble me either. . . .

For *Breathless* I had wanted first of all to respect the rules of the police genre, like Hawks in *The Big Sleep,* because this was my first long film, a commercial film made for a producer. I gave up on this, a bit out of laziness: to express oneself through standard conventions demands very lengthy elaboration of the rules and I don't like to work. If I wanted to show consistent characters, they had to act and talk like the people I know act and talk, including myself, and that one can hardly do a priori. Hence, *Breathless* goes outside conventions.

But none of that is of any importance. You always do the opposite of what you say, and everything comes out the same anyway. I am for classical montage and

From *Arts,* March 1960. Translated by Dudley Andrew.

yet I've created the least orthodox style of montage. My next film, *Le Petit Soldat*, will on the contrary fastidiously respect conventions. It will displease those who admire *Breathless* and vice versa. The cinéaste, in contact with life, discovers that theoretical oppositions between contraries fall apart and are baseless. It is false to say that there exists the classic and the modern, or fascists and progressives, or atheists and believers. There exist only those people concerned with religion, with politics, and with literary problems, and those who aren't concerned at all. That's all. Look at [Luis] Buñuel, [Roberto] Rossellini. Some see in them the helpers of the Vatican, others, helpers of Satan. But they are both at the same time.

By its subject and its expression, *Breathless* accentuates this confusion in a relatively clear manner. "Am I unhappy because I am free, or free because I'm unhappy?" asks Jean Seberg. It's at one and the same time a Catholic film because it shows us that human beings play with their lives, and every second, stage their own executions in one way or another, and it's a Marxist film, more Marxist than *The Salt of the Earth* [Herbert Biberman, 1954] . . . because it shows the state of moral decadence of young people in a capitalist country. Besides, Catholicism and Marxism, they're the same thing; it's just a matter of how you are engaged in life. *Breathless* is a film about the necessity of *engagement* . . . I wanted above all to make a film on death.

Interview with *Films and Filming*

A standard technical way of telling stories was found by the American directors before the war, and since then films have been made in the same way with no imagination, and in France they were doing movies as if they were routine office workers. It was not interesting. When Truffaut, Chabrol, and I were only writing as critics we said just that, and as soon as we had money to do something we quit articles and tried to do some shooting. We never considered ourselves as literary critics but as future directors, and as such we would always comment on the directing and cutting, whether it was good or bad. Although we had no practical experience we learnt from watching films. . . .

. . . The success of the young directors in France is not because they make films in a cheap and fast way, which is a good way to begin, but because of the handling of their subjects.

The term *la nouvelle vague* was the result of an enquiry by one of the big French papers. It was an enquiry not about movies but about young people in general, painters, financiers, and so forth, and they called them *la nouvelle vague*. Then suddenly it became identified with new directors. But in France now there is *nouvelle vague* in everything, even ping-pong. I think we are all waves.

With *A bout de souffle* I had a three-page manuscript written by Truffaut, and I went to a producer and asked whether I could find some money on Truffaut's name, and he said yes. It was comparatively easy then because Truffaut had just won a prize at Cannes. This producer was rather poor, he had no money coming in and he had to do something, so he had nothing to lose. Truffaut's was just an idea for *A bout de souffle,* I changed everything and did the dialogue myself.

It was a fictional story, but I tried to make it in a documentary style. It was a story about a killer, but with a flighty point of view. What I discovered when making the film was that nothing is technically impossible unless you have tried it. For instance, it is generally accepted that you can't paint walls in white, you have to paint them in yellow, well I wonder why? There are a thousand things like this. In *A bout de souffle* I took out everything like this just to prove that it was possible, although the result was sometimes exaggerating. The completed film was two and a half hours in length, which was much too long, and I discovered that when a discussion between two people became tedious and boring you may

From *Films and Filming* (September 1961).

as well cut between the dialogue. I tried it once and found it went fine, then I did the same thing right through the film. But it was done in the style of the movie. But in my next two films I never did such a thing.

My producer gave me freedom the major French producers would never allow me, and I was able to do what I wanted. I consider Resnais's *Hiroshima* and Bresson's *Pickpocket* as New Cinema whereas I consider my *A bout de souffle* as being the end of the old Cinema, destroying all the old principles rather than creating something new. It's more like Picasso's work, destroying everything rather than creating in a new direction. . . .

Interview with *Cahiers du Cinéma*

Int.: Jean-Luc Godard, you came to the cinema by way of film criticism. What do you owe to this background?

Godard: All of us at *Cahiers* considered ourselves as future directors. Frequenting film societies and the Cinémathèque, we were already thinking in strictly cinematic terms. For us, it meant working at cinema, for between writing and shooting there is a quantitative difference—not a qualitative one. The only critic who was one completely was André Bazin. The others—[Georges] Sadoul, [Bela] Balazs, or [Francesco] Pasinetti—are historians or sociologists, not critics.

While I was a critic, I considered myself already a cinéaste. Today I still consider myself a critic and, in a sense, I am one more than before. Instead of writing a critique I direct a film. I consider myself an essayist; I do essays in the form of novels and novels in the form of essays: simply, I film them instead of writing them. If the cinema were to disappear, I'd go back to pencil and paper. For me, the continuity of all the different forms of expression is very important. It all makes one block. The thing to know is how to approach this block from the site most appropriate to you.

I think, too, that it's very possible for a person to become a cinéaste without first being a critic. It happened that, for us, it went as I said, but it's not a rule. Rivette and Rohmer made films in 16mm. But if criticism was the first echelon of a vocation, it was not so much a means. It is said: they availed themselves of criticism. No—we were thinking cinema and, at a certain moment, we felt the need to deepen that thought.

Criticism taught us to love Rouch and Eisenstein at the same time. To criticism we owe not excluding one aspect of the cinema in the name of another aspect of the cinema. We owe it also the possibility of making films with more distance and of knowing that if such and such a thing has already been done it is useless to do it again. A young writer writing today knows that Molière and Shakespeare exist. We are the first cinéastes to know that Griffith exists. Even Carné, Delluc, or René Clair, when they made their first films, had no true critical or historical formation. Even Renoir had very little. (It is true that he had genius.)

From *Cahiers du Cinéma*, December 1962. Translated by Rose Kaplin in *Jean-Luc Godard*, ed. Toby Mussman (New York: Dutton, 1968).

Int.: This cultural basis exists only in a fraction of the New Wave.

Godard: Yes, in those from *Cahiers,* but for me that fraction is the whole thing. There is the group from *Cahiers* (and also Astruc, Kast—and Leenhart, who are somewhat apart) to which must be added what we might call the Left Bank Group: Resnais, Colpi, Varda, Marker. Also Demy. These had their own cultural basis, but there are not thirty-six others. *Cahiers* was the nucleus.

They say that now we can no longer write about our colleagues. Obviously, it has become difficult to have coffee with someone if, that afternoon, you have to write that he's made an idiotic film, but what has always differentiated us from others is that we take a stand for a criticism of praise: we speak of a film, if we like it. If we don't like it, we exempt ourselves from breaking its back. All one has to do is hold to this principle.

Int.: Your critical attitude seems to contradict the idea of improvisation which is attached to your name.

Godard: I improvise, without doubt, but with material that dates from way back. One gathers, over the years, piles of things and then suddenly puts them in what one is doing. My first shorts had a lot of preparation and were shot very quickly. *Breathless* was started in this way. I had written the first scene (Jean Seberg on the Champs Elysées) and, for the rest, I had an enormous amount of notes corresponding to each scene. I said to myself, this is very distracting. I stopped everything. Then I reflected: in one day, if one knows what one is doing, one should be able to shoot a dozen sequences. Only, instead of having the material for a long time, I'll get it just before. When one knows where he is going, this must be possible. This is not improvisation, it's decision-making at the last minute. Obviously, you have to have and maintain a view of the ensemble; you can modify a certain part of it, but after the shooting starts keep the changes to a minimum—otherwise it's catastrophic.

I read in *Sight and Sound* that I was improvising in the Actors' Studio style, with actors to whom one says: you are such and such, take it from there. But Belmondo's dialogue was never invented by him. It was written: only, the actors didn't learn it—the film was shot silent and I whispered the cues.

Int.: When you started the film, what did it represent for you?

Godard: Our first films were purely films by cinéphiles. One may avail oneself of something already seen in the cinema in order to make deliberate references. This was the case for me. Actually, I was reasoning according to purely cinematographic attitudes. I worked out certain images, schemes with relation to others I knew from Preminger, Cukor, etc. . . . In any case Jean Seberg was a continuation of the role she played in *Bonjour Tristesse*. I could have taken the last frame of that and linked it with a title: "three years later." . . . This is to reconcile my taste for quotation, which I have always kept. Why reproach us for it? People in life quote as they please, so we have the right to quote as we please. Therefore I show people quoting, merely making sure that they quote what pleases me. In the notes I make of anything that might be of use for a film, I will add a quote from Dostoievsky if I like it. Why not? If you want to say something, there is only one solution: say it.

Moreover, the genre of *Breathless* was such that all was permitted, that was its nature. Whatever people might do—all this could be integrated into the film. This was even my point of departure. I said to myself: there has already been Bresson, we just had *Hiroshima,* a certain kind of cinema has just ended—well, then, let's put the final period to it: let's show that anything goes. What I wanted to do was to depart from the conventional story and remake, but differently, everything that had already been done in the cinema. I also wanted to give the impression of just finding or experiencing the processes of cinema for the first time. The iris shot showed that it was permissible to return to the sources of cinema and the linking shot came along, by itself, as if one had just invented it. If there weren't other processes, this was in reaction to a certain cinema, but this doesn't have to be a rule. There are films where they are necessary: from time to time one could do more with them.

What is hardest on me is the ending. Is the hero going to die? At first, I was thinking of doing the opposite of, for example, *The Killing*. The gangster would succeed and leave for Italy with his money. But this would have been a very conventional anti-convention, like having Nana succeed in *My Life to Live*. I finally told myself that since, after all, all my avowed ambitions were to make a normal gangster film I couldn't systematically contradict the genre: the guy had to die. If the descendants of Atreus don't massacre each other any more, they are no longer descendants of Atreus.

But improvisation is fatiguing. I am always telling myself: this is the last time! It's not possible anymore! It's too fatiguing to go to sleep every night asking oneself, "What am I going to do tomorrow morning?" It's like writing an article at twenty-to-twelve at a café table when it has to be delivered to the paper at noon. What is curious is that one always arrives at writing it, but working like this month after month is killing. At the same time there is a certain amount of premeditation. You say to yourself that if you are honest and sincere and in a corner and have to do something, the result will necessarily be honest and sincere.

Only, you never do exactly what you believe you're doing. Sometimes you even arrive at the exact opposite. This is true for me, in any case, but at the same time I lay claim to everything I've done. I realized, at a certain point, that *Breathless* was not at all what I believed it to be. I believed I'd made a realistic film and it wasn't that at all. First of all, I didn't possess sufficient technical skill, then I discovered that I wasn't made for this genre of film. There are also a great number of things I'd like to do and don't do. For example, I'd like to be like Fritz Lang and have frames which are extraordinary in themselves, but I don't arrive at that. So I do something else. I like *Breathless* enormously—for a certain period I was ashamed of it, but now I place it where it belongs: with *Alice in Wonderland*. I thought it was *Scarface*.

Breathless is a story, not a subject. A subject is something simple and vast about which one can make a resumé in twenty seconds: revenge, pleasure . . . a story takes twenty minutes to recapitulate. *The Little Soldier* has a subject: a young man is confused, realizes it and tries to find clarity. In *A Woman Is a Woman* a girl wants a baby at any cost and right away. In *Breathless,* I was looking for a subject all during the shooting; finally I became interested in Belmondo. I saw him as a sort of a façade which it was necessary to film in order to know what was behind it. Seberg, on the contrary, was an actress whom I wanted to make do many little things that pleased me—this came from the cinéphile side I no longer have. . . .

Statements

Georges de Beauregard, Producer

Jean-Luc Godard is my friend. We have known each other for a very long time. Together we lived through a difficult period: there is no better way to learn to appreciate someone.

I met him at a time when French cinema was suffocated by conformity. Films were made according to a fixed routine. Godard had ideas. He wanted to break with this standardization, create a modern cinema, in tune with our time. I provided him with the means to do what he wanted to do. He has revealed himself to be the surest talent of our generation. He is very close to the public, he has a feel for the public, even if certain of his films have failed to meet with commercial success. Today, he has profited from all his experiences. His style is that of a man who has assimilated a great deal. He is in complete control of his medium.

As a human being, I appreciate him a great deal, and I like what he does. It is my principle, by the way, never to separate work and friendship. I try to make films with people who might also become my friends. To produce a film, for me, comes down to a sort of moral compact. My task is to discover young people in whom I can place this confidence. We must know each other over a period of several months before working on a film.

I appreciate in Jean-Luc Godard his absolute honesty, in his work as well as in his personal relations.

He has very personal methods of filmmaking. We prepare the film together through free and amicable discussion. After that, he organizes everything as he sees fit: he shoots on certain days and on others, he stops, reflects. Sometimes he overshoots a deadline, but never a budget. Lately, as a matter of fact, he has adopted a comfortable rhythm. He shot *Contempt* very rapidly. One senses that he is very sure of himself.

Raoul Coutard, Cameraman

The first time I saw J.-L. Godard he was working on the scenario for *Pêcheur d'islande:* hirsute, smoking a pipe, entrenched behind his dark glasses, silent.

Originally published in 1963, translated by Ciba Vaughan in *Jean-Luc Godard, an Investigation into His Films and Philosophy* by Jean Collet (New York: Crown, 1970).

Second contact, preparation of *Breathless:* he was more talkative.

From day to day, as the details of his screenplay became more precise, he explained his conception: no foot for the camera, no light if possible, traveling shots without rails. . . . Little by little we discovered a need to escape from convention and even to run completely counter to the rules of "cinematographic grammar."

During the shooting he dug even more firmly into his position; the shooting plan was devised as we went along, as was the dialogue.

The film took shape from moment to moment, as he viewed the screenings. Having come to a basic idea of the characters, he relied on the actors for all the details.

Godard maintains this freedom with the script even in those films, like *Les Carabiniers* or *Contempt,* that have a written screenplay.

Similarly, he could never say the evening before, or even a moment before, what would be done next—the decision would be made during the rehearsal of a scene and sometimes, after having shot a sequence, the entire scene would be reconstructed from a different angle.

Godard takes time out to reflect, chewing his thumb and forefinger.

He is never very talkative, and in order to find out what to do, it is more useful to establish a basic communication than to ask questions. Even then it is very difficult to imagine what might, in his eyes, be important; sometimes we had to start a scene over four and five times because of certain details that were not apparent to the rest of us.

The freedom he achieves with the absence of a prepared script permits an enormous flexibility in shooting, and it often happens that, if he doesn't have a scene completely worked out in his head, he decides to shoot something entirely different, in an altogether different setting, at the last minute. Occasionally he stops for a day to catch his breath and to think. . . .

But during the entire shooting, he is preoccupied by the schedule and budget. Although money is of no importance whatsoever for him personally, it matters for the production, and he modifies his directing as the need arises in order to economize in one scene what he may have overspent on other sequences.

What points of reference might help one to understand him?

His humanity, which glows through in the unreserved support he gives to his friends and in the sincere need he feels to give pleasure to those who surround him and work with him. And though he will occasionally leap down someone's throat, he keeps apologizing until he is sure that the pain he has caused has been erased. He, too, has need of friendship, and he couldn't conceive of making a film with a producer who wasn't also a potential friend.

His good faith in everything that he does, which is manifest, for example, in the fact that he readily admits his errors, to the point that sometimes he will bear the blame for his collaborators' mistakes.

Truth is a necessity for him. For example, his need for truth is such that he will not fake an exterior, he will refuse to light a room if shooting is possible without it, and he uses direct sound under any and all conditions.

François Truffaut

. . . Of all Jean-Luc's films, it is *Breathless* that I prefer. It is the saddest. It is a heart-rending film. In it there is deep unhappiness and even, as Aragon says, "deep, deep, deep" unhappiness.

Breathless won the Prix Vigo.

In effect, *Breathless* is an heir to *L'Atalante*. Vigo's film ends with Jean Dasté and Dita Parlo locked in an embrace on the bed. That evening they surely conceived a child, and that child is the Belmondo of *Breathless*.

The miracle of *Breathless* is that it was made at a time in the life of a man in which normally he would not make a film. One doesn't make a film when one is sad and destitute. Making a film means that you're living in a hotel or an apartment, that you are disengaged from material worries, and that you make your film without any distraction from your present thoughts.

In the case of *Breathless,* the man who made it was almost a pauper. Therein lies the miracle. It is rare that being so unhappy and so alone, one can still make a film.

In this connection, Jean-Luc said a rather cruel thing to me, during the shooting of the film: "I don't feel comfortable in this story of a killer. I was wrong to ask you for your scenario. I should have written one myself and then asked you to sign it. . . ." I would have done it, too, of course. But I believe that the scenario, such as it was, did help him. Jean-Luc's career has demonstrated that he is successful each time he deals with a situation like the one in *Breathless*. With *Vivre sa vie,* there is a girl. She is in a fixed situation, desperate straits, and from the beginning and at the end of the road lies death. Between these two poles, he can do what he pleases, the train rolls along without a hitch.

Personally, I divide his six films into two categories: two sets of three films each. The group I prefer consists of *Breathless, Vivre sa vie*, and *Contempt*. Their point in common is that they take off from a principal character whom they follow as if the film were a documentary. These are his three sad films. They are the most rigorously constructed. The part played by autobiography in each is greater than the role of invention.

Let's say, for the sake of simplicity, that in *Le Petit Soldat, A Woman Is a Woman*, and *Les Carabiniers*, Godard was focusing on his thoughts. In *Breathless, Vivre sa vie*, and *Contempt*, he was filming his feelings.

Reviews

Breathless was immediately the target of a barrage of critical response, the intensity of which has seldom been matched in the history of cinema. From the scores of published opinions and expressions, I have chosen to sample some rather standard French responses and a number of the more articulate English-language reviews.

The French material should illustrate the way the film was taken by the critical establishment. Except for Marcabru's piece, these reviews all appeared in papers and magazines with very large circulations aimed at the average citizen. I have not included the inflated meditations on the film by Godard's friends nor the attacks on the film by his open enemies—at *Positif* and elsewhere. In other words, I have stayed away from the discourse of the cinéphiles. Nevertheless, it is fascinating to note the rather poetic tone of these standard reviews and the philosophical and stylistic descriptions they attempt. All of the French reviews were translated by Dory O'Brien and myself.

In going through the English-language press, I was discouraged by the generally dull quality of the writing and the often pedestrian concerns of the reviewers. I have picked out those reviews that seemed most worthy and diverse without regard to source or to the fame or notoriety of the reviewer. Nevertheless, a good many of these reviews were penned by notable figures in film journalism.

The reader is urged to ferret out more reviews by consulting *Jean-Luc Godard: A Guide to References and Resources,* prepared by Julia Lesage.

Le Monde

Jean de Baroncelli

That *Breathless* should come to the movie screens of Paris a few days after *Purple Noon* [René Clément, 1959] is clearly only a coincidence. But this coincidence is too striking not to tempt one to compare the two films, that of the veteran and that of the newcomer, especially since the subjects they treat offer a certain similarity. *Purple Noon* is the work of a man who has achieved mastery over his art; a work of exceptional intelligence, rigor, and plasticity. Yet the very classicism and (over)refinement of the film seem to me to fit imperfectly with its subject. *Breathless* is, on the other hand, the work of a newcomer who, by taste as much as by necessity (having been given precarious means to work with), has turned up his nose at the rules of film narrative. Over against these rules he has preferred his instinct. This was the right move, for as a result he has found the exactly appropriate tone for the romantic chaos of his story. Speaking the other day of *Purple Noon,* I regretted not having felt, despite my admiration for the work of Clément, that small artistic spark that provokes enthusiasm. Whereas the frequently flawed film of Godard has made this small spark constantly flicker for me. My preferences are clear enough.

Another thing. *Breathless* arrives in time to regild the emblem of the New Wave, which we all know doesn't exist but which these last months everyone has consented to subject to obloquy. The absurdity of generalizations. Because three or four films in succession have let one detect the excessive influence of the most brilliant of our authors ("in the beginning was Sagan"), we rush to condemn, "en bloc," a movement of renewal which has just begun to bear fruit. By replacing, in his film, the play of wit with the movement of the heart (even if this movement is at first disconcerting), by mixing tenderness with violence, sensitivity with cynicism, and the freshness of emotions with the cruelty of words and actions, Jean-Luc Godard has delivered a masterstroke of extraordinary power. And by means of the same strategy he has traced an exact portrait of a certain modern romanticism.

Another sordid tale of debauchery, they will claim. Yes, certainly. But the real-

From *Le Monde,* March 18, 1960.

ism here is not artificial, nor the sordidness gratuitous. The hero of *Breathless* is not a criminal automaton. He is a lost kid in whom we can detect a heart and a soul—enough human depth to make us feel intimate with and even sympathetic to him. His madness, his brutality, his cynicism, his sudden outbursts of tenderness and hope, that need for "something else": so many exacerbated signs of the old malady of youth, of an eternal romanticism. . . .

I have already alluded to the technique of Jean-Luc Godard: *Breathless* was entirely shot—exteriors and interiors—in natural settings. As did Rossellini in the time of *Open City,* Godard hid his camera in the crowd and blended his actors with passersby. The result is that, if the photography is not as slick as the aficionados of pretty pictures would wish it, a prodigious impression of truth emerges from the film. One literally follows the traces of the protagonists. One loses oneself in their existence. It goes without saying that they do not cease to be fictional.

I know I've been only praising the film. There are clearly reservations to articulate. *Breathless* is far from being an absolute masterpiece. But it is almost as good: it is a film that gives us confidence in a young director. . . . Let us emphasize the fact that the scenario carries the signature of François Truffaut, and that Claude Chabrol supervised the production. But there is no point in fooling ourselves: this film carries the mark of an auteur. And this auteur is Jean-Luc Godard.

Arts

Pierre Marcabru

J ean-Luc Godard has understood that the outside world comes to us in suc-
cessive jumps, that the eye and the ear never cling to continuity in the act of
seeing or hearing. On the contrary, the succession of visual perspectives and
of sounds is an up-and-down process, thus demanding irregular attention from
the camera, a sequence of seemingly disorderly glances. This makes for a cinema
of tension, that is, of impulses of the gaze added one on top of the other, of
constitutive characteristics essential to the significance of a given situation.
Hence a sort of phenomenological observation of the characters, which makes
Breathless the most important movie we have seen since *Hiroshima, mon amour.*

Now if I wanted to overwhelm Godard, I would say that in its morality his
work is Nietzschean and in its mode of observation, it is Husserlian. But let us be
serious. Quite simply it seems to me that his work provides a fresh start to a
behavioral cinema. It is this that is most important.

From *Arts,* March 19, 1960.

Le Figaro Littéraire

Claude Mauriac

ean-Luc Godard quotes Griffith. He makes use of a time-honored method of punctuation, the iris, to which he returns the freshness and value it once possessed. A recourse, one among many, to an art of which he knows all the possibilities. But let's listen to his profession of faith: "With *Hiroshima* and with *Pickpocket* something begins which is essentially new, as with Klee in painting."

Hiroshima, mon amour was, until *Breathless*, unquestionably the only recent film to offer a new future to the art of the screen. One of the major interests of this work was that Marguerite Duras had as much to do with this, even in the opinion of Resnais, as the director himself. What's truly important is this collaboration of "authors" who make use of the cinema in order to write the work of their choice. Whether one approves or not of the style is another question. Literary criticism is possible because there are texts. Perhaps before *Hiroshima* criticism had very little to do with films. A work as ambitious as this one, a creation this free, is too new to the screen for the question of whether or not we approve of the form to come up in our reviews.

In citing *Pickpocket*, Godard likewise situates his work in its true context. His reference to Klee is, as well, most illuminating. In painterly terms, Bresson would be abstract, while Godard representational. False dichotomy: in painting as in cinema reality is always both the point of departure and the terminus of a work. The artist reconstructs what he sees in order to portray it in terms of what appears to him to be the essential truth of reality. Forms are first deformed before they are reformed: we may or may not recognize the object, but it is always there. We are speaking of the only art that matters: that without gratuity.

In search of their most secret and true voices, the Bresson of *Pickpocket* makes his characters speak with apparent artificiality. The tone is that which unmediated consciousness would have if it were possible to record the murmur of its meanderings. Jean-Luc Godard proceeds in the opposite manner to achieve the same result: one of the innovations of *Breathless* resides in the natural quality of the dialogue. It seems to us that for the first time we were hearing real speech on

From *Le Figaro Littéraire*, March 19, 1960.

the screen. But this naturalness was only apparent. It had been entirely re-created.

The writing of the film exhibits a surprising liberty. Syncopated rhythm, broken, then taken up again, but continuing in a prescribed cadence, with never a dead space, even when the filmmaker consciously transgresses the rules. His hero is, like each of us, obsessed by certain ideas and certain words, always the same ones. It is in repeating himself that he expresses in the only way he can that which is inexpressible in him.

The deftness of Godard is visible in his having chosen the most classic and the most commercial of themes: a criminal in flight. Good strategy. I have never understood those directors who would refuse to make thrillers because they preferred not to compromise their noble ambitions. With any theme, in films as in novels, one can say everything. It is with joy that we salute the coming of age of a new cinéaste who brings us the happiness of a rich, violent, poetic work that in no way resembles any film ever made before.

Le Figaro

Louis Chauvet

L et us go, for a bit, "against the current." In such an endeavor we will do nothing other than observe the sacrosanct principles of the new school. Little has been said until now about the flaws of this first film by Jean-Luc Godard. Let's consider them. We will then be better able to praise the film. After all, haven't the persons concerned clearly proclaimed their phobia of perfection?

[One.] All young film writers assume the affectation of despising their subject. So be it.

If the characters exist after their own fashion, sometimes delirious, sometimes stupid, even in a *nonexistent* story, this is quite acceptable. But why is it that we always find, in New Wave society, the same types of characters, the likeable hoodlums (this "likeable hoodlum" is becoming, it would seem, a "modern hero"), the neurotics, the decadent young bourgeois, unbalanced and unsatisfied, who give themselves up to apparently desperate erotic adventures, living by the same philosophy and forever delivering almost the same lines? Is this not a summary view of the contemporary world, of the new humanity?

Two. The method; it's no longer very original. In 1948, Sydney Myers produced, with equal technical "Jansenism,"[1] *The Quiet One,* in the streets of Harlem—an unforgettable film that was not well received. Unlucky *Quiet One*! It came out twelve years too early!

Three. Contempt for conventional rules—montage, continuity—that tries to justify itself. The deception would be to present as a personal style an "I don't give a damn" style. [D. W.] Griffith would say that to make the contrary succeed is more difficult, and Euripides and Bernanos,[2] with whom Godard is compared, would not deny this.

Four. The movement of the camera. Does the camera move? Bravo! This must

From *Le Figaro*, March 18, 1960.

1. Jansenism was a seventeenth-century Roman Catholic religious movement characterized by excessive austerity, eventually condemned by the Church as heresy.—Ed.
2. Georges Bernanos was a polemical Catholic novelist best known for *Diary of a Country Priest.* He died in 1948.—Ed.

be the golden rule: when the camera lurches, so does the spectator; he becomes seasick.

It was necessary, I believe, to point out all of this so that we can accurately determine the qualities of the author's flaws. And then go on to positive qualities.

Godard endeavors to *create* a language through an alliance of humorous or seductive images and dialogue (sometimes transformed into simultaneous monologues with an undeniable realistic lilt). This constitutes the film's true novelty.

The *limits* of the endeavor appear when what is said reminds one too much of the nasal tones of a tape recording reproducing the conversation of some wild kids bent on saying anything that comes to mind.

But these utterances, energetically zany, purposely crude, vulgar (pathetic, nonetheless, to the degree that their futile strategy hides some profound anguish), creates a sort of charm, a secondary poetry out of flashes of wit and paradoxes, which cannot be ignored.

The scenes recorded, whether in the street, on the Champs Elysées, in the middle of an apparently inattentive crowd or in the intimacy of a room, prove that Jean-Luc Godard is not only an inspired documentarist, but also an analyst who is intrigued by the states of the soul and their unceasing effects on facial expression. He scrutinizes these faces with a powerful exactitude.

There. I think one must exaggerate nothing—and underestimate nothing.

That Jean-Luc Godard has talent, ability, a sense of humor, a sarcastic wit (to which the spirit of provocation doesn't add much), a belief in cinematography, an active desire "to open new avenues," revealed in his first film . . . this is already a great deal.

The film seems assured of commercial success (certainly . . . certainly). The author will adjust to this, I suppose.

Let us not close without noting how much the beautiful, touching, and, this time, very astonishing Jean Seberg contributes to the charm of the feminine lyricism that accompanies the narrative; as well as how effective is the presence of Jean-Paul Belmondo.

Variety

Gene Moskowitz

This film emerges as a summation of the so-called "new wave" trends here in that it is a first pic by a film critic, it shows the immediate influence of Yank actioners and socio-psycho thrillers. Also the film has no big French names, but has the Yank name of Jean Seberg and has its own personal style.

All of this adds up to a production resembling such past Yank pix as "Gun Crazy," "They Live By Night" and "Rebel Without a Cause." But it has local touches in its candor, lurid lingo, frank love scenes, and general tale of a young, childish hoodlum whose love for a boyish looking, semi-intellectual American girl is his undoing. Gal, incidentally, sells papers in the street.

Pic uses a peremptory cutting style that looks like a series of jump cuts. Characters suddenly shift around rooms, have different bits of clothing on within two shots, etc. But all this seems acceptable, for this unorthodox film moves quickly and ruthlessly.

The young, mythomaniacal crook is forever stealing autos, but the slaying of a cop puts the law on his trail. The girl finally gives him up because she feels she does not really love him, and also she wants her independence. Film does not engender much feeling over the ironic death of the petty thug in the street, but none of the characters rarely feel anything.

There are too many epigrams and a bit too much palaver in all this. However, this does give a new view of a certain type of fed-up, stagnating French youth. It is picaresque and has enough insight to keep it from being an out-and-out melo-dramatic quickie. With the Jean Seberg name, plus the action, this could be a playoff possibility even worth dubbing.

But it looms more of an arty house bet. A "wave" film, with its grabbag mixture of content, satire, drama, and protest, this will need the hard sell. Technique is okay but somewhat grimy because of the spot shooting. But this very grayness may be rated an asset. Miss Seberg lacks emotive projection but it helps in her role of a dreamy little Yank abroad playing at life. Her boyish prettiness is real help. Jean-Paul Belmondo is excellent as the cocky hoodlum. Though the revolt may be a little hazy, this is a fairly vital off-beater worth special handling.

From *Variety,* January 27, 1960.

Sight and Sound

Louis Marcorelles

ean-Luc Godard, who was born of Swiss descent 29 years ago but who is
Parisian by adoption, made his first feature film, *A bout de souffle,* on a
modest budget of some £30,000. He was lucky enough to be able to work
without any external restraint, in spite of the fact that his star was the fairly
important young American actress Jean Seberg, borrowed from Columbia Pictures to whom she is under contract. The male lead, Jean-Paul Belmondo, appeared in Claude Chabrol's *A Double Tour* and had earlier played in an extraordinary short feature, *Charlotte et son Jules,* also made by Godard. The credits of *A
bout de souffle* list François Truffaut as screenwriter and Claude Chabrol as "artistic supervisor"; but this was done for the benefit of the technicians' union and,
in fact, Chabrol had little more to do with the film than to lend it his name, while
Truffaut's contribution was the discovery of a news snippet which became the
starting point of the plot. *A bout de souffle* is therefore a genuine *film d'auteur*—
more so than either *Les Quatre Cents Coups* or *Hiroshima, mon amour,* to which
the screenwriters made powerful contributions. Godard is a lone wolf; he expresses himself with the absolute independence of a novelist, yet with a disci-
pline and style, in the literary sense, which make his film perhaps the most
perfectly realised screen novel produced to date.

Many spectators, especially English ones, may not take his film very seriously
when they see how much it owes to American techniques, to comedies and gangster movies. (The film is wryly dedicated to Monogram Pictures!) The serious
filmgoer in London or Oxford, New York or Boston, may well be shocked by the
ingrained vulgarity of the theme and by the characters Godard has chosen to
portray. . . .

The film is wildly cruel and pitilessly anarchic. The social order is violently
repudiated; love is impossible; death is imminent . . . the film takes on a tragic
coloration, but this is achieved without embroidery or affectation. Godard, who
admires the work both of Nicholas Ray and of Mizoguchi, rejects traditional
techniques, sets out to be provocative, plays continually on shock effects. He
uses a form of montage which could be irritating if overworked, but which is

here held under strict control and achieves miracles: Patricia is talking to Michel; the camera never leaves her face, but by cutting and closing up this single sequence, Godard takes the viewer into a breathless, tumbling daze of a scene.

At the end, Michel is on the ground, dying in front of the policeman who has shot him down. Patricia rushes up to him, and his last words are: *"Tu es dégueulasse."* The final shot is a close-up of Jean Seberg frenziedly asking the policeman: *"Qu'est-ce que c'est que dégueulasse?"*

Vulgar language which may well raise a few pious eyebrows; but it is exactly in keeping with the situation, and this is made many times more effective by the scrupulous care given to photography, acting and direction. We are in the world of the unreal, outside literature, outside sermonizing: in a world of total immorality, lived skin-deep. This is the opposite pole, obviously, from the Brechtian concept of committed art; and Godard is himself explicit about this. "For the artist, to know himself too well is to give way, to some extent, to facility. The difficult thing is to advance into unknown territory, to be aware of the danger, to take risks, to be afraid. . . . The cinema is not a trade. It isn't team-work. One is always alone while shooting, as though facing a blank page."

Like *Les Quatre Cents Coups, A bout de souffle* was filmed entirely in Paris, a modern, largely Americanized Paris. One can challenge the irresponsibility of this kind of cinema, but not the talent of a young artist whose revelations are so startling that they demand attention. The dialogue is dense and highly literary, but it does not aim at effects for effects' sake; and it indicates that Godard, who in his articles as a critic writes a language worthy of Giraudoux, is up to the standard of the uncommitted *"Jeune Droite"* novelists, writers such as Antoine Blondin, a recent prize-winner for his excellent *Un Singe en hiver.* Instead of writing a novel, Godard *writes* a film. . . .

The New York Times

Bosley Crowther

As sordid as is the French film, *Breathless* (*A bout de souffle*), which came to the Fine Arts yesterday—and sordid is really a mild word for its pile-up of gross indecencies—it is withal a fascinating communication of the savage ways and moods of some of the rootless young people of Europe (and America) today.

Made by Jean-Luc Godard, one of the newest and youngest of the "new wave" of experimental directors who seem to have taken over the cinema in France, it goes at its unattractive subject in an eccentric photographic style that sharply conveys the nervous tempo and the emotional erraticalness of the story it tells. And through the American actress, Jean Seberg, and a hypnotically ugly new young man by the name of Jean-Paul Belmondo, it projects two downright fear-some characters.

This should be enough, right now, to warn you that this is not a movie for the kids or for that easily shockable individual who used to be known as the old lady from Dubuque. It is emphatically, unrestrainedly vicious, completely devoid of moral tone, concerned mainly with eroticism and the restless drives of a cruel young punk to get along. Although it does not appear intended deliberately to shock, the very vigor of its reportorial candor compels that it must do so.

On the surface, it is a story of a couple of murky days in the lives of two erratic young lovers in Paris, their temporary home. He is a car thief and hoodlum, on the lam after having casually killed a policeman while trying to get away with a stolen car. She is an expatriate American newspaper street vender and does occa-sional stories for an American newspaper man friend.

But in the frenetic fashion in which M. Godard pictures these few days—the nerve-tattering contacts of the lovers, their ragged relations with the rest of the world—there is subtly conveyed a vastly complex comprehension of an element of youth that is vagrant, disjointed, animalistic and doesn't give a damn for any-body or anything, not even itself.

The key is in the character that M. Belmondo plays, an impudent, arrogant,

From the *New York Times*, February 8, 1961.

sharp-witted and alarmingly amoral hood. He thinks nothing more of killing a policeman or dismissing the pregnant condition of his girl than he does of pilfering the purse of an occasional sweetheart or rabbit-punching and robbing a guy in a gentlemen's room.

For a brief spell—or, rather a long spell, for the amount of time it takes up in the film—as he casually and coyly induces his pensive girlfriend to resume their love affair, it does look as if there may be a trace of poignant gentleness in him, some sincerity beneath the imitation of a swaggering American movie star. But there isn't. When his distracted girl finally turns him in and he is shot in the street, he can only muster a bit of bravado and label his girl with a filthy name.

The girl, too, is pretty much impervious to morality or sentiment, although she does indicate a sensitive nature that has been torn by disappointments and loneliness. As little Miss Seberg plays her, with her child's face and closely cropped hair, she is occasionally touching. But she is more often cold and shrewd, an efficiently self-defensive animal in a glittering, glib, irrational, heartless world.

All of this, and its sickening implications, M. Godard has got into this film, which progresses in a style of disconnected cutting that might be described as "pictorial cacophony." A musical score of erratic tonal qualities emphasizes the eccentric moods. And in M. Belmondo we see an actor who is the most effective cigarette-mouther and thumb-to-lip rubber since time began.

Say this, in sum, for *Breathless*: it is certainly no cliché, in any area or sense of the word. It is more a chunk of raw drama, graphically and artfully torn with appropriately ragged edges out of the tough underbelly of modern metropolitan life.

The New Republic
Stanley Kauffmann

In addition to her function as aesthetic conscience of the Western world, France has always been a pioneer in moral matters. I don't mean things like the so-called "French farce," which has as little relevance to French life as to anyone's; I mean, for instance, the fact that *Madame Bovary* was published in the same year [1858] as *Little Dorrit* and three years before *The Marble Faun*. The French continue to explore in both areas. Much of the result can be written off as mere excursion, like dadaism and the anti-novel, still they *do* it.

The penalty of this virtue is high expectation, which is why the much-discussed New Wave of French films has been disappointing. Although several good films emerged from it, it has been more a Young Wave than a new one. But now, with the appearance of *Breathless,* we have a film that is new, aesthetically and morally.

The director—whose film this is in a way that no American film belongs to its director—is Jean-Luc Godard, who is 30 and who wrote the screenplay from an idea suggested by François Truffaut, of *The 400 Blows.* This is Godard's first full-length film, and it quickly establishes that he has a style of his own and a point of view. He tells here the story of a restless, dissatisfied young man, and his camera follows the protagonist about like a puppy, wheeling and reversing and crowding up close; switching abruptly (without dissolves) as abruptly as the young man himself loses interest in one matter and goes on to the next. Form and subject are perfectly matched in this work.

That subject is the anti-hero—not to be described by the favorite cavil word "amoral" but immoral and living in an immoral world. He may have got there because of his revulsion or our exclusion of him, but that is where he now lives by upside-down standards. Already familiar to us through numerous works from Jarry through Céline to Camus, he now appears on the screen: stealing, mugging, murdering—and engaging us. We do not bleed for him as the child of uncongenial parents or as an underprivileged waif. He is not to be cured by any of the cozy comforts of psychoanalysis or social meliorism. The trouble with this

From *The New Republic,* February 13, 1961.

young man, although he doesn't specifically know it, is history. If we understand him, it is because we know that he is contemporary society *in extremis:* that the dissolution of religious foundations and conceivable futures are in him carried to the ultimate, short of suicide.

Yet this film is not a bid for sympathy, it is an assault on those who can be lulled by thinking that the leak is at the other end of the boat and anyway we're only one-quarter under water. The film says, as have many French novels and plays, that if we concentrate on hoping for a revival of the past, we will all drown. What we must find is another boat—and what it is, Godard presumably doesn't know, any more than the rest of us; but (to change metaphors) at least he knows that it is fatal to cling to the bosom of the dead mother just because she is not yet stone cold. . . .

The style is all. The first two minutes make you think this is going to be a breezy Gallic comedy about crooks. A shapely girl-accomplice signals Michel when to snatch the car. Then, as he speeds out alone through the country, he sings, talks to himself, comments on the beautiful weather, finds a pistol in the glove compartment, plays with it as he drives, going "pop!" at the sun. He is soon cornered by a policeman and the gun does in fact go "pop," but the actual shooting is not much realer to Michel than the pretended one. This playful violation of the bases of civilized behavior is typical of the film.

Although it exists in an anti-conventional world and although Michel's hero is Humphrey Bogart, this is not a hard-boiled film. It is the epic of a romantic outlaw, as egocentric as romantics and outlaws always are, whose life seems the only natural one to him. It is a film of flawless consistency and uncompromised truth. It may not be *your* truth, but that, of course, is not the primary point. . . .

Time

Breathless is a cubistic thriller that has an audience because half a century of modern art and movies have rigorously educated the public eye. Filmed on the cheap ($90,000) by an obscure, 30-year-old film critic (Jean-Luc Godard) of the French New Wave, *Breathless* would seem to offer little to the average star-struck spectator—it features a Hollywood reject (Jean Seberg) and a yam-nosed anonymity (Jean-Paul Belmondo). What's more, it asks the moviegoer to spend 89 minutes sitting still for a jaggedly abstract piece of visual music that is often about as easy to watch as Schoenberg is to listen to. Then why, in the last year, has this picture done a sellout business all over France? Belmondo explains some of the excitement. A ferally magnetic young animal, he is now being called "the male Bardot." But more important than Belmondo are the film's heart-stopping energy and its eye-opening originality.

Breathless has no plot in the usual sense of the word. The script of the picture was a three-page memo. Situation, dialogue, locations were improvised every morning and shot off the cuff. By these casual means Godard has achieved a sort of ad-lib epic, a Joycean harangue of images in which the only real continuity is the irrational coherence of nightmare. Yet, like many nightmares, *Breathless* has its crazy humor, its anarchic beauty, its night-mind meaning. . . .

. . . The hero, though such ideas are far beyond his merely physical preoccupations, behaves like a personification of Gide's *acte gratuit* ("an action motivated by nothing . . . born of itself"), and his story can be seen as an extemporization on the existentialist tenet that life is just one damn thing after another, and death is the thing after that.

But Godard does not pose his philosophical questions very seriously; he seems chiefly concerned with developing an abstract art of cinema, in which time and space are handled as elements in a four-dimensional collage. Camera and performers, moving at random and simultaneously, create the cubistic sense of evolving relativity. Foregrounds and backgrounds engage in a characteristically cubistic dialogue of planes. Similarly, noises and images, words and actions conflict or collaborate in amusing, revealing or intentionally meaningless ways. At one point the screen goes black in broad daylight while the characters go on talking—they are really in the dark.

From *Time*, February 17, 1961.

More daringly cubistic is the manner in which Godard has assembled his footage. Every minute or so, sometimes every few seconds, he has chopped a few feet out of the film, patched it together again without transition. The story can still be followed, but at each cut the film jerks ahead with a syncopated impatience that aptly suggests and stresses the compulsive pace of the hero's doomward drive. More subtly, the trick also distorts, rearranges, relativizes time—much as Picasso manipulated space in *Les Demoiselles d'Avignon*. All meaningful continuity is bewildered; the hero lives, like the animal he is, from second to second, kill to kill. A nasty brute. Godard has sent him to hell in style.

Film Quarterly

Arlene Croce

Alors, qu'est-ce que "la nouvelle vague"? We had begun by elimination, as one production after another failed to bear out the notorious *Cahiers* tastes ("But they don't *make* that kind of film!"). *Breathless* shows what the modern French version of "that kind of film" really looks like, and the result is one of the most genuinely novel films of the lot. As parody, it is as subtly intellectual as *Kiss Me Deadly* was exaggeratedly visceral; as improvisation, it is as unified and witty as *Beat the Devil* was chaotic and arch; and as an example of new-wave camp, it is a beaut. The 89 hectic minutes of *Breathless,* in fact, constitute something very close to a publicity release of the whole *Cahiers* metaphysic: the cult of America and the *film noir américain,* the theories of pure cinema, etc. To this it specifically contributes the new celebrity, not only of what the French press has already labeled *"Belmondisme,"* but *Sebergisme,* and *Godardisme* as well.

To take *Godardisme* first: "I was out to attract attention," he recently told the New York *Times.* The dedication to Monogram Pictures, like the proffered copy of *Cahiers du Cinéma* that gets within camera range (yes, again), is an earnest joke—*acte gratuit* combined with a bit of inside Hip. This two-ways-at-once approach characterizes the entire film. Both ways have equal weight and are equally serious. *Breathless* at once assimilates and canonizes the Monogram tradition; that is its epochal service. It was Cocteau who said: "The principle of novelty becomes very difficult to recognize when our age forces us to remove from it its usual attributes of strangeness." It was also Cocteau who, with Sartre, proclaimed *Breathless* "a masterpiece." The principle of novelty, in *Breathless,* lies in its acceptance of an exhausted genre—the Hollywood grade-B crime film—as a simulacrum of reality. Its plot is little more than that of the quickie digest: Footloose Killer on the Run Tangles with Double-dealing Broad as Cops Close In—Big Paris Manhunt. These mediocre clichés are played out in the

From *Film Quarterly* 14 (Spring 1961): 54–56.

deadpan style of an *actualité,* producing a dual impression of great moral wit and intense neurotic despair. The term "romantic nihilism" which critics have applied to many of the New Wave films and to *Breathless* in particular is apt enough. But the trouble with it is that it tends to make a genralizing cultural analysis of what are essentially cinematic fun and games. I wonder that these same critics do not take more notice of the far more explicit cultural analysis that the film itself makes.

In so far as it is the perennial function of art to reveal, compare, and criticize cultural and moral preference, *Breathless* accomplishes much that is necessary for our present. Classic parallels are uncovered in the commonplace and are witty beyond any since Cocteau's own historic rummagings on behalf of another generation. As she appears in *Breathless,* the gangster's classic nemesis (Double-dealing Broad) would have astonished Diaghilev. The new fatal woman appears for the first time in the unremarkable person of one of those American college girls who wear slacks and yellow T-shirts and hawk the *Herald-Tribune* up and down the Champs Elysées. The writing, casting, and playing (it is Miss Jean Seberg) of this part, not to speak of the whole psychological conception of the character and its function as the film's moral focus, are of such deadly perfection that, if we were as alert to the results of cultural export as we are to its necessity, picket lines and reprisals from the American Legion would seem to be in order. After all, here she was Joan of Arc.

The French love of the free-style American idiom isn't artificial; if it reflects local ethos and tempo in the American Age, that idiom is also fascinating in itself. *Breathless* is a mannerist fantasy, cinematic jazz. Watching it, one can hardly avoid the feeling that Godard's intention, above all, was to produce slices of cinema—shots, figments, iconography—what the *Cahiers* critics talk about. His reality is always cinematized; the camera is always "there," as it were, with its short jabs or long looping rambles of celluloid. There are few dissolves and almost no smooth cuts; and the cuts are often so fast that for moments at a time the spectator is thoroughly dislocated. For example, the arrival of Belmondo in Paris is shown thus: a long shot of the city / a car pulling up / Belmondo entering a phone booth, making a call, getting no answer, leaving / Belmondo somewhere buying a paper / Belmondo on the doorstep of a pension, with some dialogue / Belmondo inside at the concierge's desk and stealing a key / Belmondo emerging, toweling, from the bathroom of the apartment. The whole truncated sequence lasts considerably less than a minute; there are no transitions, no "continuity." Often there are cuts made within the same shot. No attempt is made, either through cutting or through the long drunken pans, at academic-style montage, composition, or meaning of any sort. It is merely movie business.

Similarly, Belmondo's performance, appearance, and manner are a totemistic compendium of movie-gangster busywork: the boxer's gait, the squint, the hat-wearing, chain-smoking, telephoning, driving, singing, shouting, mugging (in both senses), and, of course, the classic thumb-to-lip gesture of reflection (after Bogart, who himself appears in appreciable closeup, in a still), are all brilliantly tabulated. Action is all. This article of faith, central to the *film noir*, is what has always made the aesthetic truth of the *film noir* seem so shallow to American and British critics; the identification of personality and behavior is both absolute and rudimentary, unpardonably so. Hence, in *Breathless*, Michel's "Burglars burgle, lovers love, murderers murder . . . they can't help it" becomes an exact reflection of the crime movie's puerile fatalism.

But it would be a shame to depend exclusively on the words in this film, good as they are. *Breathless,* from beginning to end, is the total expression of its own meaning. If action is all, spontaneity, improvisation, is the only possible style. It is the style cultivated by Michel as an expression of impermissible masculine virtuosity. He at least is the hero of his own life, even if his life is a cheap film and, in the end, not worth living. *Breathless* sees an art form as a life-style and vice versa; quite logically, it ends with its hero's death.

Sebergisme is the logical destruction of *Belmondisme.* Patricia, the American, irretrievably square, emotionally immobile, centerless, complacent, and uncomprehending, touches Michel, the Frenchman, at all those points where he is most vulnerable. She is the triumphant actual artifact of a culture of which he, in his delusion, is the copy, the dupe. He is the dynamo, she the void. Their long magnificently impromptu scene together in and out of bed inaugurates a dialectic of contemporary national manners that is almost Jamesian in its proportions. Their mutual assimilation of each other's backgrounds is as comically and painfully incomplete as it is conscientious. After she betrays—or, more accurately—disposes of him by calling the police, who shoot him down in the street, his bitter and just pronouncement upon her as a human being, *"Tu es dégueulasse,"* is as far as the film goes. No one says, *"Tu es New York"*; *"Tu es Paris,"* although it is implied at every second. *Breathless* shows, with power, irony, and precision, what great cultural convulsions have taken place in our time. Again, as of old, the megalopolis frames the last spasm of the fleeing killer. Paris, beautiful, for centuries dedicated to an ease of individual enterprise, was created for deaths larger than this.

Esquire

Dwight MacDonald

I have always had a great faith in intellectuals, and so I was not surprised when Einstein predicted where that planet would be or when Trotsky organized the Red Army or when Eisenstein and Pudovkin created a great cinema on the basis of some extremely abstract ideas. But I must admit I was unprepared for the emergence from the chrysalis of *Cahiers du Cinéma,* an uncompromisingly highbrow, avant-garde and far-out Parisian magazine with the usual tiny circulation, of a whole school of critics-turned-creators which would revolutionize the French cinema. Alain Resnais (*Hiroshima, mon amour*) and François Truffaut (*The 400 Blows, Shoot the Piano Player*) were the first masters to emerge. Now they are joined by Jean-Luc Godard, who at thirty has become famous with his first feature-length movie, *Breathless (A bout de souffle).* He was helped, as should be the case with any new school in the arts, by two senior members who had been impressed by his short films: Truffaut, who wrote the original story, and Claude Chabrol, who supervised the production.

The story-line is familiar to the point of banality: a young bum (French, male) steals a car, kills a cop, shacks up with another young bum (American, female) in Paris, who finally betrays him to the police, who kill him. The point is there is no point—cf. Truffaut's *Shoot the Piano Player*—that things happen because other things have happened and not because of any human volition or cunning. The male steals the car because it was there and shoots the motorcycle cop (who was only after him for speeding) because there chanced to be a gun in the car and pursues the female because he has a twitch for her which obsesses him because it is the only positive feeling he has. She turns him in because she finally decides she must extricate herself and can't think of any other way—though "decides" is wrong; her behavior, and his, is as planless as the reactions of paramecia who are bumped together or pulled apart by eddies in the culture fluid. And the police kill him because he fires at them with a gun that has been slipped into his hand by a well-meaning pal. It is all subhuman, without either will or feeling. There are interesting similarities to the current "objectivist" novels of Sarraute and Robbe-

From *Esquire* (July 1961). Reprinted in *Dwight MacDonald on Movies* (Englewood Cliffs, N.J.: Prentice-Hall, 1969): 372–375.

Grillet, which Miss Sarraute has described as concerned only with what "might be called 'tropisms,' after the biological term, because they are purely instinctive and are caused in us by other people or by the outer world and resemble the movements by which living organisms expand or contract under certain influences, such as light, heat and so on."

Yet the effect of *Breathless* is not depressing, as one might expect, but exhilarating. This is partly because movies are better at "objectifying" than words are. And partly because Godard has cast Jean-Paul Belmondo as the male and Jean Seberg as the female. Both are limited as actors—I predict that his aggressive ugliness and her torpid prettiness will become cinematic clichés—but they are just right here. A director should use his stars as ruthlessly as a painter his colors; he should be the subject, they the object. As Stroheim in *Greed* converted Zasu Pitts from her previous comedy gray into tragic black, so Godard has used Seberg's blank, vapid face—the kind that has launched a thousand bad movies— to get just the effect he wanted, which was that of a Bennington girl in Paris, seeking thrills and a career (both on a high, or Authentic, level) but childishly sucking her thumb in moments of crisis. A Daisy Miller of our time, the American Dream turning into nightmare.

What is especially interesting is the original style that Godard has devised to tell his story: jerky, discontinuous, staccato, perfectly adapted to render the convulsive style of this kind of life. There are no transitions, no developments; the montage often skips like a needle on a record. Again the resemblance to what the French objectivists are trying to do in the novel. . . . Godard uses his camera with the freedom of the gifted amateur who is innocent of all the conventions that the professionals have developed to take the edge off visual reality. In *Breathless* one sees the world not as it is—who knows what it "is" after all—but as an individual with a fresh eye sees it, which is the next best thing. Belmondo's drive from Marseilles in the stolen car, for instance, is a lyric of freedom, full of exuberance and humor. Its opposite, equally well done, is the long, aimless bedroom scene, in which it becomes evident, through many small touches of dialogue and expression, that each lover is so bound by childish ego as to be unable to make contact with the other, that they are emotionally impotent. This is the necessary prelude to the catastrophe.*

*When I saw *Breathless* a second time, in 1966, this famous scene still seemed long and pointless but, alas, only that. Godard's style was new in 1961 but by 1966 it had been imitated so much by others, and by himself, that the originality was less apparent than the new conventions its success had established. The whole film had dimmed, and I was irritated—and bored—by the same artifices that had delighted me when Godard first invented them. Much the same thing happened, for me, when I reread the early Hemingway 35 years later (see my *Against the American Grain*, p. 175).

When one adds *Breathless* to *L'Avventura, Hiroshima, mon amour,* and *Shadows,* I think it not premature to say that the sound film, after thirty years of fumbling around, is beginning to develop a style of its own. This new international school varies from improvisation to stylization—the difference is not as great as one might imagine—but it has three qualities in common: it subordinates plot to character; it uses images and sound to suggest a mood rather than tell a story; and it has restored montage and the camera to the dominance they had before they were dethroned by stage dialogue in 1930.

The Times (London)

Breathless] is in the fashionable idiom, a *nouvelle vague* film, a production of the *Cahiers du Cinéma* group. . . . It is the group's "intellectual manifesto." In that it preaches the doctrine of social and moral disengagement, this may well be so. It is a film in the veins of which runs not the healthy, turbulent blood of anarchy but the thin, grey fluid of nihilism.

Yet it would be a mistake to treat *Breathless* entirely in terms of intellectual generalizations or to think of it as something new and revolutionary. There are moments when it follows the classic lines (classic as the cinema understands the term, that is) of *Le Jour se lève,* only in the place of the forces of conscience and retribution that were there at work, here there is only futility, the sense of waste, loss, purposelessness.

In that last word lies, perhaps, the clue to what it is in the film that attracts and holds the imagination. It is not moral purposelessness that is here the issue, but rather those random acts and words which form the patternless pattern of everyday human existence. Scriptwriter and director are determined to break out of the all too predictable formula which encloses in the embrace of death the average big-scale commercial film from its opening to its closing sequence, and it is this determination which gives *Breathless* its stature as a serious film.

From *The Times* (London), July 7, 1961.

Films and Filming

Gordon Gow

Watching *A bout de souffle* is like riding with an L-driver, moving in short, compulsive jolts. The first time I saw it, a year or so back, I assumed that the erratic editing, the deliberate disjointedness, expressed the central character's state of mind. Michel is a petty criminal who has entered the big-time by killing a policeman, compulsively, and is now on the run, with stolen cars and a fairly free American-in-Paris girlfriend. Being *A bout de souffle*, he is all a-jitter. So I thought.

However, just recently I had the salutary experience of interviewing the director, Jean-Luc Godard, and when I asked him exactly what he had in mind his answer was that he doesn't hold with rules and he was out to destroy accepted conventions of filmmaking. *Hiroshima, mon amour,* he said, was the start of something new, and *A bout de souffle* was the end of something old. He made it on real locations and in real rooms, having no truck with studios (although more recently he has worked in a studio and found it advantageous). He employed a hand-camera because he is impatient and when he is ready to shoot he doesn't like waiting about for complicated camera setups. And having finished the shooting, he chopped it about as a manifestation of filmic anarchy, technical iconoclasm. He didn't see this especially as representative of Michel's muddled mentality, although he admitted that he wouldn't have used the same technique if he had been dealing with a level-headed character. His method seems to be largely instinctive, with the minimum of premeditation.

Even at the second viewing, the general jerkiness of *A bout de souffle* retains its power to mesmerize. It draws you in and keeps you agog. Raoul Coutard's flexible camera gives each shot an immediacy and fluidity, while the off-beat editing propels attention from point to point. Like Truffaut, Godard has seen the advantage of putting the camera in a car and the initial ride away from Marseilles toward Paris is at first a lyrical jaunt. A jubilant Michel fires gunshots into sun-pierced woods. With the appearance of the police, the tempo increases suddenly. From the killing of the policeman, the picture cuts abruptly to a distant view of

From *Films and Filming* (August 1961).

Michel running fast across open country. Here the cutting seems far from destructive; creative, in fact. Elsewhere, more than once, it looks wilful; one
closeup of Jean Seberg hops hectically about the screen, a fixed shot whose
position is shifted a number of times in the editing.

Often there is a sharp sense of urgency in this kind of cutting: Jean Seberg rises
from a sidewalk table and steps toward Belmondo's waiting car, then suddenly
they are both in the car and already it has progressed some distance along the
street. This sort of time-jump is akin to several in *Hiroshima, mon amour,* but
rougher, less orderly. A lively bed-romp is so jolted in the cutting-room that
when Belmondo and Jean Seberg are writhing blissfully beneath a sheet a censor
who felt inclined to trim a saucy frame or two could do so without interrupting
the rhythm.

Sentimentally, Godard closes two sequences with an iris, in homage to Griffith
perhaps. Slyly, he sets his principals walking through busy streets while passersby ignore both them and the hidden camera. Thoughtfully, he catches a
splendid vista of the Champs Elysées at the precise moment when the lights are
turned on. And far from being gimmicky, all these things merge into a form that
lifts the characters and the plot above themselves. . . .

Nowadays when enthusiasts in America as well as France are hopping hectically aboard a bandwagon called *nouvelle vague,* and sometimes missing their
footing pretty badly, it is far too easy to claim that any departure from the
machine-tooled, glossy norm is commendable. Change in itself is no safeguard
against decay. But this extreme effort to break with cinematic conventions is one
that works well, and by the time it has arrived galvanically at its climax, and
Belmondo has taken his long death-run down a real street, observed with interest
but without much concern by passersby, the feel of tragedy is strong and the
inherent sense of Cinema is undeniable.

Commentaries

One of the most talked-about films in the history of the medium, *Breathless* has nevertheless been subjected to very little intense analysis. Many brief reviews exist; very few extended essays. Moreover, the nature of serious film study has changed dramatically in the past two and a half decades, so that, unlike *reviews* of the film which may disagree in opinion but generally share a set of concerns, those *essays* that *Breathless* has occasioned do not fit together or maintain a dialogue. They speak at cross-purposes or they do not speak to each other at all.

To exploit the potential insights that makes this situation a symptom of our cultural history, I have chosen four essays spanning more than twenty years. The first two appeared in the guise of long reviews, Luc Moullet's in Godard's home journal *Cahiers du Cin-*

éma, and Jean Carta's in the unlikely forum of a Catholic weekly, *Témoignage Chrétien.* Together they suggest the range of thought about style, character, and morality that the film occasioned in its first year of exhibition. At the end of the sixties Charles Barr contributed a chapter on *Breathless* to an anthology on Godard put out by *Movie* magazine, the seat of British auteur studies. His essay draws on Godard's later films as it seeks the hidden Godardian system informing his first feature. Barr's essay is directed at the cultured filmgoer and also at university students who were just then beginning to study the cinema in a scholarly way.

The final selection is taken from Marie-Claire Ropars's lengthy essay, "The Graphic in Filmic Writing: *A bout de souffle* or the Erratic Alphabet," which was first given (in French) as an address to the conference on Film and Textual Analysis organized by the American avant-garde journal *Enclitic*. The editors of that journal immediately translated and published the piece in 1982. The full French version appeared in *Littérature* 46 (May 1982). Ropars's writing permits us to see in an instant just how far serious film discourse has traveled. The film's moral premises interest her not at all. Characters become functions (she labels them "M" and "F," as in algebra) of an enterprise of representation. Nor does she find that enterprise to be related to the personal expression of the director as Charles Barr had. Instead, *Breathless* becomes a contested site where male and female functions contend via images, sounds, and writing. The dissociation of images and sounds (particularly in the sequence in the Napoléon theater) allows her to bring to bear on this film the vocabulary of Jacques Derrida, of which she is a master. Cinematic "writing" cuts through the text in innumerable ways: visible words, spoken words, the break between signs and what they signify, the way some signs refer to other signs, and so on. Reproduced here is the least theoretical portion of a remarkable essay.

Breathless is not only extremely amenable to this sort of study, it is itself one of the guideposts that has led to such a poststructural, post-modern approach to films. It self-consciously stages the tension all films feel between what Ropars, following Jacques Lacan, refers to as the realm of the "symbolic" (language, reason, signification, representation) and the realm of the "imaginary" (force, the unconscious, drives, primary unification). The full essay ingeniously discovers fragments of signification scattered across the body of the text in a way that is both dream-like and perversely ludic. For example, the sounds of the French title *A bout de souffle* remind her not only of the way we say the alphabet (A, B, C, D) but also of the title of the Maurice Sachs novel Michel picks up at the end of the film, *Abracadabra*. The question of intentionality, of Godard's awareness of this maze of (partial) meaning, is irrelevant to her, as it is to most current theorists. Signification, in cinema as in writing, has its own reason and effects.

In its technique of attending to minute details of possible signification, and in its goal of not just understanding but of participating in a project of cultural writing, Ropars's essay is at the forefront of modern criticism in the arts. That *Breathless* is a film to sustain such discourse so long after its appearance testifies to its complexity and its allure. We shall have more articles on *Breathless,* of that I am sure.

Jean-Luc Godard

Luc Moullet

The first of the many innovations of *Breathless* is the conception of its characters. Godard did not follow a very precise line in painting them, but rather he consciously worked out a series of contradictory directions. Godard is an instinctive creator, and rather than logic per se (which he used in his first timid attempts, which he was too lazy or not interested enough to follow), he follows the logic of his instinct. He explains this in *Charlotte et son Jules:*

> I seem not to care what I say,
> But that's not true at all. Not that.
> From the mere fact that I say a sentence,
> There is necessarily a connection with what precedes.
> Don't be bewildered,
> It's Cartesian logic.
> But yes,
> That is exactly how I speak in the theater.

A film is not written or shot during the approximate six months allotted it, but during the thirty or forty years that precede its conception. When the filmmaker types the first word of his script on the typewriter, he only has to know how to let himself go entirely—to let himself be absorbed in a passive labor. He need only be conscious of himself at each moment. That is why Godard doesn't always know why a certain character does this or that. But after thinking a little, he always discovers why. Certainly one can always manage to explain even a contradictory behavior. But with Godard it is different: thanks especially to the accumulation of small details, that Godard imagined naturally by using himself as his subject, everything manages to hold together. The psychology is more effective because it is freer and almost invisible.

Our two heroes have a moral attitude new to the cinema. The decline of Christianity since the end of the last century (Godard, of Protestant origin, is very conscious of this) left man free to choose between the Christian conception of a relative human existence and the modern worship of the individual. Each choice

From *Cahiers du Cinéma*, April 1960. Translated by Roberta Bernstein in *Jean-Luc Godard*, ed. Toby Mussman (New York: Dutton, 1968). Amended by Dudley Andrew.

has its good aspects, and our heroes, feeling a little lost, oscillate between one and the other. Because of this the film is marked with the seal of the greatest of philosophical schools—the Sophists.

Breathless (like Euripides's plays) is an attempt to surpass Sophism by adapting it to reality; from this, happiness can result. Belmondo says to Charlotte [in *Charlotte et son Jules*—translator's note]:

I'm not upset with you, yes, I am upset,
No, I'm not upset with you, I mean I am, yes,
Upset with you. I don't know.
It's funny, I don't know.
I'm upset with you for not being upset with you.

And Patricia says:

I don't know if I am free because I am unhappy or unhappy because I am free.

Partly because she loves Michel, Patricia denounces him; partly because of the novelty involved and to have the last word, Michel wants to give himself up to the police. The changing attitudes of our times can sometimes determine a complete reversal of conventional psychology to its exact opposite. One of the results of this perpetual changing is the accomplishment of the mise-en-scène, usually found in all great films, since the authors of them are also directors. Our heroes, fascinated by the madness of their behavior, detach themselves from themselves. They play with their detached selves in order to see what this will yield. The last scene is filled with supreme irony: Michel before dying makes one of his favorite comic faces and Patricia responds. Thus the ending is both optimistic and heartrending—heartrending by the intrusion of the comic into the core of the tragic.

Critics have already remarked upon the differences between the behavior of the male and the female. . . . Patricia is a little American intellectual who doesn't really know what she wants and ends up informing against the man she loves. She is full of radiance and constant jabbering, with an astonishing lucidity through her childishness. But like Charlotte, her character is much less appealing than the masculine character. Could Godard be a misogynist? No, because this dislike of women is only external and limited to the subject alone. It reflects the contradiction at the basis of true love of man for woman: the more relative admiration of amused contempt of those who, in the encounter of reason and taste, prefer man to woman. Certain filmmakers who want their films to be "the work of a man who loves women, who says it, and who shows it" are really the misogynists. They give women the advantage by choice of external subject; they hire the most beautiful actresses, but they don't direct them or they direct them poorly because they don't know how to reveal their essential qualities. Always this ambivalence between what is and what one wants to be: "I am not what I am," said Shakespeare. Whereas the association of Godard and Seberg yielded magnificent results, undoubtedly because in Seberg we find that dialectic so dear to Godard. With her seemingly masculine life-style and boyish haircuts, she is all the more feminine. As is well known, a woman is sexier in pants and short hair because these permit her to purify her femininity of all superficial elements.

Patricia, however, becomes more admirable when she telephones the police. It is an act of courage. She decides to get out of the terrible intricacy in which she is entangled. But like all acts of courage it is a facile solution. Michel reproaches her bitterly for it since he can assume complete control of his character and play the game; he doesn't like Faulkner nor halfway things and he follows his perpetual dilemma all the way to the end. But he plays the game too well: his death is the natural sanction called for by logic, the spectator, and morality all at once. He went too far: he wanted to set himself apart from the world and the things in it in order to dominate them.

It is here that Godard detaches himself very slightly from his heroes (whom he otherwise sticks to literally), thanks to his cruel and entomological second personality of the objective filmmaker. Godard is Michel, yet he isn't, since he is neither murderer nor deceased. Why this superiority of author over character that bothers me slightly? Because Michel is only virtually the double of Godard: he makes actual what Godard thinks. A scene like the one where Michel lifts the Parisian girls' skirts shows this difference well. Certainly the cinema begins or ends with psychoanalysis, but when the filmmaker is conscious of the oddities of his soul and their vanities, they can become a source of beauty. *Breathless* is an attempted liberation. Godard is not—is no longer—Michel because he made *Breathless* and Michel did not.

Notice that the form of the film is always in the image of the hero's behavior as seen by the heroine; even better, she justifies this behavior. Michel, and to a greater extent Patricia, is overriden by the disorder of our times and by the perpetual moral and physical developments and changes peculiar to our era alone. They are victims of disorder and the film is thus a point of view on disorder—both internal and external. Like *Hiroshima* and *400 Blows,* it is a more or less successful effort to dominate this disorder; actually a rather less than successful effort since if it had been successful, disorder would no longer exist. If a film about disorder becomes disorderly itself, it must, I think, be condemned for that reason. What is most admirable in *400 Blows* is that the disorder fully resolves itself by means of order, thanks to the detachment of Truffaut and the perfect ending of the final sequence; and that Truffaut is a young man and an old man of about seventy at the same time. But there is a little more illegitimate trickery there than sincerity: the artist can only be one person at the moment he is making the film; also all evolution in the heart of the work, whether at the beginning or the ending, is a forced affectation. In this regard Godard is superior to Truffaut: while Truffaut with an applied effort forces the civilization of our times into a classical framework, Godard, more honest, searches to justify our epoch from within itself.

According to some people, order in art is valid, disorder is invalid. I don't think this is true since the uniqueness of art is that it is bound by no laws. Even the respect of the public for art is a myth which should at times be denounced. The mise-en-scène recreates the impression of disorder by two different voices, as Godard always does, by naturalness, freedom, and boldness of invention. Godard takes all that he perceives in life without selecting; more exactly he selects all that he sees and only sees what he wants. He omits nothing and tries simply to show what signifies all that he sees or that passes through his head. Incessant, natural disruptions of tone create the impression of disorder. It is not at all necessary to be shocked at the sudden shift from Faulkner to Jean of Letraz, during a love scene.

Likewise, when Godard makes a play on words, whether good or bad, we laugh because of his intentional banality. Godard shows us the profound unity which results from disorder, from permanent and external diversity. Some critics have said that the film and its characters do not evolve, except in the last half hour, and even then only slightly. But this is because Godard is against the idea of evolution. The same is true of Resnais, who arrives at the same conclusion, but by the totally opposed means of a tightly constructed work. This conception is in the air in our times: the camera is a mirror led along a path, but there is no longer a path. Like *Hiroshima*, *Breathless* could last two hours, and it lasted effectively for two hours at the first editing. The very remarkable *Time Without Pity* (Joseph Losey, 1957) shows a very precise construction and a constant progression, but it all seems arbitrary somehow. Godard follows the superior order of nature—the order in which things present themselves to his eyes or his mind. As Godard said: "From the mere fact that I say a sentence there is necessarily a connection with what precedes."

The film is a series of sketches, of interludes unrelated at first sight, like the interview of the writer. But from the mere fact that these episodes exist they have a profound relation to each other, like all phenomena of life. Parvulesco's interview clearly poses the problems our lovers must resolve. Like *Astrophel and Stella* (Sir Philip Sidney, 1581), *Breathless* is formed out of little isolated circles which are rejoined by identical hinges at the end of each sequence or sonnet: with Sidney it is Stella, with Godard Patricia or something else. The nature of the effect doesn't matter, but each scene must have an effect—that is realism. . . .

. . . Godard observes reality meticulously, but at the same time he tries to recompose it by means of flagrant artificialities. All novices, fearing the hazards of shooting, have a tendency to plan out their films carefully beforehand and to make grand stylistic configurations. For example, in *Charlotte* we find a scientific usage of extended scenes, as with Lang. This explains the style of editing in *Breathless,* where the flash cutting alternates with the very long scenes in an intelligently conceived manner. Since the characters' conduct reflects a series of mistaken moral junctures, the film will be a series of mistaken junctures. Only how beautiful and delicious are these mistakes!

But, in fact, the systematic, simple expression of the subject in script, shooting, editing, and angle shots is exactly what is least new in the film. It is not particularly clever to shoot a tilt shot every time a character falls down. Aldrich, Berthomieu, and Clément did it all their lives and it is rarely effective. All the same, this method works when in the same pan shot we jump from Seberg and Belmondo on the Champs Elysées to Belmondo and Seberg on the same Champs, walking by the shadows of De Gaulle and Eisenhower who are marching past. This shot means that the only thing that matters is yourself, not the exterior political and social life. By cutting out the scenes where our generals appear, the censors reduced the generals to mere entities, to ridiculous puppets: what will remain of our times is *Breathless,* not De Gaulle nor Eisenhower, pitiable but necessary figures as are all statesmen. This method is also effective when, very differently from that of *Vertigo* (Hitchcock, 1957) and *The Cousins* (Chabrol, 1958), the camera of the great Coutard films rolls on and on, and at the same rate as the soul of the hero. That has precise meaning. It is the classic expression of modern behavior.

With Godard, spontaneity prevails over formula, completing and recapitulating it. This makes for the slight superiority of *Breathless* over *Hiroshima,* where Resnais is concerned with spontaneity only in directing the actors. Another superior feature of Godard is that he only deals with concrete things. Remembrance, forgetfulness, memory, and time are things which are not concrete; they do not exist and like Christian didacticism or communism they are not serious enough to be treated by a language as profound as that of the screen. . . .

. . . Godard . . . makes us admit that this modern universe—metallic and terrifying like science fiction—is a marvelous universe full of beauty; a universe magnificently represented by Jean Seberg, less vivacious here than with Preminger, but more lunar in the decomposition of her existence. Godard is a man who lives with his times. He shows the utmost respect for the landmarks of uniquely modern civilization, e.g., automobiles, the comic strips of *France-Soir*. The civilization of our times is not the rightist, reactionary one of *L'Express* or the plays of Sartre, characterized by sullen intellectualism and the rejection of the realities of modern life; rather it is the leftist, revolutionary civilization represented among other things by these famous comics.

That is why it would be wrong to associate Godard with Rousseau under the pretext that they are the greatest Franco-Swiss artists. If Jean-Jacques offered us nature against artificiality, Jean-Luc claims back the city and the artificialities of modern civilization 100 percent. Following the American tradition (in the best sense of the word) of Whitman, Sandburg, Vidor, and even Hawks, he has accomplished the highest mission of art: he has reconciled man with his own times and with this world, which so many constipated bureaucrats—often in too poor a position to judge, knowing nothing else —take for a world in crisis that crucifies man. As if man were no longer capable of understanding himself in a world which seems to menace him. For Godard the twentieth century is not an enormous affront facing the creative man; it is enough to know how to see and admire. The power and beauty of his mise-en-scène, imposing an image of serenity and optimism, enables us to discover the profound grace of this world, terrifying at first contact, through its poetry of mistaken junctures and perdition.

On *Breathless*

Jean Carta

Breathless, the first full-length film by *Cahiers du Cinéma* critic, Jean-Luc Godard, is a work at once complacent and provocative, artful and sincere, which bears witness to an authentic revolt against the hypocrisies of our epoch at the same time as it portrays a moral anarchy that leaves one perplexed about the intentions of the author, about his ideas and his myths.

One certainty, in any case: he is a true cinéaste: the film's tone is as modern as have been the other recent products of the new generation. The dialogue and the compositions combine to give us exactly the sentiment of the world in which we live now in 1960. The way the director has integrated into his narrative real events (Eisenhower's visit) and certain aspects of contemporary technology (neon signs, the photo of the hero in *France-Soir*) increases the impression of veracity. The dialogue, written with a tremendous liberty, contributes to the realism of the whole.

Surely you would applaud it without reserve, this very spontaneous dialogue, if it weren't spoiled by a number of crass appeals to the audience that are disappointing, at least at first glance.

Just as we applaud the dialogue despite its dross, we admire a mise-en-scène that is so full of vivacity and rhythm and that owes less to French cinema than to the numerous ancestors in Hollywood whom Godard venerates. As effective and free as is this mise-en-scène, as a matter of fact we must admit—in opposition to certain flatterers—that it situates itself at the crossroads of various traditions and that there is nothing here that is absolutely new or which revolutionizes the language of the screen. On one point, however, it does permit us to note the extraordinary evolution of cinematographic grammar in the last few years: *Breathless* marks the end of the sacrosanct "continuity of action." When, in a classic film, you want to move from one shot to the next, you strive to tie the two moments via a connecting gesture. Let's say it's a man drinking in a café. Establishing shot: he lifts his beer; closeup: he puts it back down. The spectator, carried along by the logic of this action, doesn't doubt for an instant that the character he saw at the

From *Témoignage Chrétien*, April 8, 1960. Translated by Dudley Andrew and Dory O'Brien.

back of the café is the same as the one who now appears in a head-and-shoulders shot, putting down his glass. He thus acquires the sense that he is certainly witnessing a single scene, only taken from a different angle, rather than a different scene. . . . This rule, which requires that shots follow one another in a logical sequence (except for the technical separation of sequences by fade outs, irises, etc.) has been under fire for quite a while by a more and more elliptical cinema: the man has barely lifted his glass when in the following shot he has already put it back down. Thus Resnais in *Hiroshima* had definitively knocked over the principle of continuity because he didn't hesitate to join, in the very same sequence, the objective with the subjective, the past with the present, the heroine's distant memories of Nevers with the life she was living right now in Hiroshima.

Now Godard doesn't go this far. Still he violates, and with evident pleasure, the golden rules of his profession, notably in the excellent sequence in the bedroom where it is constantly necessary to make an internal adjustment so as to explain how Belmondo can leave the bathroom when we are sure he's in bed. More than this—and this is what's crucial—it seems that *the refusal of logical continuity prolongs the imaginary duration of the film.* As soon as there is no longer a coherent connection between shots, we restore this logic: we interpolate between two images that fit badly together the invisible shot that reconciles them: we saw Belmondo in bed; we see him coming out of the bathroom: in our minds a third shot slips between these two, one where Belmondo goes from the bed to the bathroom. We have added to the film a few imaginary seconds, thus prolonging its duration.

Sartre reportedly said of *Breathless,* "It's very beautiful." I have not heard with my own ears this terse judgment, but we ought to be astonished that such a prolific philosopher could only come up with this naive formula to describe such an ambiguous and complex film by Jean-Luc Godard.

What does it recount, this story? The unhappy idyll of a killer, half hoodlum and half child, with an American student, the few hours they spend together before the police bring the young murderer down. "All the tension of *Breathless,*" writes René Guyonnet, in *L'Express,* "resides in the futile effort made by Michel and Patricia to reunite, to find each other, to understand one another." It seems to me that he has misunderstood and that the film is much more likely constructed on a Manichean opposition between the two characters in which the first, Belmondo, is in effect utterly intent upon understanding the other; but in which the other, Jean Seberg, slips away and, for her part, refuses to give over her precious personality to a love without bounds, without escape, total. In love as in friendship Belmondo insists upon the necessity of the absolute: one must go *to the end,* beyond laws and social structures, unless one is a "coward." And Seberg in fact will turn out to be a coward, not because she fears the laws and the police—she scoffs at them several times over—but because she does not want to lose her liberty, because her concept of independence prevents her from abandoning or forgetting herself and from giving herself, ultimately forbidding passionate love. Belmondo would like to see her break all her ties with her life to follow him to Italy. It is that which she refuses, the great leap to the other side of rationality. The failure of the couple becomes concrete in the denouement when each partner speaks in monologue without hearing what the other is saying.

Of these two portraits, executed with equal success, one an absolute temperament and the other its opposite, both served by remarkable acting, it is perhaps Jean Seberg's that is the more fascinating. Godard has admirably traced this type of narcissistic psychology that begins with physical complacence ("Do you think [this Renoir] is prettier than I am?" "Do you like most my eyes, my mouth, or my shoulders?"), a complacence that also expresses itself in front of the mirror, in the photos tacked up on the wall, only partly hidden by a false sartorial simplicity: a narcissism that is pursued on the intellectual plane—as we see the heroine ruminate over her problems, analyze herself, question herself about her happiness, her destiny, without ever understanding that her life will never find the significance that she searches for in vain until she projects it toward others; a narcissism, finally, that inexorably emerges in the most hideous form of egoism, when the Other becomes nothing more than a pretext, the instrument of one's personal vibrations, a means of titillating oneself, of making oneself feel good or bad, with no interest in the self of the Other, in his very existence. Seberg reaches this extremity when she turns Belmondo over to the police. She didn't want to fall in love and hadn't found a better way to break off. She is here no more than a praying mantis, destroying the destiny of a man who loves her, for the sole purpose of protecting herself from her own temptations.

One can gauge the abyss that separates this romantic conception of the couple, for which Belmondo is the real symbol, from that epicurian conception that we see in the recent [New Wave] films of Pierre Kast or Jacques Doniol-Valcroze. Here the hero is not satisfied by merely epidermic contact. All that a Kast character can dream of, Belmondo obtained from Seberg. But he asks of her a real passion and not simply a night. This "hoodlum" has amorous requirements to which the "intellectuals" of Kast's film, *Le Bel Age,* do not have access. You can feel in Godard a visible recoiling before those beings who mix emancipation with a dullness of heart. This is the type of person that he thrashes in the character of the French-American journalist for whom sexual relationships are a mere pastime, a gesture of professional sympathy toward women, whereas by contrast, for Belmondo the failure of love justifies death. A sentence from Faulkner, cited by Seberg, announces the end of the drama: "Between grief and nothing I will take grief . . ." to which Belmondo hurls back that he chooses death because grief is a compromise. And in fact it certainly is death that he will choose in refusing to flee.

A violent protest against contemporary hypocrisy, a brutal demand for the right to do anything and to crush all in order to live in full contact with the absolute: this is what touches us in Godard's film. But this is also what we can dispute. Between the rejection of mediocrity and modern mendacity and the rejection of all social necessity there is a distinction that the auteur does not seem to make. He stands with his hero against all order, against all society because it limits the expression of an exceptional personality. Before such "intellectual anarchy," which crops up also in his statements, we have mentioned how uncomfortable we feel at the uncritical exaltation he bestows on this antisocial character. Now any method is worthwhile that succeeds in making a criminal into a human being for us, upending our usual perspective and making us identify a hidden despair in the impetuous act of a young murderer. Society would guillotine him and think it had done with him. But this scenario is not new to the cinema: look at *Chicago Nights* [*Underworld*] by Sternberg (1927). It abounds in the American cinema, most notably in the character of Humphrey Bogart (Wyler's *Dead End,* 1937, for example), and you see it in the French school of the thirties in the character of [Jean] Gabin. But here Godard won't at all try to explicate his character's conduct. He does exactly the opposite. He posits the fatal act as a sort of incident or abstraction, as if no one had really pulled the trigger. Then he moves on from this "regrettable action" in order to weave a long psychological plot between two characters in a dramatic situation. The murder is put in parentheses, conjured out of existence. It is only a pretext, in the same way that the hatred of Clytemnestra is a pretext bringing about the bloody plot of Orestes. It may seem that an action this fatal ought to have its own weight. However hardened one may be—and Belmondo is not a professional criminal—to have on one's conscience the corpse of an innocent man should lead one to think pretty deeply. But in the description we get of this sympathetic and unhappy fellow, the murder (along with a number of other scenes: thefts of cars, wallets, etc.) becomes a rather picturesque element in a folktale. It loses its tragic aspect to become a mannerism of behavior, a bad habit, a simple inconsiderateness, one of his character traits. In this fashion [Godard] presents Belmondo on the one hand as a pitiable human being while on the other his shooting of the cop has left not a single trace on him. This is where the contradiction lies, transforming the touching young man into a disturbing killer. How are we supposed to sympathize with and admire this character for whom the life of another doesn't count? He loves, we are told, and is not loved in return. Isn't this sad? The sympathies of the author are directed at him. He doesn't urge us to excuse him, but rather to find in him a true grandeur which is missing in our sordid epoch. In making the cop's body evaporate, [Godard] suggests to us in the name of I don't know what kind of haughty Nietzscheism, that the death of a man is not very important, that it is quickly forgotten as a means of full self-realization, when one is aiming at the absolute.

But by means of an apparent contradiction that ensconces itself in the very heart of the character and contributes to its authentic rendering, Belmondo is also haunted by a contrary feeling: this same man who is presented to us as ready for anything, if it means that he can reach the peak of passion, is gnawed by a fatigue, a taste for death which he expresses at several points and which explains his rootlessness, his "exile" in the midst of a society from which the absolute and love have been banished, where money rules, where no one invites him to find a place. This notion engenders a fatalism, a refusal to consider the world as capable of being changed: "It's normal: informers inform, burglars burgle, lovers love." Life is this way and no one can change it. And when, by misfortune, one has ideas of the absolute in one's head, it is better to lie down and die.

Beyond its incontestable cinematographic mastery, the message of *Breathless,* intentional or not, is anarchism, Nietzscheism, fatalism: to reject all. But it also reveals in its creator, under the gloss of self-assurance and of paradox, a false "lucidity," which is endearing because it bears witness to a disillusioned love of the world and to a poorly effaced confusion.

A Bout de Souffle

Charles Barr

G odard himself makes a brief appearance in *A bout de souffle*. He plays the
man who first points out Michel to the police.

Both Michel and Godard are wearing dark glasses. Godard peers out
from behind a newspaper (in which he has seen Michel's photograph) as Michel
did in the first shot of the film. He walks very obviously in front of Michel's
stationary car, comparing the face with the photo, yet Michel doesn't notice him.

In a way, this implausibility is just a sign of Godard's indifference to surface
naturalism, like the passersby who stare at the camera in the street scenes and the
passersby who *don't* stare when Michel is dying. This convention he extends into
a method of analysis, detaching people from the external world in order to study
them more clearly. Bruno in *Le Petit Soldat,* hesitating whether to kill the man he
has been ordered to, drives his car level with that of his target, aims the gun, and
continues alongside, 'frozen'; yet the man never looks at him. On a naturalistic
level this is ridiculous, but what might otherwise seem a rather suspect device, a
shortcut, is justified by its aptness to Bruno's dreamlike state of mind. Likewise the scene from *A bout de souffle* is not simply a cartoonlike compression of
the action, but a sign of Michel's indifference to danger, amounting to a self-
destructive urge; it seems almost as if it were Michel himself acting as informer.

This is valid whether or not one recognizes Godard playing the part. The scene
takes on a greater resonance when one reflects that Godard, the creator of
Michel, is intervening in his story, guiding it toward its end. He intervenes quite
arbitrarily; wanders around, like a director on set. It is Godard who points out
Michel to the police (like a director giving instructions) at the moment that he
drives away—as if, for story purposes, calculating to let him get just out of
immediate range. The iris-out on Godard which ends the sequence—a deliberate
archaic device, used once earlier—again reminds us of the director's hand. The
scene is a concentration of the devices by which, here and in later films, Godard
reminds us that he is putting together the story for us. Objections to the ar-
bitrariness of his endings are undercut by this emphasis on the convention, on the

From *Jean-Luc Godard,* ed. Ian Cameron (New York: Crown, 1969).

fact that we are watching a film. At one moment in the love scene of *Alphaville,* Lemmy and Natasha look out at us like two stars posing for a publicity picture (compare that of Bogart which Michel confronts in *A bout de souffle*), and Godard illuminates their faces alternately as though preparing to light a shot. The subsequent happy ending in *Alphaville,* ridiculed by some critics, is consciously a 'film' happy ending, a sort of wish-fulfillment: though Godard makes us aware that he is imposing it willfully, it is nevertheless organic in that Lemmy is persuading Natasha to behave *like* a heroine—to live up to the conventions of 'legend.' Similarly at the end of *A bout de souffle,* the arrival of Antonio with a gun for Michel, at the same time as the police, is arbitrary. Michel refuses to escape or to take the gun; Antonio throws it directly into his path. It seems to be an image of an external fate intervening, yet Michel's act of picking up the gun, which causes the police to shoot, is a free acceptance of this fate. Moreover, he has already chosen his fate, ultimately, by staying with Patricia instead of leaving Paris. As Lemmy emulates one kind of film star, Michel emulates another: Godard the storyteller provides the ending which each invites. This sort of interdependence between will and fate is nothing new in drama; what is modern is the characters' self-consciousness about their roles, and the sophisticated attitude of author and audience to the patterns of 'legend.'

The contradictions of Godard's own appearance—a narrative scene but a director's intervention; an arbitrary intervention yet one at which Michel seems to connive—are central to the film, and foreshadow his later films.

At the risk of seeming to load more on to this scene than it can take, I want to suggest a further association. There is a strong tradition that Shakespeare in *Hamlet* acted the part of the ghost—the figure of an 'objective' morality pressing in upon the confused individual whom he has created. It is almost as though he had poured so much of himself uncritically into Hamlet that he had symbolically to get outside him. Shakespeare 'is' both Hamlet and the ghost; Godard 'is' both Michel and the informer (the follower of official morality). Both confrontations, and both works, give an odd sense of an author's private debate or experiment, which is not yet fully resolved in dramatic terms. This whole parallel could be extended much further. The standard revenge play is behind Shakespeare as the gangster film is behind Godard. The theatrical references in *Hamlet* have a range and function similar to the cinematic ones in Godard's films. Hamlet himself, with his intellectual jargon, travel, paradoxes, practical jokes, self-dramatization, world-weariness, obsession with death, and, not least, his ambivalence toward women, is the type of a Godard hero (Michel, Bruno in *Le Petit Soldat,* Ferdinand in *Pierrot le fou*). The tension between contemplation and action, and between ideal and real, are recurrent Godard themes, notably in *Pierrot le fou*. Such parallels are not superficial, and one may be more able to grasp the orientation of *A bout de souffle* (particularly in the context of Godard's later films) if one sees that Godard's relation to Michel is something like Shakespeare's to Hamlet. In this film Godard's concern is, like Shakespeare's, to sort out, from a confrontation between rebellion and rigidity within a closed society, some stable values, as well as a more meaningful dramatic pattern to work with subsequently.

Obviously Shakespeare in *Hamlet* gets much further. *A bout de souffle* is only the start of the *Hamlet* which Godard is still making. (One suspects that Godard's view of the modern world would prevent him from producing anything that is more serene than *Hamlet*.) Though there is a strong continuity with his later films, *A bout de souffle* is a tentative work.

Michel's shooting of the policeman, near the start, is presented in a remote, stylized way: closeup of Michel's gun, a rather beautiful longish shot of the policeman (whose face we don't see) falling back into some bushes, long shot of Michel running away across a field. Then he is in Paris. This abruptness conveys how he is able to shut himself off from any feeling of shock. His other actions, stealing cars and money, are done and shown in the same casual manner. Borne along in exhilaration by the film, one can easily slip into identifying too easily with Michel, his freedom and 'honesty.' But freedom from what? The context of his actions is very thin; his impulses lack an 'objective correlative.' In case this seems a stale and irrelevant criterion, it is worth considering how firmly in his later work Godard supplies just this, relating the main action to a politically and socially turbulent world by which the characters are oppressed. In *Pierrot le fou* not only is there the continual weight of reference to, for instance, Vietnam, but the oppressive social milieu which Pierrot flees is presented with a sharpness which colors the whole of the action that follows. *Alphaville* presents the same world in a diagrammatic form, a world where emotion is eliminated or prostituted and where violence is normal. Lemmy's first killing, of the man in the bedroom, is done in the same stylized way as Michel's, and his subsequent violence is similarly casual, but the moral overtones are quite different. Nor is it conclusive to argue that Lemmy is one sort of hero, Michel another, and that they meet appropriately different ends: the distinction exists, but the links between the two men are strong also.

The films have in common the theme of imagination versus logic. Michel trying to get Patricia to Rome is like Lemmy taking Natasha to the Outerlands.

Patricia is committed to society and its values: she must work at the Sorbonne, take her chances as a journalist, etc. Early on she asks Michel, when he mentions horoscopes, *"Qu'est-ce que c'est l'horoscope?"* Her French isn't too good, but this is hardly a difficult word . . . the exchange is schematized to set Patricia's blankness against Michel's concern with the future, which he goes on to explain. Her failure of verbal understanding stands for a failure of moral understanding. Her vision doesn't extend beyond the present (she can't respond to his impulse to go to Rome). Likewise her final question, *"Qu'est-ce que c'est dégueulasse?"*, followed by her abrupt turning away, implies the lack of a whole moral dimension: her betrayal 'means' nothing to her. The challenge to her of Michel's personality resembles the data with which Lemmy confronts Alpha-60; she tries to cope by using logic, and the results are disastrous.

In this sense Michel stands for love and vision (it is clear where Godard's own sympathies lie) but he does so only in a pathetically tenuous and compromised way. This in itself doesn't make the film incoherent—it is the pattern of many gangster films—but it is notable that Godard doesn't use this pattern again: his films since *A bout de souffle* have shown intelligent men reacting violently against their environment to seek love and freedom (Bruno, Lemmy, Ferdinand, and Pierrot), or, sometimes, brutish heroes (those of *Les Carabiniers,* Arthur in *Bande à part*) whose conditioning by society is acutely analyzed. Michel was an awkward mixture. A hero coming from nowhere; a pattern of questioning, from the POURQUOI spelt out in cigarette packets on a bedroom wall, through all Patricia's questions to the final line; a dead end. It is the only Godard film which seems at all vulnerable to the charge that his deep concern about civilization is something read into his films by admirers who, in Raymond Durgnat's words, "impregnate his blandness with their pain." The final impression is of a tentative film, a 'run through' of ideas, characters, and styles which Godard is testing in action, fitting together in a slightly makeshift way: his own brief appearance to guide the action can be seen, in retrospect, as a sort of cryptogram admitting this. Clearly Godard learnt a lot simply from the act of making this film, whose relation to his later work is hinted at by the opening words of Bruno's narration in *Le Petit Soldat:* "The time for action is past. I have grown older. The time for reflection has come."

The Graphic in Filmic Writing

Marie-Claire Ropars

Marie-Claire Ropars begins her long essay by alluding to Jacques Derrida and his insistence that the hieroglyphic nature of writing takes precedence over the phonetic, and that we should think of language literally as a material production of concepts made by physical inscription. With this in mind, she dares to approach *Breathless* for the actual written signs found within it, and beyond these, for its own work in dissociating image and word. Thus the film is shown to contain texts and to function as a text. To begin her analysis she breaks the film into a dozen sequence units and she identifies the characters as M (male) and F (female). Punctuation marks, such as the iris, the fade out, and the dissolve, mainly determine the units. The most important moment of the film for her occurs when "the cinema itself is named," when Patricia and Michel (F and M) go to see a western. To get to that moment she begins to notice all those moments when the cinema, as a concept and institution, intrudes into the film as a text.

. . . Let's go back to where cinema first intrudes into the film. An enunciative break, occurring in sequence 4,[1] just after Michel and Patricia meet, attracts our attention first; whereas M and F's long stroll was filmed in one shot, the separation of the two protagonists starts a brutal modification of the frame (high angle shot and long shot), sustained musically and immediately followed, in a dynamic, nondiegetic cut, by a short return to M passing in front of a poster which he doesn't look at, but which is shown by the camera: it is of an American film starring Jeff Chandler. At the end of sequence 4, when Michel has escaped from the police, another poster stands out behind him, and this time he stops to look at

[1] Ropars breaks the film into twelve sequences: sequence 1 corresponds to shots 1–12; sequence 2, 13–49; sequence 3, 50–73; sequence 4, 74–94; sequence 5, 95–123; sequence 6, 124–212; sequence 7, 213–256; sequence 8, 257–271; sequence 9, 272–314; sequence 10, shot 315; sequence 11, 316–372; and sequence 12, 373–407. Each sequence ends with an emphatic form of filmic punctuation: a dissolve, a fade, or an iris out. Note that sequence 10, to which Ropars gives so much importance in this essay, is the only single-shot sequence in the film.—Ed.

From *Enclitic* 6 (Fall 1981/Winter 1982).

it: it too shows an American film, but starring Bogart, whose photo M contemplates in shot/reverse shot. The sequence concludes right there with an iris-out and -in, encircling the two policemen who are chasing M.

More and more insistently, cinema penetrates the film's fabric. The old-fashioned punctuation, which temporarily closes off this infiltration, also emphasizes what kind of circuit is involved: detective films, actor's films, action films—a classic production model lines Michel's path, as if to nostalgically reflect its framework. Born in America, this kind of cinema is relayed into France: right after the first poster, M suddenly encounters a girl who tries to sell him, or rather shows him *Cahiers du Cinéma,* well-known for its auteur principle, especially for auteurs from across the Atlantic. Beyond the historical wink, which dates Godard's first feature film referentially, we can note the system taking shape: posters, photos, magazines; the cinema comes in here as a distribution process, for which the face-off with Bogart indicates what is at stake, before the outdated punctuation, removed from its object, can drive it out. The repeated shot/reverse shot editing plays with alternating the closeups of two faces, Michel's and the actor's. During this double exchange, M removes his dark glasses and his cigarette, then runs his thumb over his lips murmuring Bogart's name, or rather his nickname "Bogey." There could hardly be a better way of designating the mechanisms of scopic projection to which the cinema invites us: the thumb movement, borrowed from Bogart, specifies M's face right from the first shot of the film, and accompanies him all along his run; the name murmured here, and the substitution of the faces, inscribe one of the dominant functions of the cinematographic apparatus: to propose the image as a place of identification for the subject. Specular image, wholly imaginary identification: Bogart's face is bare, with neither hat nor cigarette, Michel is only partly bared. The actor doesn't look like M, but like his friend Tolmatchoff whom Michel has just left; the resemblance escapes the one who is mimicking it, the image of the double slips away, but the identity doesn't. Cinematographic language, clearly marked off here, is staged in its illusory dimension: to identify Bogart, while identifying with him.

Sequence 10 means to get away from the illusion, which is taken apart in the end of sequence 4, by interposing another form: no diachronic editing, thus no exchange between a look and that which is looked at; and especially no coincidence between name and image, between representation and signification. M and F went to see a western, but their faces in closeup take the heroes' place on the screen, while the flickering light seems to transform their kiss into a screen on which a deferred projection, with far-off images, would leave its trace. As for the text murmured off, it also contains an echo of the western: "Be careful Jessica," begins the man's voice; "You're making a mistake, Sheriff," continues the woman's voice further on; but as you can see in the dialogue to shot 315, this echo can be found scattered over two poems, one by Aragon ("On the edge of kisses," the man's voice will carry on) and the other by Apollinaire ("Our story is noble and tragic," the woman's voice will continue). Diverted in this way, the western only intervenes to divert the present image in its turn, by pulling it toward a space outside, which is both absent and penetrating, which empties the representation of its presence; and the double voices, rooted in the image by means of their masculine and feminine sonorities, sustained semantically by the figuration of the kiss they prolong, cannot, however, merge into the faces they accompany: the sheriff lies in wait for these voices, but they are caught up in a poetic network of assonance, homonymy or homophony (*trop vite, évite, tragique, magique, pathétique*), and they make the signs opaque by making them glide from one text to the other. Inner voices perhaps, but foreign to M and F's language; outer voices, thus, but with no roots nor future in either of the two films. Voice-*offs*, to be sure, but for a brief moment, the *off* itself is doubtful.

So two semiotic phenomena converge in this short passage: instability of the image, both representation and support, film and screen, fiction and cinema; disconnection of the voices, parted from what it designates, torn apart by two equally impossible references. The divergence of the figurative and linguistic network stems from the relativity of their disjunction: a play of traces and cross-references, the text is directed at an image which comes undone under the pressure of another image itself reflected in the text; the editing circuit, having become reversible, sets up an open system of refusal between figure and sign.

Refusal of illusion, refusal of signification as well—both equally inscribed in the cinematographic model displayed throughout sequence 4: aren't the *Cahiers [Notebooks] du Cinéma* also the cinema-turned-notebook, the book spread open, offered in the place of vision? Let's come back to the occurrences of American films. The first poster, the one that follows the encounter with F, offers only graphic inscriptions: "*Vivre dangereusement jusqu'au bout*—les productions Hammer Films présentent Jeff Chandler" ("*Live dangerously right to the end*—Hammer Film Productions present Jeff Chandler"). No picture here, except in the typography; only a written phrase, a play of signs. Just after the poster and the *Cahiers du Cinéma,* a sign bearing the abbreviation "Roneo" (Mimeo) appears at the top of a shop-window, under which an injured scooter-rider drops dead. Sign of the cross—M keeps going by, opens his newspaper, finds in it that "the police have already identified the RN7 murderer." Written word, printing works, press—from the cinema to the newspaper, signs are linked by death to formulate the identity, the actor's, the murderer's. But the article headline, which can be read in closeup on the screen, is illustrated by a photo of the two motorcycle cops and not of M; the identification, both inquisitory and scripturary, seems foiled by the missing image—the cinema's last resort against the sign? This image—imaginary—is what the second poster offers as a delusion, with Bogart's photo taken from the ads by the camera and substituted for M's face. In spite of the subtraction done by the editing, the images remain generated in the space of the sign from which they try to escape: "*Plus dure sera la chute*—cette semaine" ("*The Harder They Fall*—this week"); if Bogart's name is not on the poster, the decipherable title responds to the call of the first written title "*Live dangerously right to the end.*" Both designate the film we are watching, predict its outcome. Delayed, diverted, M's face finally gets framed by the image; his identity is revealed, albeit through the breakdown of the deceptive mechanism on which it is based.

The cinema in its double semiological dimension is introduced starting in sequence 4: analogical figuration, and linguistic signification, written before being spoken. One of them—the analogical—brings identification into play in the imaginary; the other—the sign—draws identity over to death's side. The two systems remain separate, and are distributed between the two occurrences; but— system of signs or system of images, they are both equally rooted in the representation; when written, a word is perceived, immobilized in a sentence like the photos which revolve around it; it too represents, albeit by substitution. Flattened out, frozen in exemplary decomposition of its components, the cinema is placed under the sign's symbolic law, whether the sign be abstract or figurative. Deprived of speech, but engendering it ("Bogey"), it intervenes here as language, with all the clues linked to the imaginary and to death which lie in wait for the subject chased by meaning; and to involve writing, with sequence 10, it will have to decenter the sign in the voice, which temporarily cracks open the question of the subject, by obliterating that of identity. So the display of the cinematographic apparatus doubles the fiction, holding up mirrors to it in which its mechanism of illusion and the deadly force which drives it will be reflected in mirror construction. The precipitation of the filmic writing disturbs the markers that punctuate this fiction, by crossing out the system of signification into which it has settled. . . .

. . . Warded off, the graphic sign still returns, both desirable and prohibited:

could this be because at first it is printed on the female body? This question leads to a new circuit: . . . When she emerges through M's seeing her on the Champs Elysées, Patricia, who is holding a pile of newspapers, is yelling "New York Herald Tribune," but she is also wearing a T-shirt with the breast-level inscription, front and back, of the newspaper's lettered title. Two readings are possible, constituting F in this film: Patricia is fundamentally connected to the press and the novel, which multiply the death signals directed at M; her voice only repeats what is already written: redundancy, therefore, and deadly monotony. But also— why not?—Patricia is joined to the letter and writing, just like the shapely girl in sequence 3 who lived in a room covered with letters. Despite Patricia's noticeable love of quotations, we cannot exclude the second reading. For Patricia's favored status is to be, to the letter, the film's foreigner, the equivocal American (girl or car?) bearing equivocality and an Italian last name, who introduces a foreign accent into the language, making the words opaque again. . . . The ambiguity of writing persists with the oralization triggered by Patricia. She can spread meaning as well as short-circuit it, and appears in turn as the body-turned-sign and the sign embodied, exerting a force of attraction mixed with repulsion: both letter and literature, writing and culture; an androgynous figure, who doubles for Michel, in the double sense of the term: because she gives him away (in French *doubler*) to the police, and because with his props (hat, cigarette, dark glasses in the beginning of sequence 5) she takes on his role as protagonist with a whole sequence for herself (7), and his function as subject, master of vision and of the viewer's interpellation (12). The desire whose ambiguous object she is thus seems inseparable from a dispossession of identity for the one who desires her, M, sought in vain by a multitude of male doubles, but who will stumble and die at the feet of a female double.

Structural more than formal, the distinctive feature of this double will first be to take over in the fiction; opposite the male hero, who is tired, overcome with the imaginary, the substitution of a female agent is asserted in the last sequence, who guarantees the return of law and order with her call to the police: at the moment of firing, the policemen are arranged in such a way that they form the symbolic figure of a triangle in the shot; the final race alternates between M seen from behind, running away, and F face-on running as if to chase him down; and the editing of his death, which continues to separate M lying in the pedestrian crossing and F standing up in front of him, grants the prerogative of point-of-view to F alone: a high-angle shot of M, but no low-angle shot of F. Far from erasing the border between the symbolic and the imaginary, the film seems to try rooting it in a victory of the female over the male. But the takeover is also turned in the reverse direction: in the last shot, once M's eyes are closed, F turns around to face the camera and passes her thumb over her lips, thus also taking back from M the gesture borrowed from Bogart, and, more importantly, the cinematographic function the film increasingly reflects: a function of imaginary identification, certainly, but we have seen how full of writing it was.

Contradictory takeover, therefore, in which the female figure hesitates between the fiction and the film, constituting a subject and decentering the viewing subject, who is appealed to directly in this last shot: "Qu'est-ce que c'est, dégueulasse?" (What does "lousy" mean?). Just as M, in sequence 2, confused the point of view, speaking sometimes to the viewer and sometimes to himself. But the scriptural interchangeability of M and F is only sketched out here, and the film stops right when this is brought up. Too many sociological indications strictly split up the male and the female in the course of the fiction, divide the sexes into men and women, as inscribed in a division of the signs themselves into "ladies" and "gentlemen": this is at least how it is written on the movie theater restrooms where Patricia flees before getting back to Michel.

The cinematographic world is indeed entered by way of a descent into the restrooms at the end of sequence 9. That is where Patricia, holed up in a Champs Elysées cinema, escapes from the policeman who followed her to the basement and who strays into the "Gents" while she is getting out the "Ladies" window. False entry, thus, into a cinema where the graphic tracing of the sign which says sex is on the watch. So it has to be left behind—before being entered again; but this time to approach the purely vocal space of sequence 10. One last time here we are back at the exchange of male and female voices, texts by Aragon and by Apollinaire, in the darkness of a kiss one shot long. What distinguishes this unit from the other eleven is precisely that it is limited to one shot, projecting the act of editing into the verticality only of the writing. A singular shot, as single as the long tracking shot in which M and F's encounter took place; a single space, like the bedroom in sequence 6 tried to be in vain. The erotic activity—hidden under the sheets during this sequence—is displaced in this shot, which offers an image of the near union of the male and the female, and in the voice-offs their denied disjunction, their poetic equivalency. . . .

The union which is realized in the image only masks the division maintained in the voices. The diachronic editing works on this division at the beginning (start of 1) and the end (end of 12) of the film when it alternates the implementation of a male figure (f in the beginning and F at the end) without connecting them: in both cases, man and woman remain apart like the shots that are repeated in two disconnected series, communicating from afar, with gestures or looks, in delayed continuity. Separation of the sexes, attraction factor; attraction of the editing, factor of writing, that is, first of tension, relative discord, reactivated dissolution: the editing consists of this never-filled gap, of this current which both approaches and displaces what it intends to reconnect. But the tension can always be broken, linearity established, writing rooted in the separation into shots, into signs, into archetypal sexes. Masculine/Feminine, Ladies/Gents—the text is inscribed underground, and we know what Lacan has made of this. So the editing has to regress into verticality—and this is the effort Godard's film makes—where writing breathes into the voice, and the voice into the sign, to try to ward off that which, in the sign's differential structure, marks off sexual difference. And there is always a risk, as we have seen, of a return to a distinction between the sexes, which has not been challenged because of the fiction's stability.

"*Méfie-toi, Jessica*" (Be careful, Jessica); *méfie-toi de Jessica* (Be careful of Jessica). In the erotization of writing a kind of feminization is on the watch, whose emblematic figure is suggested in the film's first shot: a closeup of a newspaper spread open; in the middle of the newspaper, on the length of a page, the outline of a woman, enticing in her short skirt, with a doll in her hand; on either side, comic strips with captions. Piercing the newspaper, off and anonymous, a male voice can be heard; the newspaper is lowered showing its name as it goes by—*Paris-Flirt;* and Belmondo-M's face appears with all his character's props— hat, cigarette, thumb movement across his lips. Of the various readings permitted by this single shot, whose editing is synchronic at first, we will only mention the sociological profile of an uncultured hero who reads scandal sheets. But we can stress the strange complex, which delays the intervention of the cinematographic image by substituting a cinegraphic image of mixed figures and signs; and which, in the same suspense, conceals the male face behind the print of a female sketch which acts as a mask. Two paths, whose networks are entangled, open before us. One, symbolic, has to do with outlines: f must be erased for M to emerge, but the trace of F stays on the edge of a film which, as we have seen, organizes the substitution of a female subject. The other, semiotic, concerns layout: there can be no cinema without the originary dissociation of voice and image, hidden from each other; no analogical image, without drawing and letter together to give it form originarily. At the opening of the film, the hieroglyph extends a polymorphous blazon, mixing up languages, and scrambling codes; writing's blazon, but it is stretched over a female body—derisive as it may be—

which screens male speech. If the latter breaks through, the male face taking shape will finish off the collapse into representation that was merely delayed, edited in a manner prompted by the separation of the elements.

The movement which lowers the newspaper also turns down the female blazon just as Michel turns down the young women and leaves alone at the end of the first sequence. Is it by accident that the tête-à-tête with himself in sequence 2 again take the form of an editing that moves apart—voice-off/voice-in of M divided from himself? Crossing the line, with the explosion of continuity and the inversion of pan shots, killing the policeman, with the simultaneous rupture of image and sound, show the transgression of the law at stake which is repeated in the editing: society's law, of course, unknown rather than contested; but first the law of the division of the sexes, perpetuated right down to the refusal of the other sex. A law that cannot be bypassed, here, because it is instituted in the equivocation of writing, in which the hieroglyphic inspiration is still permeated with exactly what it challenges; in *A bout de souffle,* the contradiction between sign and letter, consubstantial with the graphic component as well as with the female element onto which it is projected, reveals a contradiction between the fiction, with its sexual models, and the writing, into which desire shifts the difference.

Filmography and Bibliography

Godard Filmography, 1954–1985

1954   *Opération béton* (short subject)
Screenplay by Jean-Luc Godard.

1955   *Une Femme coquette* (short subject)
Screenplay by Hans Lucas [Jean-Luc Godard], based on a short story by Guy de Maupassant, *Le Signe* (*The Signal*).

1957   *Tous les garçons s'appellent Patrick* (*All the Boys Are Called Patrick*, short subject)
Screenplay by Eric Rohmer.

1957–58   *Une Histoire d'eau* (short subject)
Screenplay by François Truffaut, narration by Jean-Luc Godard.

1958   *Charlotte et son Jules* (*Charlotte and Her Jules*, short subject)
Screenplay by Jean-Luc Godard.

1959   *A bout de souffle* (*Breathless*)
Screenplay by Jean-Luc Godard, based on an original treatment by François Truffaut.

1960   *Le Petit Soldat* (*The Little Soldier*)
Screenplay by Jean-Luc Godard.

1960–61   *Une Femme est une femme* (*A Woman Is a Woman*)
Screenplay by Jean-Luc Godard, based on an idea by Geneviève Cluny.

1961   "La Paresse" ("Sloth"), an episode in the *Les Sept Péches capitaux* (*The Seven Capital Sins*)
Screenplay by Jean-Luc Godard.

1962   *Vivre sa vie* (*My Life to Live*)
Screenplay by Jean-Luc Godard, based on a book by Judge Marcel

Sacotte, *Où en est la prostitution?* (Paris: Buchet-Castel).

1962 "Le Nouveau Monde" ("The New World"), an episode in *RoGoPaG*
Screenplay by Jean-Luc Godard.

1962–63 *Les Carabiniers (The Riflemen; The Soldiers)*
Screenplay by Jean-Luc Godard, Jean Gruault, and Roberto Rossellini, based on a play by Benjamin Joppolo, *I Carabinieri,* adapted for the French stage by Jacques Audiberti.

1963 "Le Grand Escroc," an episode in *Les Plus Belles Escroqueries du monde (The Beautiful Swindlers)*
Screenplay by Jean-Luc Godard.

1963 *Le Mépris (Contempt)*
Screenplay by Jean-Luc Godard, based on a novel by Alberto Moravia, *Il Disprezzo (A Ghost at Noon).*

1963–64 "Montparnasse-Levallois," an episode in *Paris vu par . . . (Six in Paris)*
Screenplay by Jean-Luc Godard, based on an anecdote told by Belmondo in *Une Femme est une femme* from *Les Contes de lundi* by Jean Giraudoux.

1964 *Bande à part (Band of Outsiders)*
Screenplay by Jean-Luc Godard, based on a novel by Delores and B. Hitchens, *Fool's Gold.*

1964 *La (Une) Femme mariée (The [A] Married Woman)*
Screenplay by Jean-Luc Godard.

1965 *Alphaville; ou, Une Étrange Aventure de Lemmy Caution (Alphaville)*
Screenplay by Jean-Luc Godard.

1965 *Pierrot le fou*
Screenplay by Jean-Luc Godard, based on a novel by Lionel White, *Obsession;* published in France as *Le Demon de onze heures* in the "Serie Noire" (Gallimard).

1965 *Masculin/Féminin (Masculine/Feminine)*
Screenplay by Jean-Luc Godard, freely based on two novellas by Guy de Maupassant, *La Femme de Paul* and *Le Signe;* plays by LeRoi Jones (*Dutchman*); and Jean Vauthier (*Les Prodiges*).

1966 *Made in U.S.A.*
Screenplay by Jean-Luc Godard, based on a novel by Richard Stark, *The Juggler;* published in France as *Rien dans le coffre* in "Serie Noire" (Gallimard).

1966 *Deux ou trois choses que je sais d'elle (Two or Three Things I Know about Her)*
Screenplay by Jean-Luc Godard, based on articles by Catherine Vimenet, "La Prostitution dans les grands ensembles," *La Nouvel Observateur,* 29 March and 10 May 1966.

1966   "Anticipation; ou, L'Amour en l'an 2000" ("Anticipation"), an episode in *Le Plus Vieux Métier du monde* (*The Oldest Profession*)
Screenplay by Jean-Luc Godard.

1967   *La Chinoise; ou, Plutôt à la chinoise* (*La Chinoise*)
Screenplay by Jean-Luc Godard, based on (probably) Paul Nizan's *La Conspiration* (Paris: Gallimard, 1939).

1966–67   "Caméra-Oeil," an episode in *Loin du Viet-Nam* (*Far from Vietnam*)
Screenplay by Jean-Luc Godard.

1967   "L'Amour," an episode in *La Contestation;* Italian release title *Amore e rabbia* (*Love and Rage*)
Screenplay by Jean-Luc Godard.

1967   *Le Week-End* (*Weekend*)
Screenplay by Jean-Luc Godard.

1967–68   *La Gai Savoir*
Screenplay by Jean-Luc Godard, based loosely on Rousseau's *Émile;* the title is a translation of Nietzsche's *Die Fröhliche Wissenschaft.*

1968   *Cinétracts* (short uncredited, unedited newsreels)

1968   *Un Film comme les autres* (*A Film Like Any Other*)
Production: Dziga Vertov Group [Godard and Jean-Pierre Gorin]

1968   *One A.M.*
Screenplay by Jean-Luc Godard and D. A. Pennebaker

1968   *One Plus One* (*One Plus One, Sympathy for the Devil*)
Screenplay by Jean-Luc Godard.

1969   *British Sounds* (*See You at Mao*)
Screenplay by Jean-Luc Godard.

1969   *Pravda*
Screenplay by Jean-Luc Godard, based on Brecht's play, *Me-ti*, and on writings of Mao Tse-tung.

1969   *Vent d'est* (*Wind from the East*)
Screenplay by Jean-Luc Godard, Daniel Cohn-Bendit, Jean-Pierre Gorin, Gianni Barcelloni, and Sergio Bazzini.

1969   *Lotte in Italia/Luttes en Italie* (*Struggles in Italy*)
Screenplay by Dziga Vertov Group (probably Jean-Pierre Gorin), based on Louis Althusser's concept of ideology, published in 1960 and later translated as "Ideology and Ideological State Apparatuses," in *Lenin and Philosophy,* trans. Ben Brewster (New York: Monthly Review Press, 1971).

1970   *Vladimir et Rosa* (*Vladimir and Rosa*)
Production: Dziga Vertov Group

1971–72   *Tout va bien* (*Just Great*)
Screenplay by Jean-Luc Godard and Jean-Pierre Gorin, based on Jean Saint-Geours's *Vive la société de consomation* (manager's monologue);

CGT Magazine, *La Vie ouvrière* (union official's monologue); "Maoist" magazine, *La Cause du peuple* (leftist worker's monologue).

1972   *Lettre à Jane/Letter to Jane*
Screenplay by Jean-Luc Godard.

1975   *Numéro deux*
Screenplay by Jean-Luc Godard and Anne-Marie Miéville.

1970–76   *Ici et ailleurs* (*Here and Elsewhere*)

1976   *Comment ça va?* (*How's It Going?*)
Screenplay by Jean-Luc Godard and Anne-Marie Miéville.

1977   *Sur et sous la communication* (*Over and Under Communication;* six TV programs)
Screenplay by Jean-Luc Godard and Anne-Marie Miéville.

1980   *Sauve qui peut* (*La Vie*) (*Everyman for Himself*)
Screenplay by Jean-Luc Godard.

1982   *Passion*
Screenplay by Jean-Luc Godard.

1983   *Prénom Carmen* (*First Name Carmen*)
Screenplay by Jean-Luc Godard.

1984   *Je vous salue Marie* (*Hail Mary*)
Screenplay by Jean-Luc Godard, based loosely on the Gospel of St. Luke.

1985   *Détective*
Screenplay by Jean-Luc Godard.

1987   *King Lear*
Screenplay by Jean-Luc Godard.

Selected Bibliography

Godard, Jean-Luc. *Godard on Godard.* Edited by Tom Milne. New York: Viking, 1972. (The best English-language source of writings by Godard up through 1968, fastidiously annotated.)

Godard, Jean-Luc. *Introduction à une véritable histoire du cinéma.* Paris: Albatros, 1980. (Transcription of an extended interview in Montreal. Godard discusses his ideas about film after consecutive screenings of many of his films and of films he requested to see.)

Godard, Jean-Luc. *Jean-Luc Godard par Jean-Luc Godard.* Paris: Éditions Balfond, Cahiers du Cinéma, Éditions de l'Etoile, 1986. (This 640-page tome contains virtually all of Godard's writings on the cinema.)

Lesage, Julia. *Jean-Luc Godard: A Guide to References and Resources.* Boston: G. K. Hall, 1979. (Indispensible as a tool and an introduction to Godard's work. This guide has served as the basis for the preceding filmography and for the "Cast and Credits." It annotates over 2,000 writings about Godard, including 136 on *Breathless.* The reader is urged to consult this guide for further information.)